D1054448

Can This Child Be Saved?
Be Saved?

Solutions for Adoptive and Foster Families

Foster W. Cline, M.D., and Cathy Helding

Produced by City Desktop Productions, Inc.

Library of Congress Cataloging-in-Publication Data

Cline, Foster W., M.D.
    Can this child be saved / Foster W. Cline, MD,
Cathy Helding.
      p.   cm.
    Includes bibliographical references (p.) and index.
    ISBN 0-9668922-2-4
    1. Family, Child Care, Relationships. 2. Health and Fitness.
    3. Medical, Nursing, Home Care. 4. Psychology.
    5. Self-Actualization, Self-Help.

                                            98-89462
                                              CIP

Copyright© 1999 by World Enterprises

All rights reserved. No part of this book may be reproduced or transmitted in any form or by any means, electronic or mechanical, including photocopying, recording, or by any information storage and retrieval system, without permission in writting from the Publisher.

World Enterprises
P.O. Box 396, Franksville, WI 53126

Library of Congress Catalog Number: 98-89462

Printed in the United States of America

printing number
1 2 3 4 5 6 7 8 9 10

Dedication

To John, Sarah, and Naomi, who shared the dream to make a difference. Without your constant support and encouragement it would have been impossible.

—Cathy

To my "Sweet Hermie" whose patience, persistence, love, and understanding helped during days of meetings and long evenings when excerpts and chapters were worked on and e-mailed back and forth.

—Foster

Contents

Acknowledgments

Our particular thanks go to our families for their willingness to endure our absence and preoccupation during the years of research and writing, and for their thoughtful editing and criticism. We are especially grateful to our adopted and foster children who taught us so much about what is really important in life.

In addition, we'd like to express our thanks to the following people:

To the many child and adult adoptees, adoptive parents, foster parents, and birth families who gave us pieces of their hearts and lives to share with others in the hope that it would make a positive difference. We have worked very hard to make sure that the tears we have shed together will make a difference.

To the numerous professionals who have given generously of their valuable time and offered wisdom and advice, sometimes even putting their jobs on the line to do so. Their experience has added tremendously to the honesty and value of this book.

To Peggy Malm and Christopher Waldmann for support and inspiration, wisdom and friendship, encouragement and love, humor and hope, and the constant reminder that "what doesn't kill us helps us grow."

To the staff and members of the America Online Adoption Forum and Attachment Disorder Support List on the Internet. Not only do you share the dream, you make it come true. The difference you have made in each other's lives has been a joy to participate in and an inspiration to witness.

To Don Taylor, for adding his unique, all-triad perspective to our research. His perceptive comments helped keep us on track.

We want particularly to thank all of the therapists and the trained foster and adoptive parents of Evergreen Consultants in Human Behavior and The Attachment Center at Evergreen. We thought seriously of adding all your names to this dedication, but we owe a debt of gratitude to too many of you. And you know who you are! Your love for children and the effectiveness of your techniques shine through the pages of this book.

A special thanks to Carole Huxel, Paula Blake, and Beth Meadows for researching and compiling many of the excellent resources listed at the end of the book.

To Karen Manthe and Julie Uher, who shared the dreams, the losses, and many of the struggles.

To Cory Tamsen, Gerry and Dan Galibinski, and Gerri Sullivan. Each of you made your own unique contribution to this effort, for which we are grateful.

To Rose Blakeman, who faithfully and cheerfully transcribed hours of audiotaped interviews, while simultaneously offering encouragement and support.

To our first editor, Genevieve Kazdin, known to hundreds of AOL kids and families as "grandma Gen." You have brightened and enriched the lives of so many through your generosity and caring.

To Sarah Helding, who spent many long, late hours patiently editing page after page, and offering valuable criticism and advice.

To the design, production, and marketing staff at City Desktop Productions, Inc., Franksville, Wisconsin: Pamela Cruzen, Stacey Edmiston, Chad Harbach, Elizabeth Johnson, Matthew Jossart, Amy Martincic, Richard Reich, Ron Schumacher, Robin Stearns, Paul Tabili, Gretchen Trautman, and Sue TeVrucht.

To Blake and Olivia Elliott, for the cookies, not to mention the wisdom and encouragement.

Many others to whom we owe a debt of gratitude wished to remain anonymous to protect the privacy of their families, or in some cases to preserve their jobs. You know who you are, and we hope you also know how much you are appreciated. This book is your accomplishment as much as it is ours.

And of utmost importance is the acknowledgment that without God's blessings and grace, we could accomplish nothing. To Him we owe the greatest debt.

Introduction

Sometime in the next two years 50,000 innocent and well-intentioned families will attempt to save a child from homelessness and a life without a loving, permanent family.[1] Some will be recruited by U.S. government directive through the "Goals 2002" effort, which seeks to double the number of special needs adoptions by the year 2002. In some cases, excited about the prospect of adding a new child to their family, they will overlook or discount negative feelings or discouraging information about the "children who wait." In many cases, they will imagine only satisfaction and success. Unfortunately, they will be given little or no realistic preparation for the huge and very specialized job of parenting a special needs child.

Most won't expect the children they adopt to reject their efforts and their love. They won't expect to be attacked and hurt by the very children they had hoped to save from . . .

- A life without birthday parties and Christmas presents.

- A life without pretty dresses and baseball uniforms.

- A lifetime in an orphanage.

- Starvation.

- Abuse and neglect.

- Drug-addicted parents.

- Poverty.

- Social and educational deprivation.

Over 40 percent of these families will open their hearts and homes to children who may not be capable of accepting . . .

- Pretty dresses and baseball uniforms.

- Birthday parties and Christmas presents.

- Warm beds and clean sheets.

- Dolls and toy trucks.

- Good food.

- Happy childhood memories.

- A neighborhood to play in.

- The love and affection that will help them grow.

Surprisingly large numbers of children have been permanently and severely damaged by their pasts and by the child welfare system. Depending on how you define *severely damaged*, it is estimated that between 40 and 60 percent of the children available for adoption fall into this category.

They may look just like any other kids. The damage is, in all too many cases, deeply hidden under a facade of "normalcy" that they display in order to survive. Sometimes it is buried so deeply that it takes years to surface. But it will. It has to. And when it does, it will do so with a vengeance that is fearsome and dangerous. Sometimes, particularly with very young children, their dysfunctions are blamed on environmental deprivation, which is often assumed to be "curable" by improvements in environment and large doses of love.

Yet the truth is, many of these children will refuse to be "saved." They will reject the love and affection offered by their new families, spit in the face of opportunity, and choose the most negative path. They will devastate their new families, destroy their carefully chosen new possessions, terrorize the neighborhood, and sexually abuse their adoptive siblings. They will refuse to open their Christmas presents, or break the ones they do open before they are ever used. They will spit epithets in their mothers' faces and falsely accuse their new dads of child abuse.

Numerous research studies clearly point to the fact that adopted children exhibit more behavioral, emotional, and psychological problems than do birth children raised in healthy families. Abuse, neglect, and exposure to environmental violence predispose children to very specific types of delinquency and adolescent criminality. It is estimated that at the present time, 80 percent of the children adopted in America come from this kind of background.[2] Adopted adolescents show greater tendencies toward depression, aggression, anger, violence, running away from home, truancy, and suicide. Abused or neglected children are more prone to become abusers themselves, and sexually abused youngsters often become perpetrators at a very young age, abusing siblings and/or peers.

Genetics plays a stronger role in certain types of behaviors than was once thought, and certainly a stronger role than most adoptive parents can feel easy about accepting. Denying this role is a mistake many families make and later regret.

Most of us live in a world with a common perspective—a world that makes sense. A world that is safe, secure, and consistent. Few have lived in the only world that many of our special needs children have known—one of fear, deprivation, abuse, abandonment, and toxins. The world these children come from does not make sense in ordinary ways, and sometimes not in any way at all. They have learned to survive, but at a great price. Often the price is emotional health. And frequently the payments are spread out over a lifetime. As unfair as it is, the price of that survival is also levied on the families who adopt. And it is extracted from them in ways that are unimaginable to most of us.

By the time they discover the harsh realities of parenting a disturbed child, the family whose only dream was to save a child may be hard pressed to save itself.

- The stress and demands of coping with the child leave little or nothing for the rest of the family. The parents' marriage may be jeopardized.

- The other children in the family may be angry and in need of counseling.

- The family home may have to be mortgaged to pay for the criminal damage judgments incurred by the adopted child.

- Extended family and friends may be unable to offer help or support.

- Isolated, alone, and unable to find respite care, the parents may well feel exhausted, disillusioned, afraid, and angry.

Moreover, they are grief-stricken at the destruction of the original dream. They question how anything that started with such good intentions could end with such devastation and resentment.

As if that is not bad enough, no one seems to believe or understand what the family is going through. Therapists, doctors, teachers, and law enforcement professionals, who lack special training in these issues, may blame the parents for the child's problems, effectively closing the door to help and hope.

This is the way it often is.

But it doesn't have to be this way. There are ways to rebuild the dream. There are things that can help. There is hope, and there are ways to find joy amidst the sorrow.

That is what this book is about. Help. Hope. Understanding. Solutions. It contains pieces of many lives, generously and often tearfully offered, often in the wake of disaster. Its wisdom is compiled in measured parts of child development theory and psychology, "love and logic," and the blood, sweat, and tears of the caring people who have labored and in many cases continue to labor to save the world's deprived, abused, and damaged children.

Much of the material in this book has been gathered over the course of several years of working with and interviewing adoptive families and professionals who work in the field of special needs adoption. The wisdom gained through sharing the heartbreaks and struggles of these families is immensely practical. There is an uncanny and often eerie similarity in the descriptions we hear—descriptions of the children's behaviors and responses to love and discipline, the effects they have on family members, and the ordeals parents endure while trying to help their children heal. As adoptive parents ourselves, we feel bonded to these families through our common ordeals and triumphs. Without exception, the families we have been privileged to meet and interview want to share what they have learned in the hope of sparing others even a small measure of the grief and discouragement they have endured, and perhaps by doing so, resurrect a portion of their original dream—"to save a child." Without their persistent prodding and constant encouragement, this book would never have been written.

Part I

Living with Disturbed Children

1

Overview of Disturbed Children

Who are the special needs children to whom we refer? Where do they come from? What causes them to behave the way they do?

They are children who:

- Have been exposed to early environmental deprivation.

- Have been exposed to toxins in utero.

- Have been exposed to excessive violence.

- Have been abused.

- Have been neglected or abandoned.

- Have fragile genetics.

- Have suffered neurological damage.

- Have behavioral disorders.

- Have attachment disorder.

- Have (PTSD) Post-Traumatic Stress Disorder.

- Have had early years characterized by inconsistent parenting or multiple moves and caregivers.

A child exposed to any one of these problems is at risk of becoming an extreme behavior and management problem for parents. Although their circumstances are different, their resulting childhood and adult disturbances are more dependent on *when* and for *how long* the abuse, neglect, or loss occurred than on the details of *what* occurred.[3] And it is estimated that approximately 80 percent of the children who enter the child welfare system today are affected by at least one of these factors.[4] At the end of 1990, according to data from the *American Public Welfare Association,* there were approximately 406,000 children in out-of-home placements in the U.S. About three-quarters of these were in adoptive or foster placements. This adds up to 324,000 special needs children already in placement by 1995.

Do All Children Belong in Families?

Life without parents is a difficult sentence to pronounce upon a child, but it's happening more and more often. According to a 1994 *Atlantic Monthly* article entitled "When Parents Are Not in the Best Interests of the Child,"

▮▮ Sometimes children have gone beyond the opportunity to go back and capture what needed to be done between the ages of three and eight. Sometimes the thrust of intimacy that comes with family living is more than they can handle. Sometimes the requirement of bonding is more than they have the emotional equipment to give. As long as we keep pushing them back into what is our idealized fantasy of family, they'll keep blowing it out of the water for us.[6] ▟▟

Unfortunately, not all children thrive in traditional family settings. Our present child welfare system, however, is designed around a goal of permanency for all children, and permanency, by default, usually refers to a traditional family setting. Institutional care has virtually been abolished as a government-sponsored option in this country. This means that even the most disturbed children often end up in families ill-equipped and unprepared to manage them.

Richard J. Delaney and Frank R. Kunstal, in their excellent book, *Troubled Transplants*, write

▟▟ Some children placed with adoptive families have been so injured by their abusive pasts that they are simply 'family phobic.' These unfortunate victims are too traumatized, their selfhood annihilated by parents who committed 'soul murder' on them. ▟▟

They go on to tell us that efforts to raise these children *in traditional families* are in vain. The children do not desire families, are uncomfortable with them, and even fear them. They defend heavily against any efforts at intimacy, and wreak havoc in their homes.[7]

Until his recent retirement, David Fanshel was a professor at the Columbia University School of Social Work. A leader in the field of social work, and foster care in particular, Fanshel was the principal investigator in two major longitudinal studies on foster children in homes and institutions.

At a time when many experts are questioning the value of residential treatment and promoting family preservation, Fanshel goes against the tide. Fanshel, for decades one of the leading proponents of permanency planning, has modified his views. He now believes that permanency placement with a family is not an appropriate goal for about a quarter of the older, more seriously damaged and criminally inclined children in the system.[8]

Is it possible, then, to determine if children are good candidates for traditional family placement? How can families determine if children offered to them will be a good match, or if they are prepared to undertake a lifetime commitment to meet the children's needs? A thorough evaluation is helpful, although not foolproof. *The bottom line is, if a family is not prepared to live with the children the way they are, regardless of whether they are able to heal or make positive behavioral changes, they should think twice about adopting.*

The Process of Building the Dream

Our dreams are so important to how we define success and satisfaction in life. The mental images that we carry in our minds of what our future should look like, do much to shape our actions and color our feelings. When reality does not match the pictures we have in our heads, we may feel anything from upset and vulnerable to resentful and angry. In special needs adoption, this can result in anything from disappointment to disruption.

The decision to adopt is a complex one. In this section, we are going to examine some typical adoption scenarios. Everyone's adoption experience is unique. Factors as diverse as the temperament of the prospective adoptive parents, the social workers assigned to the case, and the area of the country they live in combine to make every story different. In the not too distant past, having other chidren put most families out of the running for adoption.

As the numbers of adoptable children worldwide multiply, and the culture insists on adoption as the only viable option for these orphaned children, more families who already have birth children are entering into the process. They often feel that they have additional resources and love to share with other children, and having already experienced success and satisfaction in being parents they may feel better equipped to cope with children who need more but give less back. They enter the process with expectations based on previous experiences—expectations that may have little to do with the reality of special needs parenting, but that have tremendous influence on the dream.

As these families begin to formulate thier dream, they may spend considerable time thinking about and discussing the possibility of adoption. In a partnership, one partner often initiates the idea, or feels more strongly motivated than the other. The exploration process ideally includes gathering as much information about the process and the children who are available as possible, but often it does not. By the time families contact an agency to begin the adoption process, they have usually been thinking and talking about it for several months. Now they have decided to go ahead, and they are very eager to get on with it. Very often the first opportunity for education is during the application process.

We cannot stress enough the need for families at this point to be given realistic education about the differences between adopting a special needs child and raising a birth child.

For infertile couples and childless singles, the dream has most likely been taking shape for even longer. By the time a childless couple decides to adopt, they may have spent several years and a tremendous amount of money on fertility treatment. Much of their emotional and physical energy has been devoted to having a child. The infertility treatment process is grueling. The pressure of time passing them by becomes increasingly difficult to bear. Bringing home a baby becomes the urgent and immediate goal that usurps all others in life.

For many of these families, adoption is a second choice option. They may struggle with whether it will be able to fulfill their dream at all. They may go through a healthy period of mourning the loss of the child they will never have, or they may try to avoid that pain by substituting an adopted child for the birth child who never will be.

As one family told us:

▮▮ We had this dream of having three children, each two years apart. We'd live on a street with sidewalks with a park on the corner. The kids would play together and eventually walk to a neighborhood school. I'd join the PTA and Bob would coach Little League. Then we found out we were infertile. By the time I was 32 we had been through half a dozen fertility clinic programs. Our relationship was suffering and all we could think about was what good parents we could be and how happy children would make us. We had so much love to give to children. Why didn't God give us any? Maybe, we thought, because we did love children so much, maybe He wanted us to give that love to children who had no one. Kids who were already here but unloved or unwanted. We began to see that is was God's plan for our lives—to adopt. Once we saw that, there was no talking us out of it. Now that we knew what we were meant to do, it seemed like it would never happen fast enough. Our focus shifted from getting pregnant to adopting a baby, almost overnight.   *▮▮*

For most families, infant adoption is no longer a possibility. There are not enough healthy infants to go around. The private adoption process—about the only timely way to adopt a healthy infant today—is expensive and emotionally draining. Many families decide that rather than take their chances with this system or wait seven to nine years for an infant through an agency, they will adopt a special needs child. This may be the second remaking of the original dream and may carry with it some grief and/or anger and resentment. The desire to have all of the struggle and waiting behind them makes these families especially eager to expedite the adoption process and accept placement of a child. Unfortunately, we have met more than a few families who feel that they were taken advantage of at this point. Social workers and agencies have a practice called "stretching" that they often use when interviewing couples who have applied to adopt. Stretching looks like this:

▟▌ Have you considered a child a bit older than infancy?

Well, not really. I mean . . . we haven't talked about it.

Well, there are so few babies available. It could take several years if you want to wait for a baby.

Several *years*? But we're already in our 40s. We thought there were so many kids out there. Teenage mothers, you know?

Well, a lot of people think that, but it's just not true. But there are lots of toddlers. Two- and three-year-olds. They are considered special needs kids because they are over the age of six months.

Two- or three-year-olds are still pretty little. And they are awfully cute at that age. I guess we'd be willing to look at some. ▟▌

This kind of subtle stretching of the family's acceptance levels over time may eventually result in a couple who originally wanted to adopt one infant taking in a sibling group of three children, ages two, three, and six. Later on, the parents wonder "how did this happen?"

Whether prospective parents are infertile, single, or want more children in addition to their birth children, the dream evolves through predictable stages that create a growing sense of urgency in the waiting family. This urgency makes prospective adoptive parents extremely vulnerable to stretching and can lead to impulsive and uninformed decisions.

A subtle and rapid shift in the balance of power takes place once the decision is made to abandon the original dream and begin the adoption process. Prior to this, the couple was able to make their own decisions and chart their own path. The timing was up to them. This will no longer be the case. Someone else has just crawled into the family bed— the adoption caseworker. A stranger now has the power to make the dream happen, and many families feel they must begin a courtship process with the agency or worker. This is not really the case at all, but having had no previous experience, most families do not know this.

The selection/approval process is understandably very intimate and one that many families find uncomfortable if not downright intrusive. There are excellent reasons for this, of course, which we will discuss later. Nonetheless, after expending enormous amounts of emotional energy trying to have a baby and coming to terms with infertility, many couples do not welcome further intimate intrusions into their lives. Families who have already successfully parented birth children may resent having to prove themselves "worthy" to strangers in that respect.

It takes a tremendous amount of courage to turn one's fate over to a stranger.

Parents describe their feelings in public forums on-line:

- "They told us it would be *six months* until the next orientation class. We can't even apply for *six whole months!* Is that fair to the kids who are out there waiting for a home?"

- "We've taken the classes and passed the home-study process, and now they say it could be up to *two years* before a child is found for us. With all these children waiting, why does it take months to find a child?!"

- "We wanted to adopt an infant but the wait in our state is seven years. And there is a rule that you can only be 40 years older than the child you adopt. I am 35. In seven years I will be too old to meet the criteria. So I guess we have to settle for an older child then, right?"

- "We have been told that if we want to wait for a normal child, we might never actually get chosen. But if we are willing to adopt a child with special needs, there is a better chance. We decided a kid with emotional problems would be better for us than a physically handicapped child. After all, with enough love, most kids can heal from emotional wounds."

- "We want to adopt one child at a time. You know, like you usually only have only one baby at a time. But there is a really cute group of siblings that are disrupting from another adoptive placement, and the worker said they would place them with us next week as foster kids while we were doing the adoption home study. Then as soon as the paperwork is ready, we could adopt them. She said there were lots of families who would take the kids, so we have to decide by tomorrow. What should we do? It all seems to be happening so fast! But we've waited for seven months already. Maybe if we say 'no' they won't call us again."

- "When couples decide to have a birth child, there are absolutely no competency, financial, personal or social requirements by the state. Anyone capable of having sex is deemed able to have and raise a child, so how come we have to go through all of this?"

The home-study process is a stressful one for many families. One mother asked Cathy, "Should I bake something special when the worker comes? I mean, are you supposed to serve tea or something? Or would that be too obviously trying to please?"

Another adoptive parent notes,

> I always keep my house neat. On the fifth home visit our worker said, 'I have some doubts about whether you will do well with children. Your house is always as neat as a pin and children need the freedom to be somewhat messy.' I thought, 'Yeah, but the kids aren't here yet! And I knew you were coming. Of course I picked up and tried to make things look nice.' How do you know what you are supposed to do? If we had a big mess when she came would she have judged us too messy? Help!

As drawn out and intrusive as the process usually is, speeding it up could have disastrous results for the children and the families who adopt them. *Fast-Tracking,* a result of curent state and federal mandates designed to clear out children back-logged in the crowded foster care system, may result in diminished screening and education of families. If the quality of placement declines, it makes sense to assume that disruptions will increase due to poor selection and preparation of adoptive parents.

In the winter of 1998, an adoption worker in Texas wrote to us, saying:

> I continue to work with pre- and post-adopt kids and their families. DHS (Department Of Human Services) here is "dumping" kids in care into unprepared and untrained adoptive families with lots of disruptions as a result. The laws in Texas have changed. The intent now is to have kids

> in a permanent placement (either return home or adoption) within one year of the date of removal. There seems to be no accountability.
>
> ▟▟

The answer is not to speed up or slow down placements, but to make better-informed placement decisions and to educate families about the realities of parenting special needs children and the impact they can have on family systems. It does not benefit children when they are placed in families ill-prepared to cope with their problems. It certainly makes little sense to fast-track a kid into another disruption and ultimately more upheaval.

If families are educated about the process and helped to establish a realistic dream and reasonable expectations, much stress and anxiety can be avoided, leaving families with some reserves to carry them through the next step in the process and beyond.

A Child at Last!

Once families complete the home-study process, the home, marriage, psychological, and financial examinations are completed and criminal background checks are done, all that is left is to wait for a call from the worker saying "we have a child for you." Usually a period of transition follows, during which families and children get together to get to know each other a little before the children are moved into the adoptive home. This is called "visitation." Many adopting families are unsure of what this time means to the final placement decision. They may feel they must first make a good impression on the child, and second demonstrate excellent child management techniques to make a good impression on the worker.

In essence, they may feel they must also pass some kind of a parenting test before the children are really theirs. However, many report that they do not feel empowered to parent, to set rules, impose standards of behavior, or consequence bad behavior. They fear that any negative reaction or disapproval from the children might lose them the placement. They feel they must demonstrate to all that they are fun people to be around and desirable parents from a child's standpoint.

Yet most parents intuitively know that this "Disneyland" approach is not a healthy way to establish a new relationship with the children. With disturbed children especially, it is important to let them know from the beginning that "we are the parents. We are in charge until you demonstrate for us that you are capable and mature enough to make good decisions for yourself."

One mother's story regarding visitation:

/// I remember when we first went to the foster home to meet our three children. We drove 350 miles with a young caseworker just out of social work school. When we got to the home, we went in, met the foster parents, and sat around the living room chitchatting about the weather, kids in general, and so forth.

In the back bedrooms, we could hear the kids laughing. We heard the door open and voices, saying, 'you go' or 'stop pushing' and then the door would slam again. All the while we continued to sit in the living room making small talk and going crazy with wanting to see the children. All of the adults seemed to be uncomfortable 'wishing' the kids would come out, and every so often the worker would make half-hearted comments like, 'They are naturally a little shy about coming out,' or 'This must be a scary experience for them.'

This was making me absolutely crazy. We did not drive all that way to turn around and go home without even seeing the kids. And the poor kids. They were too little and too uncertain to muster up the courage to come out by themselves. Why didn't someone go get them for heaven's sake? So finally, without knowing if I was breaking some unwritten rule or not, I went down and played around in the hall, and started to play a little game with the kids who were on the other side of the door: 'You-know-that-I-know-that-you-are-in-there'; and soon they came running out a tumbling mass of giggles and squirms.

I do firmly believe that if I hadn't taken the initiative, we would have driven another 350 miles home that day and the case worker would be saying, 'These things take time.' She was heavy into the theory that says you have to respect kids' timeframes. But heck, they were only two, three, and six years old and facing a meeting with a bunch of strangers. What would they have thought about our ability to manage and take care of them if we couldn't even get them to come out of the bedroom?

Parents should be made to feel empowered from the moment the children are selected for them. From that point on, they must have all of the rights and privileges of "real" parents, including the right to decide what is the best way to handle visitations.

Our daughter was in treatment in Texas. We lived in Colorado. The agency wanted us to make three visitation trips to Texas to 'transition' her into our home. Luckily, we weren't in the position of many adoptive parents—'needing' a child. This was a child we were willing to work with and adopt if we felt we could be helpful to her. So we just refused to make two more expensive and emotionally draining visits. She wasn't seeing the real us anyway. She was seeing people who 'lived' at a Holiday Inn. So we told them we would only make one trip and if that was not going to be good enough they could look for another family to adopt her. What do you know?—it turned out that one visit was sufficient. She's 25 now and doing just fine.

▇▇

Parents must act like parents from the start. This includes giving the children reasonable expectations and discipline.

▟▌ Because it was so far to the foster home, we always met our kids at a hotel between our town and theirs. Whatever the kids wanted to do, they got to do. Hotels can be a lot of fun. When they first came to our home, their first question was, 'Hey, you live here? Where's the swimming pool and hot tub?'

And chores? Forget it! They expected nothing but play plans and room service. When I showed them the coat pegs that they were to hang their coats on when they came in the door, they threw them on the floor and said 'you do it.' It took many unhappy weeks of doing daily battle to undo the damage those visits did to our authority.

▇▇

Following placement, there is often a period of time when children and parents are both looking each other over, and all are on their best behavior. That time, when it occurs, is often referred to as the "honeymoon period." But therapists and parents wise to the ways of disturbed children have half kiddingly referred to it as the child's time of "stalking the prey."

Disturbed children, because of the inconsistent and unreliable responses they have received in their early life, almost always attempt to be in control of things. They will test the limits in every new situation, and try to establish dominance and control. Because prospective adoptive parents do not always feel as empowered as they should be during the initial visitation, the children (consciously or unconsciously) begin to feel that they have all the control. This locks in unhealthy family dynamics that are very hard to change after the children move in.

◢◢ Our worker said that having another child in the home would change the tone of our family. Change the tone!!! Those kids changed the whole musical score! What surprised us was that we all turned into sour notes with those kids around. But I think our being prepared with a few specialized parenting techniques, and knowing that we must be open to their feelings while showing them that we have expectations and will set and stick to firm limits, helped us get back on key sooner.   *◢◢*

Greg Keck, a well-known child psychologist who works with attachment disordered children, tells parents to assign chores to children during visitation and establish the same expectations and authority you intend to make a regular part of family life in your home. Making the visitation or honeymoon period akin to a trip to Disneyworld is a big mistake according to Keck. Good teachers "like to joke that they never smile until after Thanksgiving." The old adage "It is easier to lighten up than to tighten up" applies doubly to children who come from inconsistent and chaotic backgrounds.

Are We Prepared?

We certainly agree with Senator and astronaut John Glenn when he says

> ▌▌ The greatest antidote to worry, whether you're getting ready for spaceflight or facing a problem of daily life, is preparation . . . the more you try to envision what might happen and what your best responses and options are, the more you are able to allay your fears about the future.   ▌▌

The very fact that you are reading this book means you are interested in doing your best to meet the needs of your family. Whether you are just thinking about adopting, or have already done so, this book and some of the resources we suggest at the end of it will prove invaluable. With realistic expectations, the right tools and techniques, the correct attitudes and philosophies, and adequate professional resources, you have as much chance at success and satisfaction as anyone.

The optimum time to prepare to be a special needs parent is before the children arrive, when most prospective adoptive parents have the time and energy to devote to reading and discussion. Although it is never too late, once the children arrive, the overwhelming nature of their needs will take precedence. We recommend that families approach this process in logical stages.

Prior to Placement:

- Assessment: Is special needs adoption for me? (See the next section, "Think About Adopting or Foster Parenting Special Needs Children")

- Assessment: How many and what kind of children am I best suited to parent?

- Assessment: What are this particular child's needs? (See the section on the CHAFCA assessment tool.)

- Assessment: Am I capable of meeting the needs of this particular child without sacrificing others in the family?

- Parenting tools and techniques

- Professional resources (physicians, mental health professionals, educators, pastors)

- Support systems (groups, Internet, respite care)

After Placement (if not done earlier)

- Assessment: What are this particular child's needs? (See the section on the CHAFCA assessment tool.)

- Parenting tools and techniques

- Professional resources (physicians, mental health professionals, educators, pastors)

- Support systems (groups, Internet, respite care)

Think About Adopting or Foster Parenting Special Needs Children: A Self-assessment Tool for Prospective Adoptive or Foster Parents

This workbook-style course is a self-examination tool that we highly recommend to families considering adoption or foster care. It is designed to be thought-provoking and to stimulate discussion in many areas of critical importance to success in parenting special needs children. Several states have now made this a part of their adoption education process. Individuals can purchase the workbook and use it on their own.

(To order call: 1-816-453-9792 or see the resources section in the back of the book for additional ordering information.)

The Cline/Helding Adopted and Foster Child Assessment (CHAFCA)

We have found that adoptive parents feel more secure and empowered to help their children when they have an accurate definition of what the children's problems are and what options they have for managing and treating those problems. A first step in this direction is a thorough evaluation.

We have developed an effective tool that parents can use to make an accurate and complete initial assessment of their children, the Cline/Helding Adopted and Foster Child Assessment (CHAFCA). It is a preclinical evaluation that can be easily taken and scored by the average parent, and also can be used by professionals as an early diagnostic and intake tool.

The CHAFCA can help determine the future therapeutic and parenting needs of the children and assess "goodness of fit" issues prior to placement.

CHAFCA consists of two parts. The first obtains basic identifying information, complete medical history of the child and the family, and background information unique and relevant to adoptive/foster children. It provides an easy way to record and remember important details that are often lost or forgotten as time passes, but may simplify diagnosis and assist with treatment decisions many years later.

The second part consists of twelve subtests specific to problems frequently seen in special needs adopted children. The CHAFCA can be taken in its entirety, or each subtest can be taken and scored individually when needed.

The CHAFCA Subtests:

Subtest 1:   Emotional Health

Subtest 2:   Reactive Attachment Disorder

Subtest 3:   Oppositional Defiant Disorder

Subtest 4:   Attention Deficit Disorder with Hyperactivity (ADHD), with Subtest for Attention Deficit Disorder without Hyperactivity (ADD)

Subtest 5:   Conflict and/or Depression

Subtest 6:   Neurological Disorder, Learning Disabilities, and/or Developmental Delay

Subtest 7:   Sensory Integrative Dysfunction

Subtest 8:   Sex Abuse Indicators

Subtest 9:   Predictors of Violent, Aggressive, or Dangerous Behavior

Subtest 10: Fetal Alcohol Syndrome (FAS/FAE)

Subtest 11: Giftedness

Subtest 12: Substance Abuse

Accurate identification of the problem and early intervention are often the keys to success in parenting and in treatment. CHAFCA can help families avoid large investments in time and money, as well as potential harm to the child that can result from a trial and error approach.

Parents and professionals alike are encouraged to adapt the use of CHAFCA to their individual needs. (To order CHAFCA, see the order form in the back of this book or call: 1-800-854-2344).

Coming to Terms with Terminology

As authors, our tools of our trade are words. Inherent in the use of words is the potential for misunderstanding. Terminology can be misleading. Both intent and meaning can be misinterpreted unless clear and precise language is used. When talking about children and emotionally charged issues, it is tempting to try to pretty up the language, to be "politically correct." It sounds less offensive that way, and it becomes easier to hide from or ignore the harsh realities. After all, when we hear about atrocities, we feel a tug of conscience if we do not attempt to do something about them. When we hear about abused children, those of us with healthy psychological makeups recoil in horror.

We have been told by child welfare workers and adoption proponents that if precise terminology were used to describe today's adoptable children, prospective adoptive families might be scared away and not consider adopting at all. As a matter of fact, we have worked with agencies to design orientation materials for adoptive families that honestly describe the children who are available and the kinds of adaptations families must make in order to parent those children. Such materials are often criticized by the very families they attempt to educate. "Why would you put negative labels on these poor homeless kids? Are you deliberately trying to discourage families? Don't you know you are scaring away potential parents for kids who have no one?" We know that if families are frightened off by terminology, they probably lack the stamina and strength necessary to raise and advocate for the difficult and challenging children of today's special needs system. No one is served by placing children in families who have been misled or deceived about the child's potential or problems. Ironically, the same families who criticize our honesty often come back after adopting and say we were not honest enough!

When agencies and organizations talk about *adoptable children*, or *waiting children* they tend to use the same ambiguous and misleading terminology:

- *Difficult to place child*: This may mean simply that there are not enough families interested in adopting any child other than a healthy, same race infant, or it may mean children who are difficult to place because they will need the energy and effort of about eight parents.

- *Children who wait*: Taken at face value, this may mean children who wait for any reason at all. Perhaps they wait because the system processes their paperwork slowly. Who knows? An ambiguous and unclear identification.

- *At-risk children*: At risk of what, or from what? At risk of abuse? At risk of not finding a family? At risk of being lost in the system? At risk of becoming drug addicts or criminals? A very vague term.

- *Vulnerable children*: Tugs at the heart, but if you think about it, aren't all children vulnerable in some situations? So what exactly this means is left to the imagination. Most prospective adoptive parents do not have the background and knowledge to imagine the unfortunate truth.

- *Special needs children*: To most people this phrase conjures up an image of a child in a wheelchair or perhaps a retarded child. Many states define any child older than six months, disabled, health impaired, or part of a sibling group as having special needs. A *very* broad definition. However, today's special needs population consists mostly of children who have been severely damaged emotionally and/or neurologically.

The Population We Refer To and the Words We Use

When writing about adopted children, we prefer not to use misleading or vague euphemisms that refer only to something *outside* the child. Instead, to make sure that our meaning is clear, we use terms that refer to what is going on *inside* the child. By using such words as "disturbed," "neurologically damaged," or "disabled," we mean no disrespect to the children. We do not wish to attach labels that will stigmatize children for life, or lock them into diagnostic categories. We do want to make sure that the reader knows exactly what type of child we mean. And we think it crucial to the best interests of the children and families affected by the tragedies of which we write that there be no sugarcoating of their problems for the sake of political correctness.

Legally speaking, adoption is tighter than marriage. You can divorce your spouse, but you cannot divorce your child. Unfortunately many adoptive parents have told us they spent far less time contemplating "goodness of fit" issues before adopting than they did before choosing their spouse.

Children are quite literal and concrete in their thinking. They know when we are attaching fancy labels to down-to-earth problems. They usually handle terminology the way the important adults in their environment handle them. If we are not afraid of words, they are not either. If we do not shrink from discussing disabilities, they do not either. When we speak honestly and with respect to our children about their disabilities and handicaps, they learn to rely on our honesty and openness, and know that they can be direct, straightforward, open, and honest with us in return. No subject is too hard to talk about. Even their disabilities.

One of our fetal alcohol affected children became involved in an effort to pass legislation mandating treatment for pregnant women who drink or abuse drugs during the third trimester of their pregnancies. At age nine, even with severe learning disabilities, this child was able to tell others "When my mom was pregnant with me, she drank a lot of alcohol and it infected my brain, so now I have trouble learning and doing things other nine year olds can do easily. That makes me have to work harder and feel different. I think this law is important so other kids don't have to be born with damaged brains like mine." This child has excellent self-esteem, is happy, and is as well adjusted as any child with her limitations could be. But she has struggled more than most, and knows it. Terminology does not worry her. She is more interested in truth and in helping others. Out of the mouths of babes . . . !

When talking about some special needs children, we may refer to them as "mentally ill," or as having a "psychiatric disorder." It is important, especially for prospective adoptive parents, to recognize and accept that this term *does* apply to many of these children. For example, children who are described as "having difficulty attaching," or "having trouble bonding," or more ambiguously "may take some time learning to trust," may have a psychiatric disorder called Reactive Attachment Disorder of Early Childhood. This is a diagnostic category found in the American Psychiatric Association's *Diagnostic and Statistical Manual*, the book used to define mental illness. Although it has its roots in early childhood, it is a serious disturbance that has lifelong implications for children and families. The bottom line is that children with attachment disorder are seriously mentally ill.

Effects of Infant Abuse and Neglect

Few Americans understand the lasting effects of infant abuse and neglect. To understand the corrective responses disturbed children must receive, and parents or caretakers must apply, it is necessary to understand the basics of how early trauma plays such a pivotal role in their problems. The importance of the first year of life for both cognitive and personality development cannot be overemphasized. It has been estimated that half a lifetime's knowledge is gained during the first year of life. During the first year the infant organizes visual perception and auditory reception, learns reciprocal response, develops loving and/or conflicted relationships, forms the basis for cause and effect reasoning, and lays the foundation for gross motor skills. What a year![9]

University of Chicago pediatric neurologist Dr. Peter Huttenlocher has chronicled this extraordinary epoch in brain development by autopsying the brains of infants and young children who have died unexpectedly. The number of synapses in one layer of the visual cortex, Huttenlocher reports, rises from around 2,500 per neuron at birth to as many as 18,000 about six months later. Other regions of the cortex score similarly spectacular increases but on slightly different schedules. And while these microscopic nerve fibers continue to form throughout life, they reach their highest average densities (15,000 synapses per neuron) at around the age of two. By the age of two, a child's brain contains twice as many synapses and consumes twice as much energy as the brain of a normal adult.[10]

This organic circuitry enables our brains to organize and use information, to produce and process the chemicals we need to remain emotionally stable and healthy. *Once in place, it cannot be rewired.* Flaws in this structure affect our ability to think, feel, move, see, and hear for the rest of our lives.[11] During the early years, there is an almost magical dance that takes place between the developing brain and the child's environment. This interaction is responsible for much of what makes us human. Studies have shown that if the environment does not provide the right stimulation, if a child is neglected, abused, or otherwise deprived at this critical time, that child will grow up functionally retarded.[12]

At each early stage of brain growth, there is neurological readiness for internalizing particular concepts.[13] Thus, in a *stage-specific* and critical window of time, the brain is ready to learn trust, to learn causal thinking, to learn language, and so on. If the developing child's environment does not provide the essential stimulation at the critical period, the optimal time for learning that concept, the ability to learn that concept may be irreversibly lost.

The theory holds, for instance, that language development best takes place in the second and third years of life. It is not that some people cannot learn a foreign language at a later time, but that it is much more difficult once past that critical window of opportunity.[14] The brain must use adaptive functioning, which is successful in varying degrees in different people. Adaptive functioning is never as good as learning something the right way at the right time.

The brain rapidly weeds out unused connections during this time as well. It is known, for example, that if Asian children do not learn how to pronounce the English *r* sound, it becomes almost impossible for them to pronounce it later, and "Roger" will always be "Lodger." The Asian languages do not use this sound, the child does not hear it spoken, and so the brain eliminates the ability to pronounce it as it structures for efficiency.

The complexity of such simple skills cannot be underestimated. For example, learning disability specialists have discovered that there are 45 individual brain functions associated with telling time, ranging from the interpretation of the visual—itself a complex task—to understanding spatial and mathematical concepts.[15] A glitch in the neural wiring anywhere along the way will eliminate that ability *permanently* and an adaptive substitution will have to be found.

The longer the environment deprives the individual of critical input, the more difficult or even impossible it will be to learn the concept or skill later. In our collective years of research and work with children and families, we have found that deprivation during the first years of life may be nearly impossible to overcome later, despite years of excellent therapeutic and educational intervention.[16] This may be one of the hardest realities for families of special needs children to face—the irreversibility of this damage.

First-year Development Briefly Explored

Contrary to what we thought in the past, the earlier the developmental year, the more important it is for later cognitive and personal development.[17] The experiences of the first three years of life are critical in this regard.[18] The first year lays the foundation for four essential and related human thought and personality traits:

1. Causal thinking

2. Conscience

3. Basic trust

4. The ability to delay gratification

The first year plays an essential role in laying the foundation of these four basic personality variables. Upon these variables, civilization is built, love is exchanged, people live happily or unhappily together, relationships last or crumble. If we meet a person walking the streets at night who lacks these, we're dead. Without these critical elements, civilization as we know it is lost! *Without these elements, critical thinking is impossible and intellectual and emotional growth is permanently stunted.*

Among the first circuits the brain constructs are those that govern the emotions. Beginning around two months of age, the distress and contentment experienced by newborns start to evolve into more complex feelings, such as joy, sadness, envy, empathy, pride, and shame. Abuse or neglect at this stage can produce heightened anxiety and abnormal stress responses that can become hard-wired for life.[19]

Causal Thinking

All of childhood responsibility and responsiveness is based on causal thinking. It is necessary for understanding and learning from consequences, and for delaying gratification. It plays an important role in respect, responsibility, reciprocity, and all tasks that call for planning ahead. It provides the foundation for most learning and for appropriate identification of and response to emotion.

Conscience Development

Conscience development can only take place with the development of causal thinking. The rudimentary foundation of conscience takes place in the first months of life when a child learns that "My actions can make mom happy. When she's happy, things turn out well for me." Conscience is based on the ability to put ourselves in another person's shoes and imagine what they might be feeling. This can only occur if there is consistent early nurturing from a mother figure. If an infant is treated inconsistently, the developing brain circuitry wires chaotically.

This is very often the case with drug or alcohol-abusing caretakers who, depending on whether they are drunk, stoned or sober, respond with appropriate love and nurturing or with inappropriate anger and abuse—to the same situation. The baby cries, and mother picks her up and feeds her. Or, the baby cries, and mother smacks her. The infant brain can make no logical sense of this input. So when the child attempts to use its 'logic circuits' later in life, the response is just as chaotic and inconsistent.[20]

Abuse and neglect destroy the development of both causal thinking and conscience without which a child cannot understand why things are right or wrong, empathize, feel remorse, have a positive self-image, feel guilt, or want to mend their ways.

Basic Trust

Eric Erickson, a noted psychologist, remarked in his pivotal essay, *The Eight Stages of Man*, that the primary task of the first year of life was the development of "basic trust."[21] This, too, can only develop in a consistent, responsive, and loving environment. Basic trust, upon which all functional human relationships are based, is the knowledge that people are generally well intentioned and worthy of trust, and that there is a logic to the world that also can be counted on. When a child, after early traumatic experiences, is unable to learn to trust his parents and rely on their logical consistency, he becomes a constant control problem. He does not trust others to make good decisions for him, or to have his best interest at heart. Therefore he feels he must *always* control things himself, must *always* do things *his* way, or he will lose (or die).

The Ability to Delay Gratification

The foundation for this is laid in the first year of life, when a mother says "Wait a minute honey, I'm coming," or when the child quits crying as he watches his food being prepared, knowing he is about to be fed. When a person has to be gratified instantly, when waiting is impossible, then almost all higher order thinking, from accepting responsibility to avoiding AIDS to planning a chore or homework, does not exist. The ability to save money and hold a job is lost.

We live in an increasingly violent society. Much of this violence stems from a need to receive instant gratification without expenditure of effort. Entitlement is rampant in schools, labor and job disputes, welfare programs, and the justice system. The nature of violent crime has changed over time, and its current state is far more dangerous to society than ever before. Today we face much more senseless violence then ever. Or, as one Denver policeman put it, "It used to be that when somebody was killed, it was because 'somebody done somebody wrong.' But now people shoot into a house simply to see the bullets fly." In the mid-1990s, for the first time in history, Americans were more likely to be killed by a stranger than someone they knew. The problem will not be solved by tighter gun control. Americans have always had guns. The root of the problem lies in the hardwiring of the brain of the person pulling the trigger, not the hardware in the holster.

In Evergreen, Colorado, at a large mental health clinic that works with severely disturbed children from all over the world, one therapist notes, "If a child has had a good first three years of life, and there is no substance abuse in pregnancy, even if the symptoms are severe we can almost always reach the kid. If there has been early abuse and neglect, even if the symptoms are mild, all bets are off."

Neurological Changes

Even more fundamental, says Dr. Bruce Perry of Baylor College of Medicine in Houston, is the role parents play in setting up the neural circuitry that helps children regulate their responses to stress. Children who are abused early in life, Perry observes, develop brains that are exquisitely attuned to danger. At the slightest threat, their hearts race, their stress hormones surge, and their brains anxiously track the nonverbal cues that might signal the next attack. Because the brain develops in sequence, with more primitive structures stabilizing their connections first, early abuse is particularly damaging. Says Perry: "Experience is the chief architect of the brain." And because these early experiences of stress form a kind of template around which later development is organized, the changes they create are all the more pervasive.[22]

Neurological changes stemming from early abuse and neglect may be even more devastating than psychological changes, and in many cases have a direct effect on emotional responsiveness. Animal studies show that mammals neglected and deprived in their infancy show neurological changes that can be seen on brain scans. EEG results appear with abnormal spiking, and the pattern is predictable.[23] Thus, children who have suffered from early abuse and/or neglect often have a combination of psychological problems and neurological deficits. Many are diagnosed with a learning disability.[24]

Second-year Development Briefly Explored

The major task of the second year of life is for the child to learn "Basic German Shepherd." Children learn to obey "Come, sit, go, no, stay" messages from loving authority figures, and to take "no" for an answer. In other words, to accept control and authority. It is only this ability to respond lovingly to the requests of others that allows parents to encourage and permit *autonomy* and *independence*, which are the goals of the second year of life.

A disobedient toddler who doesn't respond to his parent's requests, lives in an anxiety-filled world where he is the boss; a world where limits are uncertain, and where parental frustration mirrors the toddler's anxiety. Knowing instinctively that he is unable to control and take good care of himself, he feels unsafe and threatened by others. Not knowing who, if anyone, can be trusted, he relies on his impulses to govern his behavior. Weighted down by stress and emotion, the child is generally slow to learn, impulsive, has no boundaries, and appears hyperactive.

Thus, the "normal" first year with its foundation of basic trust, and a "normal" second year with its essential elements of control, limits, and rules which the child must internalize, are essential for the development of a child who can focus, learn, and interact normally with others. At the end of this time, if all goes well, the foundation for socialization, productivity, and civilization is set. The seeds of responsibility and respect have been planted.

Poor experiences in the first two years may be at the root of many problems faced by our schools today. These problems include learning disabilities, behavioral disorders, ADD or ADHD, and to a lesser extent many control issues, impulsivity and attention problems, and motivational deficits. Input very much equals output during these years, and it behooves us to look closely at the quality and consistency of input our children receive long before they enter Head Start or other types of early childhood programs.

Many such children live in poverty-stricken neighborhoods where poverty erroneously gets the blame for the dysfunction in the family and the disability in the child. In our fairly extensive experience with impoverished parents, we have seldom found a lack of monetary resources to be the primary problem. These families are *socially* impoverished, and the financial poverty that is so easily recognized and measured is merely a secondary problem. It arises from the parent's own inability to focus and sustain attention, think causally, take responsibility, and maintain lasting reciprocal or loving relationships. It is a generational cycle that is being repeated in the child.

2

Appearance and Demeanor of Disturbed Children

Children who come from either domestic violence settings or community violence settings survive by becoming *hypervigilant* and *hyperreactive*. They must constantly scan the environment, looking for potential danger, and feel as if they must be ready to act in an instant to avoid or defuse situations that threaten their survival. Their "fight or flight" reflex is overdeveloped and their ability to trust is underdeveloped. They pay much more attention to nonverbal signals than to words. Words lie. Actions seldom do. In order to survive, these children learn at a very early age to act *before* they are acted upon. These behaviors are not adaptive for the normal home or school situation, and can cause myriad problems for adoptive and foster parents.[25]

Brad's mother was a cocaine addict who funded her habit by engaging in prostitution and small scale drug pushing. Her circle of "friends" included a heroine-addicted pimp and several big time drug dealers, who often dealt with customers by "beating the s—t out of them" when they didn't pay on time. It was not unusual for Brad to see or hear his mother being treated in a similar fashion for not turning enough tricks to pay her pimp what he felt he deserved for a night's work. Brad witnessed much of this "back alley consequencing" in person, and it became a normal part of his life, since it often took place in his own home. He had no other frame of reference or role model. He finally came to the attention of social workers when a shoot-out occurred in which Brad witnessed one of the drug dealers fire a pistol shot into the head of a "client" at his kitchen table. He had been watching TV in an adjoining room and took cover under the coffee table, a place of protection from which he also had a clear view of the action. Brad was six years old at the time. He was taken into state custody and placed in a foster home. He brought with him the things he had learned at home. After several foster placements and a stint in a residential treatment center, where he was the youngest by far of all the residents, the social workers involved felt he needed "permanency." He was placed in an adoptive home with a family who felt that love was the key to undoing the damage his past had inflicted upon him. His adoptive family and his therapists worked very hard to erase the effects of his violent past, and for a time seemed to succeed. Then in adolescence Brad became violent toward his adoptive mother and began running away from home. He became involved in drug use and violently assaulted a much younger child. Brad suddenly found himself back in the "system," this time as a juvenile offender. After all the efforts of his adoptive family and community, it appeared as if he was going to follow in his mother's footsteps anyway. His adoptive parents alternate between wondering if there was something else they should have done, or could have done better, and feeling sad and resentful of the time and emotional investment they made in him.

Qualities of Children Exposed to Violence Early in Life

It is estimated that as many as 80 percent of the children in out-of-home placement today have been physically abused or exposed to domestic or environmental violence.[26] Children who witness domestic violence display various emotional, physical, and behavioral disturbances. Their problems are similar to those of physically abused children.

Witnessing parental abuse produces feelings of anger, fear, guilt, shame, confusion, and helplessness. When the community fails to offer protection and support, children also feel undervalued and worthless.

Children may express these emotions as:

- Withdrawal

- Low self-esteem

- Nightmares

- Regressive behavior

- Aggression against peers, family members, and property

In addition, child witnesses of domestic violence often suffer physical problems, such as bedwetting, insomnia, colds, and diarrhea.

Children often suffer developmental delays in verbal, cognitive, and motor abilities when they live in homes with domestic violence. Learning disabilities are common. Children older than five or six tend to identify with the aggressor and lose respect for the victim. They learn to equate anger with violence and believe that violence is justified.

There is evidence that child witnesses of domestic violence carry violent and violence-tolerant roles into their own intimate relationships. Domination is viewed as the appropriate role for men and subordination the role for women.[27]

Some qualities of children exposed to environmental violence are:

- Difficulty sleeping
- Clinging behavior
- Constant questioning, or none at all
- Hyperactivity
- Hyper-vigilance and watchfulness
- Acts first-thinks last (impulsive)
- Aggressiveness
- Mistrust
- Difficulty concentrating
- Sneakiness
- Tendency to be overly secretive
- Hypersensitivity or hyposensitivity to pain
- Anger
- Fear
- Inability to express needs
- Inability to allow others to take care of them
- Inability to show pain or illness
- Attempts to meet own needs inappropriately for age
- Lack of empathy[28]

Attachment Problems

Attachment disorder is an increasingly recognized diagnosis that applies to many children who have suffered early neglect and/or abuse. Because such a large number of special needs children come from this type of background, Reactive Attachment Disorder of Early Childhood, as it is officially listed in the American Psychiatric Association's *Diagnostic and Statistical Manual (DSM IV)*, is overrepresented among this group of children. Although there are still a few therapists who feel the diagnosis should be rare, and fewer still who doubt its validity, thousands of adoptive parents, and the therapists who work directly with them and their disturbed children, have no doubts about the reality. Attachment disorder is a physical and emotional impairment that forces children to sabotage intimacy in relationships. They will not allow others to get too close to them. Caretaking and loving adults are not associated with love and affection in the child's nervous system, but rather, through thousands of repetitions of neglect or abuse, are associated with pain, fear and anger. Because the children lack the ability to love and trust they often have one or more of the following problems.

Severe Control Issues

No one would voluntarily follow the directions of another if they thought the other could not be trusted. If the world is an unsafe place, and *it* cannot be trusted, one would have to control just about everything and everyone to feel secure and safe. Some children go so far as to try to control their own bodily functions by such means as retaining stools until they have a bowel impaction. They will not be ruled by their own bodies' rhythms. They will control *everything* and *everyone*.

Low Self-esteem

Low self-esteem may or may not be evident. These children go through life feeling like victims, which in most cases they were at one time. Because they manipulate others and have little feeling or concern for others, they have poor peer relationships with children who know them well. On the other hand, they can be charming and attractive to newcomers. This lack of long-term friends bothers some children more than others. They have trouble accepting praise, and may be unable to feel deserving of good things, because inside they feel fraudulent and worthless. They may sabotage the efforts of adults who try to provide those things, thus recreating the cycle of deprivation and rejection they are used to.

Anger

Anger and rage attacks are often frequent and occur with minimal provocation as the child subconsciously feels hopeless, helpless, and angry, feeling that others are uncaring and untrustworthy. They feel victimized, blame others, and want to "get back" at them. They may incorrectly label their anger as sadness, or may try to get others to express the deep rage they feel inside but are unable or afraid to express themselves. Often, when they "push someone's buttons" until that person explodes in anger, they look smug or satisfied and may seem temporarily relieved.

Delayed Emotional Development

These children didn't get their early needs met appropriately, and didn't get the thousands of positive responses an infant needs for normal development. At age two, children need reasonable limits. At three, they internalize those limits and their role models. Children deprived of these basics are eventually going to have to redo their early stages or remain locked up in them as adults.

Negative Attitude

The child's relentless negative attitudes wear the parents down. When parents talk of being drained of energy, they are often most exhausted by the ubiquitous, relentless, and grinding nature of the problem.

Signs and Symptoms of Attachment Disorder

- Inability to give and receive affection in a real way; lack of eye contact on parental terms; indiscriminate affection with strangers

- Marked control problems; extreme defiance and anger

- Tendency to be destructive to self, others, animals, and material things; accident-prone

- Tendency to be manipulative and superficially charming

- Stealing

- Hoarding or gorging food

- Preoccupation with fire or gore

- Lack of impulse control and cause and effect thinking

- Learning and speech disorders

- Lack of conscience

- Tendency to lie about the obvious

- Poor peer relationships

- Persistent nonsense questions and incessant chatter

- Tendency to be inappropriately demanding and clingy

- Parents appear hostile and angry[29]

Daniel A. Hughes is a therapist in Waterville, Maine who specializes in treating children with attachment problems.

Many of his clients are foster children. In his book, *Facilitating Developmental Attachment,* (Jason Aronson Inc., 1997) he notes:

▟▌ Because the poorly attached child has had a tragic personal history, he most likely takes pleasure in, strives for, or strives to avoid, many things which have little or no value to another child. A closely attached child may take pleasure in pleasing his parents, while a poorly attached child may take pleasure in upsetting his parents. A closely attached child may work hard to get a gift; the poorly attached child may become anxious when given something and work to sabotage receiving the gift. Common incentives for 'good behavior' may have little impact on the poorly attached child. Also, a positive incentive may be mildly desirable to the child, but the act of opposing and frustrating his parents may have an even higher incentive value.[30]   ▟▌

Newly adopted children cannot be expected to have an attachment to their new parents, and most adoptive parents do not expect this immediately. After all, they are virtually strangers to each other. But most parents expect that, given time and loving interaction, the children will develop trust in them and a reciprocal relationship based on mutual caring will develop. Many families express distress over the baffling behaviors children with attachment problems display, and the fact that the child seems neither to want anything from them nor to give anything back. Parenting these children is a challenge, as parents try to remember that ordinary reinforcers are meaningless or undesirable to these children.

Hughes goes on to list some examples of what actually may be positive incentives for the poorly attached child:

• Being in control of the feelings and behaviors of others

- Engaging in and winning power struggles

- Saying "No!"

- Causing emotional and physical pain to others

- Maintaining a negative self-concept

- Needing no one

- Avoiding emotional engagements with others

- Avoiding experiences of mutual fun and laughter

- Avoiding having to ask for favors and help

- Avoiding being praised for actions

- Avoiding feeling loved and special to someone[31]

These factors make poorly attached children highly resistant to traditional behavioral and therapeutic interventions.

Children with attachment disorder are extremely sneaky and manipulative. Their cleverness in these areas often seems to exceed their cognitive functioning abilities in other areas. In addition, they often present themselves quite differently to outsiders than they do to family members, especially parents, and even more especially, mothers. The press for intimacy in a family is more than the children can bear, and they often do anything they can to avoid closeness and cooperation. They make themselves as oppositional and unlikeable as possible in the hopes of keeping family members at a distance. This often causes problems for parents who have a great deal of trouble explaining why they respond to the child the way they do. When teachers, neighbors, friends and the like see children who exhibit charm, trustworthiness, an eagerness to please, and then observe parents who are seemingly too strict or are exhibiting negative emotions about the children, they are likely to believe that the children are what they seem and that it is the parents who have problems. The rule of thumb when dealing with an unattached child in the classroom or elsewhere, is

Believe the parents, not the child.

It is true that when parents make emotionally healthy children "good and mad" they are usually wrong. The converse is true with a disturbed child. When parents make them "good and mad" they are usually right! This is particularly true with attachment disordered children. A wise teacher will recognize this and stay in close communication with parents to give the children the message that all of the adults in their life are on the same page.

How Old Is the Child, Really?

Children are usually defined by how they are "packaged"— by their *chronological* age. But many special needs children have a very different *psychological* age. There are children who are packaged as teens, but are really toddlers in terms of emotional development and maturity. The disparity between appearance and psychological age may cause older children to sometimes appear low-functioning, and younger children to appear especially bright. Adaptive and survival skills developed in early years often make these very small children take on a facade of maturity. They may act parentified or seem advanced in maturity by having been forced to take on those roles with younger siblings in the absence (physical or psychological) of their moms and dads. Although they look and act mature, their developmental needs have not been met and there are usually large holes in their emotional and psychological makeups that must be filled if they are to function as healthy adults.

When a child's psychological age is out of synch with his chronological age, predictable patterns of problems exist at specific stages of life. An especially volatile time is late adolescence, ages 16 to 18. At age 16, the average child has become ready to drive, not only signifying a readiness for responsibility involving the life and limb of others, but symbolically indicating a readiness for emancipation. A child who is emotionally locked in early to mid-childhood is still very dependent on adult decisions and subconsciously knows he is not ready to go out into the world on his own. A child who has never completely attached to his parents cannot begin to detach in an age-appropriate way. Internal panic ensues, and this manifests in all kinds of outrageous and dangerous behavior. Anger, aggression, and attachment issues that may have gone temporarily underground or appeared "cured" resurface.

Common behaviors at this time include

- Running away or prematurely leaving home

- Drug and alcohol abuse

- Truancy

- Falsely accusing adoptive parents of abuse

- Delinquency

- School failure

- Violent or aggressive behavior towards self, family members, and others

It is often at this point that parents feel most discouraged and hopeless. In a short time their child will legally become an adult. Many report feeling that all of their efforts have been for naught. The child appeared to be doing well, and then, disaster strikes—again. One mother wrote,

███ You know, I wonder sometimes if placing these kids in families is not just a giant cop-out by the system/society, etc. We 'hide' them in families, expecting the families to work the miracles or at the very least keep them out of public trouble. When they do get into trouble, which they inevitably do, the family is blamed. When the family looks for help, there is none. Your problem—your dime.

One of the Ellingson's sons—the one who was doing well, not the one who was so obviously disturbed, became violent in January. They had to call the police. The police admitted him to the hospital, who could only keep him three days. After three days the insurance would not allow him to remain under that kind of admission, so some medications were given and David was sent home. The pattern repeated until Mr. Ellingson said they no longer felt safe with David in the home. Nobody would keep him long enough to help him. He didn't 'fit' anywhere. He was too violent and destructive to be at home.

So the next time he was taken in by the police, they refused to go get him. The police informed them that if they did not pick him up, they were guilty of abandonment. To make a long story short, a CHPS [child in need of protective services] hearing was held and David was taken from the Ellingsons by the county. The ironic thing here is, the hearing should have been called 'parents in need of protective services.' *They* are the ones who need protection, not the kid! So David is now a foster kid—again—in a group home with a bunch of other unmanageable kids. He is 16. The county will now initiate stopgap measures and dink around with him until he turns 18 and then turn him loose.

Brian and Carol Ellingson are pretty upset, to say the least. Brian is hoping that David will become like the prodigal son, realize how good he had it at home, and mend his ways. I doubt it. David *did* know how good he had it at home. This is not about that at all. These kids are mentally ill. David can no more control this than a schizophrenic can control his episodes of craziness. That is my take on it, anyway. They do have issues and behaviors that they *can* control, and those we must provide training for.

But some of it is not within their ability to do, it seems. Every developmental stage seems to bring about a reoccurrence of their problems. I am hearing all too often about these kids who at age sixteen or seventeen blow right out of the water. Kids who look 'cured' or 'normal' for years suddenly knock the rug right out from under their parents. It comes as a complete shock. You have to wonder, are we doing any good?

Outcome studies should take this into consideration. It ain't over til it's over. And that might be at about age 40! Look at Kristy Waters, the Grove kids, the Ellingson's son. That's three in my immediate circle of friends. I know there must be countless others in families all over the country. ▰▰

Many children, because of neglect, deprivation, or intrauterine exposure to toxins, are physically small for their age. One of the most common results of fetal alcohol syndrome is short stature and slowed growth. Most FAS/FAE persons remain very small, even as adults, regardless of nutritional input. Children who have suffered early nutritional deficits or severe emotional trauma may take time to catch up to normal size for their age. And all children who have experienced early neglect or dysfunctional environments will have developmental lags.

Some children are both small for their age and psychologically immature.

▰▰ On Amy's sixteenth birthday, she walked around the house and said, several times, 'I can't be sixteen. This all must be a mistake. I know I'm a lot younger.' And then she asked me, in all seriousness, 'Mom, could they have gotten my birth certificate messed up? I can't be sixteen. I don't feel sixteen, I don't know how to act sixteen.' And I thought to myself, 'Well, her recognition of that is some indication that there might be light at the end of the tunnel. She really is growing up.' Maybe it was her own recognition of her psychological age that allowed us so easily to put off her driving until she was eighteen.

In many cases, parents can come up with creative strategies to allow children to act their emotional rather than chronological age. Kids who have missed out on an important developmental stage need safe and appropriate ways to make it up. We all know adults who don't act their age at times. When their lives are examined, it is often found that they are playing out something they missed or didn't get enough of at an early developmental stage.

Often physically small and developmentally young children are happier and do better academically when placed in a lower age/grade situation. School systems are frequently loath to retain children, because "retention doesn't help the problem." For many children, that's absolutely true. But when the problem is caused by developmental immaturity that may, with time, catch up to the norm, the situation can be enormously helped by retention in a regular classroom setting. In spite of this, retention may be hard to carry out, as many school systems prefer placing children in special education classrooms, often with disturbed or learning disordered children, instead of simply holding them back a grade or two. (Remember, most districts receive additional funding for special education students.) Many an eight-year-old in a regular first grade classroom has been able to cope better and acted closer to 'normal' than he or she would have acted in a third grade special education classroom while being mainstreamed into regular classes for part of the day. Flexible thinking and judgments made on a case-by-case basis are essential to making educational decisions that meet children's best interest. Parental involvement and support are extremely important. Parents should not be afraid to advocate for their children and insist on programs that meet thier needs rather than the school or school district's. Many schools will agree to an unconventional program on a trial basis if they are given an "out" if it doesn't seem to be working for them. The key to working with schools (or anyone for that matter) is, as well-known educator and speaker Jim Fay likes to tell his audiences, "You can't make someone mad and sell them something at the same time."[32]

> Joyce had repeated kindergarten and first grade before we adopted her at age eight. But she had such a hard time in every class that we decided to talk her into repeating fifth grade. It was a slightly hard decision because she would be two years behind. Not that she failed fifth, but school was becoming such a stretch for her academically, and she had few friends because of her immature behavior. About three months into the second year of fifth, which was, by the way, her happiest school year ever, she came home crying with happiness. 'Today I got the top feather award and I never thought that would happen to me.' Everyone deserves to be 'top feather' sometime in their lives!

At age ten, an additional year in a grade will seem far more crucial than it will at age 30. It can mean the difference between years of struggle and not "fitting in" and being able to make normal progress, albeit at a slower pace. It might help some children feel successful enough to remain in school and graduate instead of dropping out as a "failure."

Flexibility is a *big* key to success with special needs children. They may continue to develop two or three years behind their peers, and always fit better with the younger kids. They may not be ready to drive at age 16, but may be at age 19. They may not go through the physical changes of puberty on time, or they may experience them earlier than normal. Fetal alcohol syndrome children often have early hormonal surges and experience premature puberty. For these children, families may need to find temporary out-of-home placement, since their sexual and aggressive behaviors can become so inappropriate, and their ability to control them so poor, that they become dangers to themselves and others. The important thing to remember is that as the child progresses through each stage, the plan can be altered or changed. We are seldom locked into a particular course of action for a lifetime. If it becomes apparent that something is not working well, families can regroup and look for alternatives. When thinking through new strategies and approaches, it may be helpful to ask, "What's the worst that can happen?" If the "worst" is simply having to find a different solution, what have you got to lose by trying?

// I wish we could put training wheels on the car, and only let him drive it in the driveway, like we did when he was learning to ride a bike. That's what he needs—developmental crutches to help ease him into the next age. Extra practice time in an extra safe environment. But since that isn't practical, all we can do is accept that he just isn't ready to move on yet, and help him fit in where he's at. He's become a master of the public transportation system. He can find his way just about anywhere on the city bus. And he knows who and how to call if he gets lost. We're proud of him and he is proud of his abilities. *//*

Are Adopted Kids *Really* Different?

Adopted kids are "different" from other children in some predictable ways. Some are more different than others. The degree to which these differences affect the children's lives varies from the barely significant to lifelong, life-threatening complications. In this book, we concentrate primarily on children who have moderate to severe difficulties related to adoption and events that lead up to adoption.

When we first began researching this book, we knew that a certain percentage of adoptive families had serious and disruptive difficulties raising their adopted children. What we were not prepared for was the reaction we received when people got wind of the fact that we were preparing to go public with this information. Because of our notoriety in the adoption community, word spread fairly quickly. Suddenly people were phoning, cornering us after workshops, writing us letters and e-mail, to tell us their adoption stories. Even more surprising were the strangers who told us their stories in airports and stores, almost anywhere we might be overheard talking about adoption. An adoptive father literally popped up out of his United Airlines seat when he overheard us talking about the book on a flight to Spokane, Washington. "Been there, done that!" he shouted, and went on to tell us of his personal experience with a very disturbed child. Many of these stories were whispered or relayed in hushed, secretive voices as if the topic were taboo or forbidden. Adoption is supposed to *save* children. Adoptive parents are supposed to *heal* them. Anything less is failure. That is the ideal, of course, but often not a possibility. It seems a pervasive attitude that when things go wrong, someone should be ashamed. That someone is usually the adoptive parent.

Almost everyone, it seemed, knew *someone* who had suffered the loss of the dream. Why, we wonder, do families hide these truths from each other and the world? If we as adoption professionals were unaware of the magnitude of the problem, we realized most others would be too, including the families who struggle with children and feel like they are the only ones. The isolation and secrecy surrounding this topic is disturbing and may do more damage to families than any other single factor.

It's time to come out of the closet with this information, face it squarely, and find ways to deal with it that *will* heal children, or at least prevent further damage to them and their families. Hiding from it is clearly not working. The problem is growing bigger each year.[33]

For any and all children, adoption is second best. As adoptive parents, we may tend to wish this were not so. Yet if we are honest we know that ideally children are raised by healthy and loving birth parents who nurture them and provide for their physical, material, educational and emotional needs. Anything else is, simply and honestly, second best.

Admitting this does not diminish the importance of adoptive parents to their children, nor does it reflect on the parents' character, the quality of life they provide for their children, or the depth of their love, or the love the children feel for them. Adopted children are generally very lucky to have parents of the highest quality who are deeply caring, loving, and committed to their best interest. They are *not* lucky, however, to have been born into circumstances that would require them to be adopted in the first place. Those circumstances make them "different" from the get-go.

That the fact of being adopted plays an important role in children's lives is often overlooked or denied by adoptive parents. Yet time and again adoptees tell us it does. Researchers Ruth McRoy and Harold Grotevant studied the role adoption plays in the lives of a clinical sample of adoptees. In an article detailing their findings, one telling paragraph quoted adoptive parents who said, of their adopted daughter, that they "didn't realize that she took the fact that she was adopted more to heart than we expected. It wasn't a big deal to us." But it was to their daughter.[34]

The fact of adoption complicates a child's development. Regardless of special needs, adoption sometimes

- Carries a societal stigma that is a throwback to the days when "illegitimacy" was a term used to judge a person's worth.

- Causes problems for the child in school, such as teasing, difficulty dealing with projects about family history or genetics, and so on.

- Causes children to wonder about their birth families and perhaps question if they might somehow be "damaged goods."

- Causes children to long for their birth families.

- Causes children to idealize their birth families and imagine that life would be much better if they could "only live with my real mom."

- Brings up issues of abandonment and loss at each developmental stage.

- Negatively affects self-esteem.

- Creates insecurity and difficulty trusting in relationships.

Although each of these things can be the source of considerable difficulty for adoptees and their families, they are usually self-limiting. There is much literature available on these topics, and agencies usually prepare families for their eventuality prior to adoption.

There are some differences related to adoption that can predispose the children to more serious problems, and for which families are not usually prepared.[35]

Do Adoptive Families Have More Problems?

All families have problems at times. Adoptive families may have no more or less than others, but the problems they do have may be unique to adoption, or to the special needs of their children. They may be especially intense, or time and energy consuming. And they may last the lifetime of the child. Because of the unique nature of the problems a special needs child brings into the home, there are often fewer support systems available to the family.

When children are made to wander from one environment to another, they may cease to identify with any set of substitute parents. Resentment toward the adults who have disappointed them in the past makes them adopt the attitude of not caring for anybody, or of making the new parent the scapegoat for the shortcomings of the former one.[36]

Sometimes simply realizing that there are common problems associated with parenting special needs children can help.

Areas families may find unique and problematic include the following:

- Accurately identifying the children's particular needs

- Determining appropriate treatment

- Finding professionals or support persons who understand the problem

- Finding and financing services

- Dealing with the needs of other family members while simultaneously meeting the needs of disabled or dysfunctional children

- Finding respite care or babysitters who can meet the children's needs

- Integrating the family into the community

- Dealing with prejudice or stereotyping

- Lack of autonomy or empowerment prior to finalization

- Negotiating the legal system

- Making educational plans for the children

- Working with professionals who do not understand the children's or the parents' needs

- Helping the children deal with adoption-related issues at each developmental stage

- Lack of support or understanding within the extended family or social circle

- Unrealistic expectations of themselves or the children

- Dealing with blame for children's problems

- Financial burdens associated with children's special needs

- Adjustments to home environment and family routines to accommodate childrens' special needs

- "Goodness of fit" issues

- Out-of-home placements

- Incomplete or unavailable records and/or medical history

- Misleading documents

Simple things often take on a complexity that would be funny if they were not such a cause of stress and distress to adoptive families. Take this mother's story, for example:

▐▐ I took Jacob down to the local elementary school to register him for kindergarten. We had a certified copy of his birth certificate with us—his amended birth certificate that is. You see, Jason is adopted, and when his adoption was finalized, his original birth certificate was destroyed and replaced with one that indicates that my husband and I are his 'real' parents. We were so surprised when it came in the mail. There on the 'mother' line was my name, and the hospital he was born in and some strange doctor's name. I've never even been to that city! Nothing on the certificate indicates that this was an adoption. As a matter of fact, it states that everything is true and accurate and is sealed by the state seal to prove its authenticity. So the school made a photocopy to put with Jason's record. A simple thing, right? Except for one thing. Jason is a special needs child. He has fetal alcohol syndrome. That meant that his mother drank heavily enough when she was pregnant with him to severely damage his brain. The first time I came to school to volunteer as a field trip driver, I was turned down flat—with a glare. The teacher was almost rude to me the few times I tried to talk to her about Jason's limitations. And then it dawned on me. His mother!!! Brain damage from alcohol consumption. Get it? According to official school records, and the state seal, *I* am his mother! It's all those constant little things that make life so complicated with Jason. Someone who hasn't lived it would never understand how draining it can be. This practice of destroying adopted children's birth certificates and creating falsified documents to replace them is done in every state. Adoptive parents should obtain an original birth certificate for their children before finalization and keep it in a safe or safe deposit box. Once the amended certificate is issued, the original is no longer accessible.   ▟▟

In addition to all of the above, adoptive parents need to know that foster and special needs adoptive parents are more likely to be charged with child abuse than other parents.[37] (See chapter 11, "Coping with False Allegations of Child Abuse.")

Adoptive families may also struggle to balance their own expectations of adoption with those of others. They make unfair comparisons between their own difficulties and the "happily ever after" stories they have read about or watched on television.

▟▟ Sometimes when I read or hear about the happy experiences of adoptive families, I get that warm, 'goose-pimply' feeling. Words like 'great,' 'wonderful,' 'fantastic,' 'superb,' dance through my mind. Then I begin to wonder about those glowing reports. Are these people real? Does anyone else have problems and heartaches because of adoption? Does anyone understand what it is like not to live happily ever after?[38] ▮▮

How Much Can Be Expected from Treatment?

Many adoptive families seek professional treatment or therapy for their children with the hope of healing the damage done during pregnancy and the years prior to the adoption. In addition to monetary cost, which in many cases runs in the tens of thousands of dollars, families also spend tremendous amounts of energy participating in and supporting the children's therapy experiences. Can families determine what kind of results might be expected from therapy for any given child? Perhaps not without giving it a try. What families *can* do is guard against unrealistic expectations, and weigh carefully the amount of time, effort, and money that is spent against the odds of specific gain.

▮▮ Since 1964 American child care institutions have been living with the good-news, bad-news results of a highly respected research project known as the Cleveland Bellefaire follow-up study. The bad news is that the benefits of residential treatment tend not to last once a child returns to society. 'Success' is defined modestly, even by those who run what are considered to be among the best residential programs in the country. Many, like Woodland Hills, gauge success in terms of recidivism. Eighty percent of the 160 young people who graduated from its peer program from 1989 to 1991 were not sent to other institutions during the year following their release. One year later, David Kern says, is a reliable indicator of future success.[39] ▮▮

It is interesting to note that in the above example, 32 of the 160 children *did* return to institutional placement within one year following treatment. Of those who did not, we know nothing further. It is probably safe to say that problems continued to exist for many of these children, but were managed through outpatient therapy or some other means. It is also safe to assume, based on our experience, that a certain percentage eventually needed to be re-institutionalized at some point after the one year follow-up occurred.

Most long-term treatment institutions run time-limited programs. They are not designed to become permanent placement alternatives for a child to grow up in. Two years seems to be an average maximum stay for most residential programs. Insurance coverage often runs out long before treatment options. A few centers are more open-ended in their policies. The Villages, founded by Karl Menninger of the *Menninger* clinic family, is one such institution. On the average, children spend about two-and-one-half years there, although about ten percent stay from three to five years.[40]

As we discuss later in the book, by the time children have spent such a large portion of their lives living in institutional programs, they may have significant difficulty integrating their institutionalized lifestyle into a normal family environment.

For children whose behaviors can be managed in a home setting, outpatient therapy is the treatment option most parents chose. The biggest problem families report with this option is finding a therapist who understands not only adoption issues, but the other problems associated with early abuse and neglect, neurological and cognitive impairment, attachment issues, special needs family dynamics, and so on. The wrong therapist can quickly make problems worse. This all too frequently happens to special needs families who think that any reputable child psychologist will know how to help, or be able to refer them to someone who can. The Outside Resources section at the end of the book provides some therapeutic contacts we have found especially valuable.

When children are accurately diagnosed and treated by appropriately trained therapists, benefits usually result. However, these benefits may be of limited value and duration. Some children are so damaged by their pasts that effecting a cure is impossible. The best that can be done, oftentimes, is to improve temporarily the children's behaviors and relationships with others. Many will need continued care and follow-up to maintain the gains they make. As the children grow older, they may need to rework those gains in the context of new developmental stages and understanding of their issues. Behaviors change with age, so it makes sense that therapy will be needed to deal with these changes. Relationships with others also change as the child matures. New ways of relating must be learned, and old, dysfunctional ways unlearned or analyzed. A 1992 *Atlantic Monthly* article described a typical senario:

/// The Vogels have had periods of tranquility lasting several months. Harold has been to Weidiko twice, but only the second visit, a three-month stay in the winter program, helped. Other therapists' efforts were completely ineffective; Leichtman's successes are of limited duration. At twelve, Harold is moving away from tantrums and violence and is into stealing and fire setting; the prognosis is still uncertain.[41]
                                                                    ///

The long-term prognosis may not be as optimistic as we would like for many of these children. Although many families do eventually seek professional help, follow-up studies of *treated* adoptive children show them less likely to be living with their adoptive families.[42] Many still end up, at some time during adolescence if not before, in out-of-home placements such as residential treatment centers or psychiatric facilities.

Unless treatment realistically addresses the problems families are likely to experience after the children return home, and in doing so provides parents with training, tools, and follow-up support, gains made in treatment are likely to be short-lived.

Genetic Influences

There is increased attention being paid to the role genetics play in behavior. Genetics have been shown to contribute significantly to alcohol-related problems, severe mental disorders and suicide.[43] In addition, a review of several studies shows substantial evidence that "heritable factors for antisocial personality disorders and criminality exist."[44]

The majority of studies are conclusive about the increased proportion of psychological problems shown by adopted children. Early environment and "fragile" genetics are known to play pivotal roles in behavior, and both appear frequently in children free for adoption. Although there are some experts who would like to say that IQ is a cultural artifact, the fact is, IQ is mainly a product of the genes. Among adoptees attending a children's mental health center, there was a greater number of professional-level fathers. In comparison with the non-adopted group, however, significantly more males in the adopted group scored low on verbal IQ on a Wechsler Intelligence Scale.[45]

It is now widely accepted by most professionals that genetics plays a strong role in:

- Predisposition to addictions

- Temperament (outlook, satisfaction with life, happiness)

- Certain medical conditions such as diabetes, some types of cancer, heart disease, and so on

- Rare genetic disorders such as hemophilia, Tay-sachs, and fragile x syndrome

- Schizophrenia

- Personality disorders

- Attention deficit disorder

- Psychotic disorders

- Hyperactivity

- Depression

- Antisocial behavior

- Cognitive functioning

- Physical characteristics and metabolism

- Autism

- Dyslexia

- Conduct disorders

- Tourette's syndrome

- Criminality

- Obsessive compulsive disorder[46,47,48,49,50]

Increasingly, genetic makeup is believed to control an individual's "set point for happiness" and general outlook on life. Some of us are predisposed to be sunny and resilient, others sullen and angry. Some are prone to reflection and thought, others to impulsiveness and reactivity. Some are active, others nearly inert. Curiosity and drive are to some extent part of our temperamental makeup, and are strongly influenced by genetics.[51]

Happiness, then, seems to be largely determined by genes, not by outside reality, thus limiting the effect that environment can have on a person's disposition and response to events.[52]

Psychological and Behavioral Disorders

Those adopted children with special needs who are most difficult to parent are those with severe emotional and behavioral problems, attachment disorder, and mental illness. Contrary to popular misconceptions, they are no more likely to come from the American foster care system than from foreign orphanages.[53]

The term "mental illness" encompasses a wide range of meanings. It includes everything from full-blown psychiatric illness to points on a continuum of well-being and satisfaction with life. It may include such factors as self-esteem or the ability to adjust to change.[54] There are, indeed, many more adoptees receiving mental health services than would be expected by their proportion of the population; these tend to be youngsters rather than adults, and the phenomenon can be explained by factors other than psychiatric vulnerability due to adoption.[55]

A Wisconsin study of children in foster care, encompassing 42 counties and 147 respondents, reported that 47 percent of the youth had received or were presently receiving mental health services in their current placements.[56] This same study indicated that 76 percent of youth surveyed had experienced some form of maltreatment prior to placement. Most common was neglect, followed closely by physical abuse. Sexual abuse was least common, reported by 31 percent. All three of these factors are strong predictors of psychological problems as well as criminality.

Many studies show that adopted children are more likely to manifest *behavior* problems than non-adopted youth.[57,58]

There is some indication that gender influences the direction of problems that develop due to early life experience. A 1983 study done in Toronto with 104 adopted children ages 8–20 found that adopted boys demonstrated a significantly increased risk of psychiatric disorder in comparison with non-adopted boys.[59] A similar study reported in 1992 found adoption to be a significant marker for psychiatric disorder among boys, and a marker for substance abuse among girls.[60]

Other well controlled and documented studies yield the following results:

1. Out of 57 adopted children referred to an hospital outpatient program, a disproportionate number (47 percent) were diagnosed with conduct disorders.[61]

2. The types of disturbance shown by adopted children are more likely to be conduct-disordered than those shown by the birth-child control group.[62]

3. 80 percent of children waiting to be adopted in Minnesota have experienced physical abuse, chronic neglect, or sexual abuse.[63]

4. More than half of the children who have experienced physical abuse, chronic neglect, or sexual abuse are diagnosed with medical or physical disabilities.[64] (Estimated to be about 80 percent of the children awaiting adoption today.)[65]

5. Youth in foster care suffer considerably more psychological distress than is typical for their age group.[66]

6. A study of 290 birth children and 380 adopted children found a pattern of dysfunctional behavior in approximately one out of four adopted children that occurred with much greater intensity and frequency than in their non-adopted counterparts. The children studied were primarily adopted as newborns, with 87 percent being adopted by 180 days. This pattern included the following behaviors:

   • Rejection of authority

   • Lying

   • Cruelty to others

- Refusal to accept responsibility for consequences or actions
- School performance below ability
- Lack of long-term friends
- Manipulative behaviors
- Difficulty with eye contact
- Stealing
- Refusal to follow parental guidelines
- Self-control problems
- Inability to give or receive affection
- Self-destructive behavior
- Phoniness
- Problems with food
- Thoughts about fire, blood, or gore
- Superficial attraction to and friendliness with strangers
- Substance abuse
- Promiscuous sexual activity.[67]

This same study indicated that problematic behaviors tended to occur in clumps, with one child typically exhibiting several difficult-to-manage behaviors.[68]

Children who have been physically abused, battered, or beaten by caretakers or other adults in their environment, or mistreated by older siblings or children in a foster home, can be expected to suffer emotional and psychological repercussions. However, research shows children don't even have to be the direct victims of family abuse to be harmed. Repeated exposure to parental fighting can enmesh kids in a cycle of violence that sets them up to be victims and per-petrators of abuse later. They learn to equate anger with violence and believe that violence is justified.[69] Boys who observe their fathers abusing their mothers seem to be at extreme risk of using violence in their own homes as adults.[70]

Predictors of Criminality

Adoption as a factor in criminality has long been ignored. David Kirschner and Linda Nagel, in their pivotal study of adoption and catathymic violence, cite the following reasons for this omission:

// We believe there are two major reasons why adoption is neglected in these highly charged cases: the pervasive pat-tern of denial found in most dysfunctional adoptive fami-lies and the vocal opposition of the adoption establishment. Some parents deny that adoption is of any psychological significance to the adoptee, let alone of relevance to the commission of rageful acts of violence.[71]   *//*

Troubled adoptees may suffer from a combination of risk factors that include genetic predispositions, disrupted attachments or the failure to form attachments at all, physical, sexual or emotional abuse, neglect, exposure to toxins—all of the factors we have discussed so far in this volume. These factors make it easy to overlook the part that adoption itself plays in the child's pathology.

Even under the best of circumstances, when birth par-ents make an adoption plan for their children, or in open adoption situations, adopted children report feelings of rejection. Based upon the studies reviewed, parental rejection (actual or perceived) appears to be among the most powerful predictors of juvenile delinquency.[72]

As hard as we try to help children understand adoption from a rational and practical perspective, they still think like children. Most of the adult adoptees we have interviewed felt a sinking sense of rejection at one time or other during childhood and adolescence. There is a big difference between *knowing* and *feeling*. And human beings are notoriously emotion-driven.

Listening in on a conversation between two eight-year-old adoptees in an adoptee support group gives us an inside look at how children think about adoption:

Group leader: "Why do *you* think your birth mother didn't keep you? Didn't she love you?"

Tony (defensively): "That's not it. She did love me. My [adoptive] mom told me she loved me *very much*."

James (challenging): "Then how come she didn't keep you if she loved you so much, huh?"

Tony (quietly, hanging head): "Well, she was too young to raise a kid, and she had to finish school and she didn't have a job, so she wanted me to have a good life and she knew she couldn't give me one."

James: "Huh! If she *really* loved you, she woulda went on AFDC [aid to families and dependent children] and gotten her GED!"[73]

Neil Feinberg, a noted attachment therapist, tells of a young international adoptee who was role-playing a conversation with his birth mother in which he was telling her his feelings about being abandoned in a cardboard box on the steps of an orphanage. Angry and sobbing, he shouted, "I'd rather have *died* with you than have had to live this life."[74] Intellectually he understood that his birth mother literally saved his life by giving him up, probably with much anguish and that her "abandonment" was an act of pure unselfish love. Although his life in America was what most would consider ideal, his deep-rooted feelings of rejection and abandonment would not allow him to accept it.

Children who are physically abused, who experience violence as a way of life, are far more likely to react with violence themselves, violence that often leads to criminal charges. It is a learned response. This is easily understood and makes sense to most people. What can be difficult to determine is why a person who was not exposed to early life abuse, and has no previous history of violent behavior, would suddenly commit an outrageously violent and brutal act. This is illustrated by the case of Patrick, who, having never committed a violent act, suddenly and without warning bludgeoned his adoptive parents to death and set fire to their bodies.

The roots of seemingly unmotivated acts of violence, often murderous acts, are of interest to both mental health professionals and criminal justice experts. This type of violence is called "catathymic violence." It is a product of sudden rage, triggered by a precipitating act that is uniquely keyed to the individual's psychodynamics. Many instances of catathymic violence have been committed by adoptees. In New York alone, since 1986, there have been at least seven occurrences of adoptees murdering their adoptive parents. In addition to catathymic acts, many serial killers have also been adopted. Some of the more notorious are David Berkowitz (the Son of Sam); Kenneth Bianchi (the Hillside Strangler); Joseph Callinger (the Philadelphia Shoemaker); Charles Albright; and Gerald Eugene Spano. The suppressed rage that leads to these atrocious acts is deeply rooted in the children's pasts, in which adoption appears to play an important and complicated role.[75] Catathymic violence occurs in *only a very small percentage of extremely pathological cases.* We include them only as important indicators of the depth of distress that can lie buried in the subconscious of some adopted children.

3

Life in the Trenches

Now let's consider what it is really like to live with a disturbed child.

"It's the most difficult job in the world," psychiatrist Michael Katz says of parenting special needs children. It's rewarding to hear a professional say that. Often misunderstood by others—even professionals who work with special needs families—parents often believe that it is only other parents of disturbed children who can truly appreciate that they have "the most difficult job in the world."

This belief is certainly understandable! For the attitudes and behaviors of disturbed children are bizarre, and incomprehensible to outsiders unfamiliar with living and working with such kids. It is beyond the realm of most people's experience to imagine a deprived child who would not respond positively to love and an enriched environment.

Most people think that very young children in particular are extremely resilient, and have the capability to heal completely from whatever trauma they experienced in their early years. This leads to much misunderstanding and heartache for special needs families, and can become a serious roadblock to obtaining help for the child.

What are the behaviors and attitudes that are so baffling and upsetting in these kids—the sources of such serious misunderstanding?

- They may consistently break rules and push limits.

- They are openly defiant and disrespectful of authority.

- They often have negative attitudes and seem to enjoy playing the victim role.

- They act out their feelings instead of expressing them with words.

- They successfully draw others in the family into their own pathology.

- They misbehave in the usual ways, but with more than the usual intensity and duration.

- They are afraid to trust, and may forcefully or covertly reject others' love.

- They may inflict physical harm on members of the family or community.

- They may torture or kill family pets.

- They may steal from family members, lie to family members, and then lie about the family to others, in attempts to get parents into trouble.

- They may act charming and compliant outside the family to fool others into thinking their parents are crazy or abusive, or as a means of controlling or manipulating others.

- They may be destructive to their own or others' possessions and property.

- They may run away from home and aggressively fight any effort to prevent them from doing so.

- They may attempt suicide or be self-injurious, requiring 24-hour supervision (or they may injure themselves and tell others they were injured by their parents).

- They can be filled with rage and hate, and make every moment others are with them difficult and unpleasant.

- Anger and rage may be directed most intensely and sometimes exclusively toward maternal figures.

- They may refuse to participate willingly in family activities, and may try to prevent others from enjoying themselves.

- They may attempt to maintain control over everything and everyone.

- They may express displeasure or anger through bodily functions such as urinating or defecating in corners, closets, dresser drawers, and so on.

- They may react to simple requests with violence or rage.

- They will try (and for a time, almost always succeed) to encourage others to see the parents as the problem.

- They manipulate and triangulate, divide and conquer.[76]

Not all disturbed children will exhibit all of these traits, but they are so pervasive in this population that a good many children will exhibit several of them.

Since many of our kids display more "normal" behaviors outside the home, it is easy to imagine that their parents are exaggerating their difficulties for some reason. Perhaps they have a pathological need for sympathy or attention. Some parents have been accused of not liking or loving their adopted child. Not only is this not helpful, and may make the parents feel crazy (again), but this accusation also inflicts deep wounds on a loving parent's heart. "If I didn't love him, *why* would I live with these outrageous behaviors, and why would I keep looking for help?"

However, this *is* an honest list, as the hundreds of families we have interviewed will testify. These traits translate into specific behaviors that can be extremely difficult to manage over time.

Terry Peudo, age nine, has been diagnosed with an attachment disorder and has not bonded with his adopted family despite years of love, effort, and therapy.

When the Wallaces talk about Terry, they sit together, their bodies turned toward each other. They finish each other's sentences so often it's almost like talking to one person. Their eyes speak volumes of sadness.

To an outsider, the Wallace's parenting techniques might seem rigid or overprotective. Terry does not sit on the couch—he would urinate on the cushions if he did—but rather is seated on a plastic tablecloth spread on the carpet. When he dashes away, his parents call him back to keep him in their line of vision. Left unsupervised in the past, he drank a huge bottle of antiseptic mouthwash, used the sink spray to soak the wallpaper and pulled it into shreds, and clogged up the plumbing with washrags.

He has destroyed several of Nancy's beautiful old quilts, picking at each quilt until it fell apart. He picks at himself, causing small sores, and has pounded bruises on his arms which he then told his teacher were caused by his adoptive dad. Caught

> misbehaving, he lies in the face of the evidence. Reasoning with Terry doesn't work; rewarding good behavior is impossible since it is so hard to find any; mild corporal punishment has no effect. In fact, it seems to satisfy him in a smug way that worries his parents more than his behavior.

Parents of very disturbed kids frequently tell us that they feel unfairly judged and misunderstood by friends, family, and professionals, around one major issue: Is their child exhibiting aberrant behavior, or is it "just a normal childhood phase," or "one of those things all kids go through at their age"? They know their child is "different," and extraordinarily difficult to get along with and manage.

They say things like

▐▐ Nothing, absolutely *nothing* seems to work.

He can act so normal when he *wants* to. Why won't he do it at home?

Nobody seems to understand what it's like to live with him 24 hours a day.

I *know* all kids his age lie, but this is a *different* kind of lying. **▐▐**

And it *is* different, even though many families cannot explain why. They are well versed in normal behavior in children and know that something is seriously wrong with their child. They also know that others do not see what they see in the privacy of their relationship with him, which makes them feel crazy.

The four most usual factors that make the determining difference are:

Difference

1. Frequency— behavior occurs more frequently and consistently than normal

2. Duration—behavior lasts longer, by far, than the normal child's behavior

3. Intensity—behavior is angry, violent, destructive, and/or dangerous.

4. Motivation—behavior falls into the pathological realm of extreme control issues, extreme anger, intent to harm, and so on.

For example, all children lie at one time or other. But not all the time, and not when faced with evidence to the contrary. Many two-year-olds go through a period of having temper tantrums. But they do not last for eight hours, every day, and result in serious damage to persons or property. Most normal temper tantrums fizzle out as the child tires. A disturbed child may gain momentum and accelerate in an attempt to draw adults into his game and get his way. It's as if draining energy out of the adults in the environment, pours energy into the child.

Many children, especially little boys, go through a stage of urinating in places other than the toilet. But not at age 11, and not in mother's dresser drawers to punish her for asking him to dry the dishes. One mother told us that her 13-year-old foster daughter would wait until the parents had guests for dinner, and she knew they were seated at the dining room table enjoying their meal. Then, down the dining room window would come a stream of urine, as the daughter held herself out her bedroom window, which was directly above the dining room, and urinated down the side of the house.

All children will at times attempt to control through behavior, but not control *everyone* and *everything all the time* as if their very lives depended on it. And finally, and perhaps most importantly, most children respond in a reasonable length of time to conventional discipline methods. Very disturbed children do not.

One would have a hard time finding a clinician more knowledgeable about extreme situations than Hugh M. Leichtman, the administrative director of Wediko Children's Services in Boston. Leichtman warns that although a child's temperament and constitution affect the way trauma will be played out, many parents who adopt traumatized children are *essentially turning their homes into a therapeutic milieu*. In essence, the parents become unpaid therapists in a pseudopsychiatric setting! Rearing these children requires a set of skills beyond those normally expected of parents, and parents should not expect their affection to be returned in the normal way. The children's multiple problems require a complicated, long-term treatment plan. Through case study, Liechtman details the not unusual situation in which a child had to be prescribed multiple medications over many years of individual outpatient psychotherapy, family-systems therapy, and residential treatment.[77] Parents of such children risk their own emotional and financial disaster against the chance that their children can heal. And in many cases, the odds are extremely poor. Marriages sometimes break up. The parents pay for services not funded by insurance or the government, and often lose considerable time from work. The children may need supervision until a fairly advanced age. Finding child care for a 14-year-old oppositional child with self-destructive tendencies and poor impulse control is nearly impossible for most families. Families are responsible for property damage costs incurred by the destructive child, or if the property is their own, may find repeated replacement expensive and demoralizing.

Many adoptive and foster parents have expressed surprise at the length of time the child tests them. Most expect and are prepared for a honeymoon period to occur for a short time after placement. Few are prepared for the fact that every time the child goes through a new developmental period, the testing often repeats. As one mom noted, "Same problem, new adventure." Why? The child's early trauma or deprivation influences each developmental stage as the child reformulates identity and coping capacities. "You have this undigested part of your life—you were traumatized. The scarring, the disconnection that comes with trauma, gets recycled as the child moves through the various life passages."[78]

Parents of disturbed kids are generally willing to share the intimate details of their family life with someone willing to accept and understand that they are doing the best they can to cope with an abnormal and difficult situation. We found families more than eager to share their experiences with others in the particular hope that families considering adopting one of these children would at least have some awareness of the potential difficulties they might face. Another hope, often expressed by families we spoke to, was that other parents would feel less hopeless and misunderstood if they knew that they are not alone in their experiences and feelings. That the behavior their children exhibit is normal given the circumstances of their early life, and not caused or exacerbated by something the parents are or are not doing.

So what does *normal* life look like for these special needs families?

A sibling group of three who had moderate problems with general out-of-control behavior in a foster home, arrive in their adoptive family and begin urinating and defecating in closets, corners, and dresser drawers whenever the parents set rules or impose limits. The family tries counseling, behavior modification techniques, and tolerance combined with lots of love, attention, and fun. The behavior continues and at times gets worse, particularly after periods of time when the child seems to be developing some closeness to the family, or after a fun family outing. The odor in the home become an embarrassment to the family who becomes isolated from friends and extended family. Grandparents say "this isn't normal, aren't you going to do something?" Nothing they try is working. The parents become angry and feel helpless and hopeless. They begin to feel like they do not even like their children, which brings on heaps of guilt. Therapists blame the parents for the children's reactions, citing parental anger and waning patience as the cause of the problem. Outsiders openly question the parents motives for adopting and their ability to parent so many children. The whole family feels crazy and trapped.

Jacob, adopted at age three from Bolivia, where he was living on the streets, had become an uncontrollable delinquent and chronic runaway by age 11. He told his adoptive parents that he hated them, and wanted nothing more than to return to his native country. He resented their bringing him to the United States, claiming he was happy in his native land and never asked them to adopt him. He refused to attend school or participate in therapy. As a last resort, and as a measure to keep him safe and out of trouble, he was placed in two locked residential treatment facilities. Neither could help him, or control him, and he managed to escape from both. A stay in a psychiatric unit at a well-known hospital resulted in a grim diagnosis but no effective treatment. He had become involved in theft and vandalism, and his parents were told that they were liable for the cost of damages as well as court costs when necessary. They were threatened with abandonment charges and possibly time in jail if they refused to let him return to their home. His last rampage cost them over $20,000. When this behavior did not win him the desired ticket to return to Bolivia, he became violent, threatening to harm family members and killing the family dog. Finally, with no better options available, at age 16, his adoptive family purchased him a one-way ticket to Bolivia and sadly bid him farewell, feeling like hopeless failures. They continued to support him by sending him money and arranging for an apartment for him in Bolivia. Six months later, after several brushes with Bolivian authorities, they were contacted and advised that they would be charged with criminal neglect of a child unless they returned him to the U.S. He was, after all, still a minor. The family felt like hostages; only in a hostage situation, the government will usually offer help and support, neither of which seemed forthcoming in this situation.

A large, previously successful adoptive family with nine children, several of them with special needs, adopted a seven-year-old child described by the placing agency as appearing to have "a little trouble trusting." In her first few weeks with the family, she appeared to have made a remarkably uneventful and smooth adjustment, and from everyone's point of view, had become well integrated into the family structure. She was charming, compliant, and played well with her new siblings. She seemed to respond to the love her new family offered, and was beginning to show sign of trusting them. Soon after her eighth birthday, a gala occasion celebrated with her first birthday party ever, she started to exhibit strong aggressive tendencies. She began hurting the other children, pushing them down stairs, opening a window and trying to force the two-year-old to jump out, stabbing her brother with a freshly sharpened pencil, and holding a pillow over the baby's face. Her adoptive parents felt that in order to protect the other children in the family they would have to place her out of their home, taking the chance of losing her trust and shaking her security. The alternative was to lock her in her room at night, which they felt was emotionally if not physically abusive, or provide 24-hour line-of-sight supervision, which was virtually impossible to provide unless they slept in shifts and sat guard duty outside her door at night. They considered putting alarms on her bedroom door, so they would hear if she was out of her room at night, but the agency supervising her placement had rules prohibiting this. (Adoptions are not final for six months in their state and the family was governed by foster care regulations until finalization.)

Steve was adopted when he was five years old. He was always a difficult child, but his acting out and behavior deteriorated badly at age 14. His family felt they had made significant progress with him only to find that as he matured, his gains seemed to disappear and be replaced by severe disorders of personality and behavior. He was diagnosed with post traumatic stress disorder (PTSD), borderline personality disorder (BPD), and major depression. The family felt he was attachment disordered, but could find no local professional trained to diagnose or treat it. He was taking several heavy-duty medications to keep his emotions and impulses in check, and although they seemed to help at times, they didn't ever help enough to make him stable, predictable, or controllable. His parents wondered if all of their parenting efforts had been wasted. They were shocked and resentful at a system that placed such a disturbed child in their home and now offered them no help. They felt they had been conned by a clever and manipulative child. Looking back, they could see many instances where he was compliant and cooperative only when he had something to gain. They wondered if his professed love for them was real, or part of that same clever con game. He didn't appear to be able to correctly identify his other feelings, and certainly couldn't express them appropriately. They became afraid that as he got even older, he would get heavily involved in substance abuse, which would only add to the list of problems, and certainly not contribute to his stability. Already they had found evidence of marijuana use in his room, and had to lock the liquor cabinet after discovering that he had watered down the liquor supply. His birth parents were substance abusers. Was he genetically programmed to repeat the mistakes of his parents? Was the generational cycle of abuse in fact impossible to break? His parents' dreams of giving him a chance at a better life were shattered.

Amanda, adopted at age three months, by a childless couple, had always been a rebellious and self-centered child. Highly controlling and oppositional, her parents found it hard to enjoy her growing-up years. Each new developmental stage was a struggle. She lied, stole money and jewelry from her mother, and by age 11 was sneaking out of the house late at night to meet boyfriends. At age 15 she ran away, and not just a few miles away to a friend's house. She was with her 19-year-old boyfriend who bought her an airline ticket and flew her to another state, where he had recently moved to find work. They were picked up twice by the authorities and the boyfriend charged with transporting a minor across state lines. Amanda was returned home at taxpayers' expense. She then stole the family van (the family filed charges), and drove it back to his house, 1200 miles away. The family was tempted to allow her to remain with the boyfriend, since they could see no practical way to prevent her from returning to him, and she made their lives so miserable when she was around. They were confused, upset, and afraid. They did not want to give up on their daughter. They loved her and wanted to help her, yet they could not force help on someone who didn't want it. And to make matters worse, their own parents were blaming them for being "too strict," and suggesting that maybe they just weren't cut out to be parents after all. Grandma even said "maybe that's why God *didn't* give you a child of your own." They wanted to argue that Amanda *was* their own in their hearts, but decided it was futile. Nobody understood. They were alone.

Hugh Liechtman, of Boston-based Wediko Children's Services recounts these details about his client Harold: Over a period of two years Harold's tantrums became so frequent that Antonia, his adoptive mother, couldn't play the piano; her wrists were constantly damaged, and they never had time to heal before the next episode. Harold was taken to a series of play therapists, whose offices he wrecked, with no positive effects. The therapists—who often said, "Harold, you must be very angry"—told the Vogels to develop Harold's self-esteem by giving him experiences that made him feel successful. "We followed their advice and things got worse and worse," Ted says. Antonia adds, "All this makes sense up to a point, but with his intelligence and the profoundness of his problems, he can keep avoiding the whole point of therapy. He'll just keep his secrets to himself and hang on to his disturbed behavior and wreck his own life—and yours while he's at it."

At twelve, Harold is moving away from tantrums and violence and into stealing and fire setting; the prognosis is uncertain. Still, the Vogels feel that Liechtman is the first therapist to grasp the problem, and that he has saved their family. "Kids like Harold are very difficult for even the most skilled of parents to manage and control," Liechtman says. "These people have admittance to St. Peter's gates already, and Harold will test them further.[79]

4

Coping with Feelings

It's amazing how one's perspective is forced to change when living with a very difficult child. Parents sometimes develop a macabre sense of humor that can be hard for others to interpret or understand. It can seem coarse, cruel, or uncaring, when in fact it is a necessary element to survival—a self-protective device—for many adoptive families. They come to expect the unexpected, and this lends an element of constant apprehension to daily life that can be very stressful. The only certain thing, they may feel, is that whatever happens next will *not* be good. They know they must cope with their feelings and respond to the needs of the child in unconventional ways, and that those efforts will be questioned and misunderstood, adding yet more stress to the situation. Ordinary child-rearing problems can seem trivial when faced with a murderous or suicidal child. Progress is measured in microsteps. Very small signs of recovery are celebrated as tremendous victories, provided the families are not too angry or burned out to recognize them and rejoice. Most impressive are the stamina and strength, the commitment and energy, of adoptive families who are beaten and battered emotionally, and sometimes physically, by the children they hoped would become a real part of their family. They give and love unconditionally, many times with little or no hope of acknowledgment or return. Many maintain their sense of humor, faith, and commitment under appallingly bleak conditions, sometimes at significant personal cost or cost to the family as a whole.

The negative emotions reported by so many parents of disturbed children are normal, predictable, healthy responses to stressful and traumatic circumstances. An Internet mailing list support group, consisting of adoptive parents of attachment disordered children, generated this collective list of emotions that the parents were *currently* experiencing. The parents felt

- Disgusted
- Trapped
- Crazy
- Bitter
- Overwhelmed
- Afraid
- Angry
- Victimized
- Sad
- Depressed
- Frustrated
- Exhausted
- Confused
- Guilty
- Encouraged
- Rageful
- Resentful
- Remorseful
- Stupid
- Used

- Hopeful
- Hopeless
- Lonely[80]

- Conned
- Deceived

Why the preponderance of negativity in this list? Are there no positives or rewards that provide balance and satisfaction in the lives of these parents? Of course there are, although they may be overshadowed at times by the very intrusive and overwhelming nature of the problems, and by parental exhaustion. Scores of books and articles have been written detailing the joys of adoption, and telling those stories that end with "and they all lived happily ever after." Most adoptive families have written their own imaginary scenarios about adoption rewards prior to adopting. We, on the other hand, have chosen to be honest about the fact that, along with the *joys* are also many *misfortunes*. We want to acknowledge that there are many hundreds of children who honestly never provide *any* of the expected rewards. These children are all too numerous in the special needs adoption world of today, so damaged by their pasts that they have little or nothing to "give back" to a family.

Yet many families, even after years of struggle and pain, continue to feel hopeful. Until every option is sought, every parenting strategy and therapeutic method exhausted, these parents continue to hope and to work. Families may report that they feel unloving, but they continue to *want* to love and to act in loving ways while facing enormous challenges and odds. The dream is alive in their hearts—the dream of finding the key to opening the hearts of their children to love. And this dream provides the impetus to continue, to struggle against the odds, to face and fight the demons. In this way, they maintain their sanity and commitment. In addition, families who report the greatest level of satisfaction and overall feeling of success have been able to make the paradigm shift we discuss in chapter 5 of this volume.

The parents who provided us with the list of emotions above are not giving up on their kids. They are not by nature joyless or depressed, but they do share the common ground of having to find joy in other aspects of their lives, and in things many others would find too tragic to bear. They work hard at finding help and hope, and have tremendous respect for others like them who struggle not only with their children, but with the misunderstanding of well-meaning outsiders who often, in ignorance, condemn them for their actions and feelings. They share the pain with each other, and in doing so it is diffused and made more tolerable. (See the Outside Resources section at the end of this book for a list of support groups.)

Families devote incredible amounts of energy, both emotional and physical, to helping their children heal, only to meet with roadblocks and resistance from the child, the community, and in some cases the professionals to whom they turn to for help. While these children sometimes appear to *want* love, their subconscious fears, early learned responses, and neurological differences do not allow them to accept it. Their fear of intimacy and inability to reciprocate causes them to push hard and then harder against loving parents who may believe that the cure lies in being more loving. The harder the parents try to force intimacy and relationships on the child, the harder the kids push them away. The more the parents do the right thing, the worse the child's behavior gets. Parenting such children can be overwhelming and exhausting, and at times physically dangerous.

Misdirected Rage

The adoptive mother often becomes the target of rage that would be more appropriately directed at the birth mother. Freud called this type of response *displacement*. The child may have never even known the birth mother. Nevertheless, because of a combination of genetics, intra-uterine events, and character, many adopted children have feelings of anger toward the birth mother.[81] While rageful toward the adoptive mother, it is interesting to note that when adult adoptees search for their birth parents, it is almost always the mother they search for first. They may later look for their birth dad, but it is the birth mother with whom they primarily wish to reconnect and resolve issues.[82]

At other times, the birth mother serves as a kind of fantasy or ideal mom, leading to further rejection of the adoptive mother. "My real mom wouldn't make me do chores." "My real mom wouldn't care if I got my nose pierced. She'd think it was cool!" "My real mom would let kids do whatever they want and give them lots of money." This is not necessarily an attempt at manipulation on the part of the adopted child. They may really believe it is so.

It is not unusual for a birth mother to promise a child in foster care that she will return for him when "I get my act together." In such cases, adoption is often the last thing the child wants, and she may feel kidnapped or held hostage by the foster family and later by the adoptive family. The adopted child begins to see the adoptive family as the source of separation from the all-loving and perfect birth parent. This can be very destructive to the adoptive family, and makes it impossible for the children to integrate and bond fully.

Permanency planning does not provide for such children. The Adoption and Safe Families Act of 1997 mandates that adoption is the ultimate goal for every child in foster placement.[83]

When such children are placed in an adoptive family where responsive intrafamilial love is expected, they are unable to give or receive it.

A foster mother whose 11-year-old foster son had been with her in long-term placement made the following observation:

// Jake just can't handle the idea of our adopting him. Every time the adoption gets close, he falls apart. And he says very clearly that he does not want to be part of any family. In our family, I call him 'my little personal assistant' and he loves it. It's only when I go into the 'son' routine that he absolutely can't handle it. He likes being a 'personal assistant.' **//**

From a social services perspective, however, this placement that worked for Jake was not allowed to continue, and he went on to an adoptive home which, of course, proved disruptive.

Anguished Notes Online

The Internet offers a valuable gathering place for parents to receive and give support to others struggling with similar issues. Families from all over the world can connect to others who understand and share their pain. And very often they report that shared pain is lessened pain. For families who were previously isolated from others like them, it is an emotional haven of understanding.

// In the six years that we have dealt with our boys it was mainly me that was their object of hate and revulsion. And of course, lots of times it would change the minute that my husband would come in the door. This is not to say that he never saw them acting out, but he was almost never the recipient of their anger and rejection. That is, until almost the end. Then, he began to get the same kind of behaviors pointed at him, and he began to see that it's almost impossible to not take it personally. In many ways, I can act somewhat dispassionate around that kind of behavior, but it *does hurt*, and lots of times I've 'run away' to the bathroom where I can lock the door, and just bawled my eyes out.[84]

Another mother writes with unflinching honesty:

◢◢ We moved from Florida to Oklahoma in January of 1994, five months after Terry came as a 7-year-old from an orphanage in Romania. Ten months after that, we added Christine, a 12-year-old from Ecuador. When I look back, I know that clearly I had no clue what was going on, as *no one in their right mind would screw up their family that effectively on purpose!* Brenton joined the family in 1989 as a 19-month-old, and he has been incredibly difficult from the beginning.

At one point, I am not sure of the exact time frame, I remember calling our adoption agency and describing our numerous problems and concerns about Terry, and the worker said, 'Find a therapist who knows about attachment disorder.'

A single adoptive mom I know with three adopted kids says she sleeps outside their bedroom door because they are so dangerous at night!

It takes years of living like this for it to really sink in. This is *not normal!* ◢◢

Yet another mom writes:

// The one I deal with is my daughter. I call her the ice princess. She is so cold to me it chills the whole house.

I have raised her six years (no contact from natural mom). I have involved her in numerous activities in the past. Lately I just co-exist in the house with her, but it is far from comfortable. She does not talk to me about anything, she does not include me in idle chit-chat, she does not listen to me when I try and talk with her, and never responds. She will just stare at me, just basically treats me like an outsider.

It hurts a lot. I have been told that in the long run she may come around. I am at a point where if she does she does, if not oh well. I can honestly say I am doing all I can for her.[85]

//

On-line discussions can help parents cope with a child who is clever enough to sustain a normal image outside the home. Neighbors and relatives see a very different child, and cannot be expected to understand. But in an on-line support group, there are others going through the same struggles. Local support groups often fail to get off the ground, since many families are tied to line-of-sight care of their children and cannot get out of the house to attend meetings. The Internet offers in-home, 24-hour-a-day, person-to-person support.

Misplaced Blame

In the community, it can be indescribably frustrating to try to explain to someone how difficult a child is being at home, when he is utterly charming in public. When no one else sees the child being hateful to his parents or exhibiting destructive or violent behavior, it is hard to believe the parent, who often seems irrationally angry or desperate, or looks and sounds unstable. The level of frustration for families is overwhelming when others can't see what is so glaringly obvious to them—that *this kid needs help!* As they fail to be understood by those around them, the rejected parents feel a frantic desperation followed by pervasive hopelessness that often transforms into a chronic low-grade depression. This does not go unnoticed by the child's therapist who, if untrained in these issues, often will suggest the parents get help, instead of treating the child.

Masters of Manipulation

Judy reported that her daughter often made her appear crazy to others, and sometimes even question her own perception of reality. After years of unsuccessful attempts to find ways to convey the truth to others, she came to a grudging acceptance of her daughter's manipulative skills.

■■ My daughter frequently states goals, mostly on the order of 'I plan to go to medical school.' The problem comes when anyone (not just us, but teachers or even other kids) tries to link these goals to shorter-term prerequisites, like 'Then you should make a point of turning in your homework in science class.' Then she becomes enraged and, having learned lots of 'self-esteem' jargon through years of smiley-face stickers and the like at school complains that people are not being 'supportive.'

This is a child who has yet to complete a single academic class in high school. I don't mean get good grades, I just mean remain as an enrolled member of the class till the end of the year. Yet she becomes furious if anyone suggests that this will have to change if, as she claims, she wants to go to 'a good liberal arts college'—another stated 'goal.'

"Two years ago, our daughter had a one-on-one paraprofessional aide (because of behavior problems at school) who took her to visit a local college that prepares students for international careers. By the end of the visit our daughter had convinced her, and everyone else she met, that this was precisely the sort of career to which she aspired. A day later she literally didn't remember saying these things—the point of her enthusiasm was to grab and hold onto their attention and warmth during the visit.

She has charmed many other well-meaning adults and older teenagers with similar bursts of enthusiasm and "goals" that just happen to match their own. But there is no depth to it. It is outright manipulative, not genuine. And the point of it is always the same—to gain attention and control in a given situation.

In fact, anyone who is actually in a position of guidance or authority in our daughter's life soon stops being a candidate for her charm, and becomes instead a target for manipulation, lies, and anger.

Expensive Kids to Raise

Mixed in with hopeless frustration is a very real resentment and concern about the monetary costs of raising a special needs child. One adoptive parent noted, "Thank goodness we applied for adoption assistance subsidy payments, although at the time we didn't think we'd need any. Now we call it 'combat pay' and sometimes 'hazardous duty pay,' 'cause that's what it is in this case! The subsidy barely covers the cost of the clothing and furniture she wrecks every month!"

In most states, adoption subsidies are fixed at the time the adoption is finalized legally. They are based on the child's needs at the time, with no way to increase the payment should unforeseen expenses arise. Rarely do they cover the extra costs incurred over time. Most states also offer Medicaid coverage as an adjunct to subsidy payments. However, many service providers do not accept Medicaid. Parents can be left with prohibitive costs such as the following:

- $30,000–$100,000 per year for residential treatment[86]

- $150 per hour for therapy

- $1000 for psychological testing

- $200 per day for trained respite care

- $4000 per semester for private schooling

Families who cannot afford such treatment may find that their only means of obtaining services for their children is to allow them to become wards of the state. By relinquishing their children into state guardianship, they force the state to pick up some of the cost of care. However, some states may still require parents to pay hundreds of dollars per month for foster care while at the same time taking away the parents' rights to make treatment decisions. Treatment may be limited to facilities that accept Medicaid payments, or may be deemed unnecessary entirely. It's a real catch-22 situation.

In addition to the often expected, and sometimes prepared for, medical, dental, and therapy expenses associated with adopting a special needs child, there can be hidden or unexpected costs that have at times forced families into bankruptcy. In some states, for instance, parents are liable for court-ordered fines or charges resulting from criminal damage restitution if their child is convicted of a crime. Legal costs to defend the child can easily run into thousands of dollars.

Parents may find they need to hire an attorney to defend *themselves* against false allegations of child abuse (more on this later) or abandonment charges initiated by the county or state if they refuse to pick a child who has been arrested or detained by police. It does not matter if the parents are afraid for their own personal safety or that of other children in the home. One family we know spent $6,000 in attorney fees to prove to the county that they had the right to place their legally adopted child in a long-term respite care home of their choice. They were told that because the child was adopted, they did not have the same right to do this as they would have had with a birth child! This was not true, of course, but they had to hire attorneys to prove this to the county, which was threatening to take the child into custody and charge the parents with abandonment.

Jim Mahoney, a therapist from Spokane, Washington and well-known speaker at adoption conferences nationwide, half-kiddingly suggests that foster and adoptive families of special needs kids ought to be able to purchase some kind of additional liability insurance to cover the costs of criminal judgments against the child that might otherwise force them into bankruptcy. Then in a serious note he adds that families really need to think about this issue when they accept placement of certain kinds of children.[87]

And then there are the day-to-day 'ordinary' expenses that special needs kids can be expected to have. Witness this correspondence that took place on the Internet between two special needs adoptive parents:

// Dear Brian,

And to top it off, Nina trashed her $300 glasses AGAIN today. Twice in two months!!! She just bent them in two until she snapped the nose bridge. I know better than to get angry—that never helps and usually just makes things worse. But I did anyway. Sigh!

Are your kids destructive to their possessions?

//

Response:

// Steven did the same thing to his glasses right before he went back into the hospital. We got off lucky—they were able to order a new frame front piece and repair it for only $55. *These kids are very expensive to raise.*

Brian **//**

Holidays and Family Outings

Holidays and family celebrations can be difficult and heart-breaking disappointments for special needs families. The expectations of family harmony, traditions, and intimacy can push everyone's stress barometers to volatile highs. Birthdays bring up abandonment and loss issues for adopted children, and remind them of perceived or actual abandonment or rejection. Holidays are occasions for musing about birth families and others from whom they have had to separate.

Since it is so profoundly difficult for disturbed children to trust, they are virtually unable to receive, and therefore benefit from, the positive feelings and wishes of others. They may reject or destroy gifts, or refuse to participate in reciprocal rituals, in part due to poor self-image and feelings of unworthiness, and in part due to issues concerning belonging and attachment. They may act out or shut down. Sometimes acting out is easier for parents to deal with, as it appears to be the more "normal" naughty response to overstimulation that many children may express at parties. Complete refusal to participate, attend, or even simply speak to others can be much more wearing and misunderstood. The child's lack of communication and reciprocal interaction can be extremely painful to parents who must watch a child remain on the periphery of a family while they desperately yearn for a close, meaningful relationship. If extended family and friends put additional pressure on the parents to explain the child's behavior, or attempt unsuccessfully to find ways to make the child participate, it may force the family into isolation.

Having little desire or ability to participate in parties and family celebrations may carry over to include family outings and vacations.

▮▮ Lucky for us, when we went on our yearly island vacation, the elderly lady who rented the other half of our duplex cottage was deaf as a post. But we still told the kids, 'Here you can't scream, can't pound on the wall, and kick for hours, can't poop or pee in the bedrooms. Because the people here get *really* mad!' I don't know what they thought all those mad people would do to them, but they never engaged in any of those behaviors there. It was hard on us to realize that they *could* control their behavior when they wanted to, but just wouldn't for us at home. It seemed so personal. It was *us* they hated, *us* they were 'out to get.' It took years of training and hard work on our part to get past the anger about this, to understand it in a different way, and especially to finally understand that there was something much deeper driving them—and that until *that* was resolved, all we could do was adapt and find ways to cope. I don't think we had a normal family outing for years. Family outings can become nightmares, and family fun a thing of the past after these children move into the home.

One day at the zoo, Jason just laid down on the pavement—flung himself down and went limp, like a floppy rag doll. He just didn't feel like walking anymore, and didn't want to see the zoo. He refused to get up. I asked him politely, threatened, cajoled and even offered a bribe, a real last resort measure. Any four-year-old can act this way. But most four-year-olds can be reached. A crowd was gathering. So we just slowly walked off, casually talking about how we hoped Jason wouldn't fall too far behind and have to run hard to catch up. Of course, we expected, like all children, he would at least try to catch up if he saw us getting too far away. Ha! All of a sudden, he started screaming, as if he was in pain, 'ow, ow, ow.' As he screamed, more people gathered, looking at me to do something. There was no choice but to pick up this screaming kid and carry him like a sack of flour out of there. All the while he yelled, 'ow, ow, ow, you're hurting me.' I was really concerned about getting reported for child abuse at the zoo![88] **//**

Normal three- to five-year-olds will rush in panic to catch up if mom walks away in a situation like this. But unattached children don't care if mom leaves them behind. They are not connected to anyone, so it doesn't matter to them one bit. They are as happy to be in the company of a group of strangers as their own family. In their eyes, they need only themselves. It puts the parent in the position of victim and the child in control, especially in today's child abuse–aware society. "Look at that poor little child. He just wants to get away from her uncaring treatment! And he's so cute and charming, too. How can she get mad at him for being too tired to walk? He's so little! She should take him home so he can have a little nap, not make him trudge around the zoo if he's tired."

▐▐ What kid doesn't like the zoo, for heaven's sake? Jason didn't, and he didn't want *us* to like it either. It would not have been fair to the other kids to leave, so we didn't go home. I carried him to a private corner and told him that he could walk, or I would 'help' him. I made sure that he was low-grade uncomfortable when I carried him, which he didn't like. His head hung down and bobbled along, and I didn't make an effort to support it. After all, he was perfectly capable of walking himself if he chose. No one really had fun after that, but we did stay and struggle, just to make the point that he could not 'make' us leave by pitching a fit. I put on a great act of having fun, and I think he was fooled. By lunch time he had come around to just being quietly angry. He refused to sit with us at the same lunch table. Since I had the lunch, that meant he didn't. So he sat at a neighboring table and sought sympathy from a stranger by complaining that I wasn't feeding him. I got a few dirty looks, but redeemed myself somewhat by loudly saying, 'Well Jason, we're having a delicious lunch *over here* if you care to join us.' Thank goodness nobody bought into his act, or it would have put him in control of every outing from then on.[89]   *▐▐*

Most families want and deserve to be able to have enjoyable outings with all of their children along, without them turning into power struggles and misery for everyone involved. Certainly all children have bad days now and then, and should be accommodated. But for some special needs families, every outing is a disaster. The drain of energy and emotion becomes more than any one family should have to bear.

It's no small wonder that parents report feeling *trapped*.

This is one of the most difficult feelings for adoptive parents to deal with. Stuck in a hopeless situation with no way out and no end in sight. And it is so hard to find support for those feelings! The usual response of family and friends is, understandably, "Well you knew he had problems when you adopted him." And yes, they have made a commitment to a child, which they intend to honor, and yet they cannot find workable solutions to living peaceably with this very same child. The normal rules of parenting do not seem to apply.

The child's intense maintenance needs make it important for caregivers to have a break once in a while, yet it is difficult to find baby-sitters who can safeguard and control such needy kids. One parent complained,

// Every time we move, we go through all the teens in the area who will baby-sit. They are all one timers, I can assure you. He terrorizes them, every one. It's not long before you run out of baby-sitters. Then you're stuck. **//**

Some parents feel trapped . . .

- By a commitment that is difficult to maintain.

- By a lack of resources for respite care or help for the child.

- By physical constraints placed on parents by the system or society.

- By emotional constraints.

- By financial worries or obligations.

- By the law.

- By the very professionals who are supposed to help.

Some parents report feeling crazy, as if their children's pathology has somehow rubbed off on them. Many seek therapy for themselves when it is the children who really need help. They forget that they were healthy and functioning normally until the disturbed children entered the home.

These feelings sometimes stem from the parents' attempt to understand their children's reactions and behaviors by imagining what they, as healthy functioning individuals, would think or do under similar conditions. In that context, disturbed children do not make sense. They are not approaching life from the same healthy base as the adoptive parent. Their thought processes are skewed by their disorders.

When parents respond to their children in healthy ways, the result is often an escalation or worsening of the situation. Unhealthy responses often seem to satisfy the children and may temporarily obtain good behavioral results, but generally make parents feel dissatisfied. This paradoxical situation contributes to that unsettled, uncomfortable, and crazy feeling that so many parents report. It also forms the basis for many of the unconventional and specialized parenting techniques we describe elsewhere in this book.

And some parents feel angry . . .

- At the child.

- At the agency.

- At friends and family.

- At helping professionals.

- At teachers.

- At themselves.

- At the government.

- At the law.

- At their spouse.

- At God.

Am I a Good Enough Parent?

The kind of person who adopts a special needs child is generally caring, loving, and giving. When a disturbed child projects his pathological emotions on an unsuspecting and unaware parent, it is often the parent who feels bad, the parent who feels guilty. Have I loved him well enough? Have I given enough? Have I tried hard enough or been understanding enough?, and on and on. We have watched parents anguish over these issues until they have convinced themselves that they are bad people who never deserved to have children at all. They begin to wonder if they are deficient in some important way.

Typical parental anguish can be seen in the following Internet correspondence:

How do we get past taking what our kids do personally?"

"My attachment disordered kid seems to direct most of her manipulation, lies, compulsiveness, etc., etc., at me! I get really upset and have at times come to not like this child of mine very much."

"I feel like I'm suffocating when she is in the room. I know this sounds awful, but that is how I feel. Of course I can't say this to others because they would think I was crazy.[90]

Response:

▮▮ Hi again. To the post about not being able to stand being in the same room as your kid, feeling like you are suffocating. *Me too.* It doesn't feel good to feel this way. I have often said to the therapists working with us that I wish I could be more 'large' or more 'saint-like' or somehow rise about this abysmal situation, but the past three years have proven to me that I can't.[91]   **▮▮**

Notes like this, when shared with a group of understanding parents, usually generate a flood of similar experiences, as the following notes indicate.

▮▮ I have also had the feeling of not wanting to be near my child. I know the guilt and fear it evokes. Even though she is in a residential treatment center, I have dreams almost nightly of her coming home!! She thinks *everything* they have taught her in residential *(although it is exactly what we taught her at home)* is the gospel, although she certainly doesn't live by it, she talks the talk, but *cannot* walk the walk! I bought a baby monitor last time she came home, as my husband does not like the room alarm. I cannot sleep knowing she is next to our four-year-old's room!! This is our life!![92]   **▮▮**

Response:

▮▮ I have felt the same way . . . and it's not 'taking it personally' to have a high level of anxiety when there is a toxic person in the room with you. I was actually feeling sorry for Amanda and missing her a lot today when I came upon a familiar scene in the drug store where a 14 to 15 year old girl bumps a display and five or six bottles fall down. No big deal! Mom says, 'pick it up,' daughter starts in about how pissed off she is and says 'give me the keys so I can sit in the car.' Mom sighs and picks up the bottles but at least doesn't give the rude silly girl the keys. I felt like hugging that mom and saying, I have one of those too.[93]

Hi folks. My daughter, age 17, who ran away about six weeks ago, just called for the first time since she left. (I located her and worked with her DHS worker to get her to a small group home.) She just wanted to chat. So she did. She told me about her new home, being back at her school, how was I doing, how is the dog, etc. How can she sound and seem to be so sweet and so entirely normal???? Does she do all this on purpose? I understand how other people think she is such a little darling child, as they get only this aspect of her, that I just got on the phone— soft-spoken, sweet, considerate, 'perfect.' My plan is to stay uninvolved (?!), let her know I care, do what I can for her without putting myself out much. Am I really that cold and uncaring? No, that is not me. It is hard for me to be like this-it is an act of will, not spontaneous at all.[94]

Hi all! I've not been posting much, have had my twelve-year-old home from residential for the past eight days (going back tomorrow). *Sigh!* I think I am coming to a very difficult decision that our daughter can no longer live at home. Even though she is only twelve, we are going to check out some group homes. I had thought that I could keep her at home a little longer if I could get some assistance in the home. Our county has informed me 'that's what the subsidy is for' and 'if I bring her home, there is no money available,' so I'd 'better move to another county.' They (and the treatment facility) support her going to a long-term placement.

After the last few days, (I have barely slept, and have turned into a raving lunatic on more than one occasion, I am embarrassed to say) I am beginning to agree with them. We have put six and a half years of parenting and sometimes two therapies per week, and have not made a dent of progress. We saw her worker of four years (weekly two-hour in-home services) yesterday, and after ten minutes, she looked at Mel and then at me and said 'Nothing's changed, has it?' She hasn't seen us for over a year, yet she could see it plain as day. Melody has severe AD, FAS, ADHD, OCD, ODD, and recently got two new labels (for all they're worth): borderline personality disorder with psychotic features and bipolar disorder.

The first time she was hospitalized was because she was hearing voices. Disassociation was the buzz word then, but she was never officially diagnosed. Severe sexual abuse by several family members, severe physical abuse and possibly satanic abuse got her the PASS. The rest just kind of came along with time.

Having her home has changed the whole dynamics of our family, and not for the better. I think if there was just one kid with problems, I might be more capable of handling it. But we also have her three treatment-level siblings with their own set of problems. Then I have the two 'normal'?? bio teenagers. I guess I bit off more than I could chew. Somewhere in my mind, I thought they'd get 'better' as they got older. Unfortunately for Mel, she has only gotten older. I really look to this list for support. *Do you all think I'm the most terrible parent on Earth?* I know I feel like it right now, but after a two hour conversation with the therapist, I think I am coming closer to the 'decision.' There is more hope for the other three, (and maybe the teens???) but it makes life so difficult on all of us when she's here. And I really don't think she is happy. She may never be 'happy' anywhere. I asked her today what 'happy' meant to her—she didn't know. She is one of those kids that can suck the lifeblood out of you from morning to night, turn around and have the audacity to smile sweetly and say, 'I want more please.' Isn't it amazing what five years of abuse can do to a human being??[95]

The difficulty of living with such children has strong and lasting influence on family dynamics. Awareness, coupled with training in specialized parenting techniques, can go a long way towards controlling the impact of the child's disturbance on the family.

Despite the difficulties, there are many families who do well with very disturbed children. After working with such families and living with disturbed children ourselves, we realize that these parents have attitudes, techniques, and tools, that have served them well. These attitudes, tools and techniques are covered in the next section.

Part II

Parenting
Disturbed Children

5

When Parents Feel Like Failures

Because so many adopted children have histories of early abuse or neglect, parents with no prior experience with adoption may understandably have unrealistic expectations of themselves and their children. Throughout America, disturbed children now are placed in families—children that in years past would have been raised in group homes, residential treatment facilities and even psychiatric hospitals.[96] Children who in the past would have been cared for by highly trained and often highly paid professionals are now being sent to live with untrained parents. They receive their training on the job, at the school of hard knocks.

At the present time, unfortunately, there are few useful training materials available for this job. There is very little parenting information available on specific tools and techniques that work with difficult and disturbed children. Most therapists are trained only in traditional methods of discipline and behavior modification, so even if they wanted to train parents in more effective strategies, they could not. Others fear the liability issues inherent in offering professional training to nonprofessional parents. Agencies who wish to provide training or postplacement help have few resources available to them.

Conventional parenting techniques work for *almost all children, almost all the time.* However, in the cases of adopted children who have suffered early psychological or physical trauma, the usual techniques must be augmented with nonconventional techniques that will encourage the growth of attachment and acceptable behavior while allowing for the children's often delayed development to proceed. The difference in these children's responses is that their behaviors reflect an underlying emotional problem. Until that problem has been identified and corrected, nontraditional methods of modifying behavior will be necessary.[97]

The problem with nonconventional techniques is that they can be misused. And they can be misunderstood even when implemented correctly. They are, in short, controversial. Nevertheless, it has been our experience that such techniques must be available to those who parent disturbed children. The parents must exercise extreme caution and discernment in their use. But they should not be denied their use simply because there is potential for their misuse. In many cases, there is greater risk in *not* using these techniques.

We are not advocating the use of any particular technique with any particular child. Such decisions can only be made by the parent in conjunction and cooperation with the child's therapist. We are simply providing options that we and others have found successful with some children.

Adoptive parents are often experienced parents and are generally well versed in traditional methods of child rearing. They may come from large families where good parenting skills were modeled. They may have done extensive reading on parenting or taken parenting courses. They are lovers of children and often have excellent instincts as well as practical knowledge. And they are committed and willing to work very hard at being good parents. They enter the adoption process with the belief that their parenting attitudes and techniques will be effective with their adopted children. Many of these parents have bought into the popular notion that parents are responsible for how their children act and "turn out." *In reality, all parents can do is provide children with an environment that encourages them to make good choices and the best decisions possible for their own lives.* Ultimately all children have free will and will exercise it for better or for worse. At that point the decision and the responsibility is out of the parents' hands.

Parents may find themselves at a complete loss as to how to handle the behavior of the new additions to their home— children who reject their love, while ignoring consequences; children whose behavior becomes so unimaginably outrageous, negative, and bizarre that the parents are reluctant to tell others about it; children who show behavior that the parents can control only by resorting to techniques that they feel reluctant to use—techniques that may appear unusual or extreme to outsiders. They may find themselves besieged with emotions previously foreign to them, such as boiling rage or seething resentment. Combined with the exhaustion most feel at this point, these emotions can be overpowering and frightening in their intensity.

Parents with high expectations for quick and full integration of the children into the family are most at risk. Their expectations for themselves and the child are unrealistic and unattainable. If their own self-worth is contingent upon the children's response, they are in big trouble. That is a very unreliable yardstick, and the parents will never measure up. Usually parents are not psychologically prepared for the children's initial (and sometimes ongoing) lack of responsiveness to them. This lack of responsiveness is a shock if it follows a honeymoon period in which parents and children initially scope each other out, and all show their best face. In some cases there is no honeymoon at all, and the family is stunned at the impact the children have on the home. Even parents who believe themselves to be psychologically prepared for the children's lack of responsiveness can find the situation draining and exhausting over time. Their initial expectations are that the adoption will work out and the children will become positive and responsive *within a tolerable time period.* After all, they reason, other adoptive parents develop close, loving relationships with their children, don't they? If indeed, as the media slogans indicate, "Adoption Works For Everyone,"[98] then why isn't it working for them?

Common Family Dynamics in Special Needs Adoptions

- Parents are angry and frustrated with their children, each other, and mental health professionals.

- Mother is most traumatized by child's rejection.

- Marriage may be troubled because mother bears the brunt of child's pathology, while father typically does not see the pathology and blames the wife.

- Children attempt to re-create former dysfunctional patterns in the new home, symbolically or concretely.

- Healthy siblings resent or even hate the disturbed child, but may not express this to parents.

- Resolved, unresolved, or unrecalled traumas which parallel the children's traumas will (re)surface in parents' lives.

- The family becomes more isolated as the children's behavior escalates.

- Parents internalize the children's problems as their own failure.

- Children relate happily to anyone outside the family, but are oppositional, detached, and rejecting within the family.

- Adolescents prematurely leave the family in negative ways.

- Children continue to love formerly abusive parents, as well as hate them.

- Unrecalled events, traumas, and relationships may be replayed or re-emerge in family/child dynamics.[99]

The Paradigm Shift

Even the correct use of both conventional *and* specialized parenting techniques may not "fix" the problem. Even with the best of parenting techniques, the children's misbehavior and control problems may continue. Unless and until the deeply rooted causes of the behaviors are discovered and healed, the child will continue to behave in an abnormal way. And for some types of disturbances, there is no cure. This is very important for parents to realize and accept. The results of certain kinds of damage are lifelong, and may continue to manifest themselves in disturbed personality and dysfunctional relationships well into adulthood.

The families who do best with this reality are those who are able to adjust their attitudes and expectations to match the abilities and capabilities of the children. We call this making a paradigm shift.

The following letter, written by an experienced adoptive parent, illustrates well the need to make a paradigm shift when parenting a disturbed child.

▄▄ I wrote the following mainly as a way of 'talking out' my own intense and distressed feelings. After I read it I realized that it might be useful to those of you who know or work with Maria, or have kids like her, or who care about and support me through my many and frequent 'kid crises.' Where would we be without you????

God bless you all!!![100]

Maria had been doing so well. She was learning to use the computer, taking a real part in many more family activities and chores than ever, communicating honestly and effectively, and showing lots of responsibility. We were so proud of her, and told her so. She was so happy with things, and pleased to be able to do so much. She was so delighted that she had not spit in her hair for such a long time, and that as a result we had allowed her to let it grow longer than it has ever been in the past. She *really* admires long hair, and wanted curls or a ponytail so badly. It was almost long enough. She was doing well with personal grooming, taking complete responsibility for it and keeping that hair shiny and clean all on her own. She wore a few simple pieces of jewelry without breaking or misusing them, and hasn't unravelled a sock or picked a seam apart on her clothing in ages. Her room has been as neat as a normal nine-year-olds, and her things as well taken care of. We were trusting her with more and more things and responsibility as she demonstrated her ability to handle it.

And then, apparently out of the blue, she went on another destructive binge. She used scissors to cut holes in her bedding, annihilate her Barbie doll's wardrobe and some of her own clothes, and collected doll cups of spit that she hid on her bookshelves (the intent of which we can only guess based on past experience). She created mounds of paper snips which I suspect used to be books, and we found amazing amounts of demolished 'stuff' like candy wrappers, wads of yarn (socks?) and other garbage items in amongst her toys. Her beloved Barbies are headless(!), and the doll furniture ruined.

When I woke up on Sunday morning, I could hear some strange sounds coming from her room. I never did find out what she was doing to make the sounds I heard. She made up many stories, none of which sounded possible. She had no trouble looking me right in the eye and making up lie after lie. That is how I came to discover the havoc she had created. I went to look for myself. Her bed was destroyed and much of the other damage was piled up around her on top of the mattress. This all had to have occurred within about a 24-hour period or less or we would have noticed it sooner.

Adoptive families all start out with a dream. It mirrors the dream we all have for all kids, really. The dream?—that we can somehow make everything okay. That we can undo any damage with love and the right kind of therapy and training. The reality? These kids are mentally ill. In addition to whatever else is going on—FAS, ADHD, etc., they have diagnosable mental illnesses—you can read their descriptions in the DSM IV, the psychiatric diagnostic manual. And you never know when that illness will manifest itself. Just like schizophrenia or any other mental illness. It can go underground for years, and then suddenly and unpredictably surface. We *do* know that there are neurological and chemical differences in the brains of children who do not receive the right kind of nurturing and stimulation in early life. But how we want to believe that we can make up for that later. And the sad and scary truth is—we can't. I hate that, and have not wanted to admit it. Yet I know it's true and have seen it clearly in other families—just not my own. The letdown from denial is very rough.

So—what do we do??? In between episodes, we give her as much of a normal life as we can, and are always prepared for it to come to a crashing halt without a moment's notice. Then we pick ourselves, (and her), up and begin again. Clean up the damage and start at ground zero to rebuild gradually what was lost in the crisis. Step by step. Until it starts all over again. Maybe each time it lasts a little longer, or doesn't get quite as bad, and maybe not. Maybe she can only have a piece of what we all have in life. A piece of a chance. A taste of love. A smidgen of 'normal.' Kind of a family. Perhaps short but cute hair and Barbie torsos are better than no hair and no dolls at all.

I, of all people, should not be surprised or caught unaware of these facts. I have watched too many families, my own included, feel they have gotten out of the woods with a child only to have a major episode of regression send them reeling with shock. Yet we all want so very badly for the progress to be permanent, the 'success' to be certain, the child to heal. And we want to have the magic or the power or the knowledge to give it to them. What they should have had in the first place. I want to have been her mother in the beginning—before.

Instead now I am forced to listen to myself talk to other families about redefining success. 'Who knows where they would be without us and our efforts. Would they ever know even those fleeting moments of normal relationships, of normal interaction??? Maybe their behavior would be *much* worse.' All true.

Will the things we work so hard for be there when they need them? (We can only hope and pray.) Will they be able to make use of them, or will their illness destine them to destroy their chances at a healthy and productive life sooner or later? (Not in our hands) They come so far, but in one fell swoop they can destroy it all. (Yes, but they may not.)

Maria is devastated. She *cares*. She is bonded to us, and us to her. She loves us as much as she can, and she lets us love her as much as she can . . . and she has a conscience. She is as confused by this as we are. And I'm sure it is frightening her. Her stress level is extremely high right now. And so is ours.

When I see the slogan 'Adoption works for everyone,' I wonder if the originator really knows what that means. I have watched it destroy many families. Not a day goes by that it does not seriously test our resources. And it is a very *humbling* experience. Most of all—it is *not* for 'everyone.'

I'm doing what God wants me to do, I am sure. It ain't always fun, and it ain't always easy, but it is His work, and that makes it a privilege. Today I pray for Maria, and for our family . . . 'May God in His goodness and mercy give us all the strength and wisdom to do His will in His way. And please God, get us through this one—again! Thank you! Amen.'[101]

There can be no disputing the fact that special needs adoption is *not* for everyone. And we do need to make the realities clear to families *before* they adopt. But for families who have taken on the enormous task of parenting special needs children, there are parenting tools and techniques that we can offer to provide practical and emotional help.

Successful adoptive parents must become extremely flexible in their responses, while accepting their children's limitations and the realities they impose. They must devise a new family model that matches the children's abilities and emotional makeup, rather than trying to force them into traditional molds.

I think if you adopt such a child you at least have to be prepared for someone with special needs that may last a lifetime. You have to be able to say, Well, I'd really like to have a brain surgeon, but if I get a kid who grows up to be a McDonald's worker who needs to be living in some sort of supportive-living setup, I'll love him just as much.[102]

And when you ask how the Eastern European adoptees are faring as a group, the relevant question is always, Compared with whom? As the Ames study concluded, when the comparison is with "children left behind in the orphanages, the answer is very clear. All of them are doing much better than they would have if they had never been adopted.[103]

On closer examination of the preceding statement we noted that, had the children not been adopted, most of them would not have survived! Studies that report outcomes in this ambiguous manner can be misleading. The impression, at first glance, is that the children are doing *well by ordinary standards,* which may or may not be the case at all.

In any event, the most satisfied parents seem to be those who are more process-oriented than outcome-driven. They enjoy the challenge of adapting to each new developmental stage and the changes that brings in the child. They thrive on finding creative ways to deal with their children's behaviors and problems. They thrive on the process of being an advocate for their children's needs, and integrating them into their family, school, and society. They say things like, "I have been the very best parent possible for these children, regardless of the outcome. My children may never even graduate high school, or may end up in prison, but I gave them the very best chance they could have had. Without me, they might be dead."

Successful parents reframe success, noting with pride each small triumph or accomplishment. Parents who are able to make this shift in thinking can find satisfaction in knowing that they have made a positive difference, even if they did not succeed by traditional standards.

As Sam Ross, executive director of Green Chimneys, a residential treatment program for troubled youth, says, "My teachers used to say to me, 'If you don't pay attention, you're going to end up being a truck driver or a garbage collector.' Now I pray each night that my children will end up being truck drivers or garbage collectors.[104]

A few exceptionally committed and dedicated families adopt not just one or two special needs children, but perhaps twelve, or twenty! These large families often succeed with children who would otherwise be overwhelmed with intimacy issues in a smaller family. Often they apply techniques of child management and daily organization similar to those used in residential centers.

To succeed with these children, they may drastically alter their lives and standard of living. Their value system often undergoes similar adjustment, especially in terms of material values, as this mother's account illustrates.

▌▌ I'll adopt again. I am a 42-year-old mama with a baby still to raise, so I'll be mothering until I'm 60 anyway. I've already been a mother for over 23 years now and I really do love it. Today Sarah is 23, Deysi 20, Cristy 20, Gina 19, Saray 19, Yolie 17, Carolina 17, Marcela 16, Sergi 15, Jesse 14, Joe 14, Monica 13, Sonny eleven, Daniel eleven, Alex, seven, Gito six, and CW is nearly one year old.

Our family has weathered many a storm, figuratively speaking it's been more like hurricanes and typhoons. We've experienced lying, cheating, fighting, stealing, shoplifting, bodily mutilation, running away, drug use, sneaking out at night, and numerous other disruptions. My house and furniture have also taken a beating. The walls are marked on, toilets have exploded, and most of the furniture has been knocked over and is barely still standing. Daniel even managed to flip over the Christmas tree at my mother's house one year. We've not had fire-setting nor pet abuse so I've probably been luckier than most. Sometimes I think I have enough disastrous experience right now to be tour guide in Hell!

Happily though we're now on the other side of most of our problems. Everyone has been with me long enough to consider themselves a firmly entrenched Bodie family member. My love for them is not in question, nor is my commitment to them. We will still have behavior problems, particularly since adolescents tend to try and get way too big for their britches. A certain lack of impulse control has also been an issue amongst my kids. I've learned that idle time is as useful as a demolition derby. Kids have to get their energy out everyday in some way or another, preferably in some appropriate manner. I've learned that family activities (and chores), church activities, school activities, sports, and part-time jobs are all necessary and help in teaching kids to set goals and live positive, useful lives. This time next year five of my kids will be in college, five in high school (if my three eighth grade boys continue to hold it together), three in middle school, two in primary school, one is married, and one still a baby. Lord, thank you, *I love my life!!!*[105]

This mom has what it takes to succeed with many special needs children. Fortunately for many children, there are families like this out there. But their kind of living is not for everyone. And there are not enough of these families to accommodate the needs of all the children who wait. When unprepared families bring home children who destroy their furniture, kill the family pets, and so on, they do so without the benefit of having made the conscious choice that the Bodies and others like them have made.

Successful and satisfied special needs families

- Measure success by how well they cope and advocate for the child's needs.

- Feel a sense of accomplishment in having been a part of a child's growth process.

- Find fulfillment by focusing on the challenge their child offers.

- Enjoy the closeness of 'being in this together,' even if the child cannot give that feeling back.

- Show love laced with an attitude of curiosity and interest rather than worry and concern.

- Remind themselves that they are the best thing that ever happened to this child.

- Remain oriented in the present rather than overly concerned with the far distant future.

- Are ready and willing to allow their child's needs and abilities to determine goals and expectations, rather than trying to force the child to fit into a predetermined mold.

- Know that what is right is not always what is easy.

- Feel a sense of being "called," or "doing what they are supposed to be doing." Have a higher purpose.

- Grieve the loss of their original dream, but are willing and even eager to replace it with another.

- Have a sense of humor, a sense of faith, and a healthy involvement in other pursuits in which they feel successful.

- Take pride and pleasure in small accomplishments.

The more difficult a situation, the more relaxing it is to have options. Great parenting techniques mean optimal response to a situation, not necessarily controlling the child.

Although a child's behavior often cannot be controlled, the parent's emotions are almost always under control when they have adequate parenting tools and techniques.

Great parenting techniques are not designed to give parents power, but peace!

Whenever possible, parents of disturbed children would be wise to find creative ways to *eliminate* the need for power struggles and control battles.

▟▟ I guess I didn't realize how much of our life had been adapted to our special needs kids until we spent a week with some friends in another state. They live in a beautiful Victorian Country home filled with lovely antiques. Unique objects of art and collectibles add to the ambience. That's when it hit me! We *used to* have objects displayed around the home, but after our destructive and out-of-control kids arrived, we found it much easier to avoid resentment and bitterness by removing the things we valued. It was too disappointing to see our carefully cared for things broken or defaced. Instead, it became obvious that change in the children would be a long time coming—if ever. So we gave many things away to friends that we knew would appreciate them and take care of them. As a survival technique, without even realizing the extent of it, we have created a more utilitarian environment that is easily scrubbed down, and has less emotional value. ▟▟

How much easier and more effective it was to alter the environment rather than do continual battle with the children over property issues.

No matter how disturbed the child, conventional parenting techniques must always be tried first.

Therefore, every parent must be well versed in the tried and true parenting techniques of giving children choices, setting up logical consequences, knowing how to give empathy without rescue, using the good neighbor policy, knowing how to use active listening, problem solving techniques, and so on.

It is also important to understand the common reasons children misbehave, before deciding which behavior modification strategies and management techniques will be most effective.

6

Common Reasons
for Misbehavior

Many adopted children have behavior problems for the
same reasons that all children have problems. Even very disturbed children can misbehave for common reasons, and
in those instances they will usually respond to traditional
parenting strategies (which should always be tried first).

The most common reasons for behavior problems in
children are:

◆ Children exhibit behavior problems because they want
   contact or attention.

Some children simply did not grow up in families where
parents or others taught them to say, "Hey, I want a hug."

Therefore, in order to get physical or verbal contact or attention, the children become behavior problems. Children want and need contact. The contact can either be positive or negative. It is the parent's job to try to make sure that the majority of contact is positive.

◆ **Sometimes children and adolescents are behavior problems because they wish to *avoid* contact.**

It is strange that children may exhibit behavior problems both to gain and to avoid contact. Nevertheless, this is true. Such children have intimacy problems. When they feel themselves getting close to a parent, or when they start caring about other people, they wish to distance themselves and attempt to bring about psychological or behavioral anguish in others. If they succeed, they validate their belief that "no one will love me!"

◆ **Children and adolescents will act out their feelings in order to be provided with structure or safety.**

When parents appear to have lost control, or when they do not provide secure structure, children may act out as a way of saying, "Do something to stop me. Tell me no. Set some safe limits so I don't hurt myself, because I can't (or don't know how to)." When some adolescents say, "You can't make me," they may secretly hope parents take up the challenge and insist on changed behavior.

Adolescents acting out because they need structure are sometimes resistant to it, and will play the "get back" game. Some adolescents become threatening to parents. If it is frightening for adults to be in a home where children are threatening, think what it must be like for the children! For some children, living in an unstructured home with disturbed siblings is almost akin to adults living in a housing project filled with psychopaths. They might start having problems, too, hoping somebody would do something to remove the threat.

◆ **Children use bad behavior as a way of expressing their feelings.**

Younger children don't naturally talk about their feelings as much as they show them in their behavior. It would be nice if children were straight about talking over their feelings. Healthy children may say, "I'm feeling pretty upset right now, can I talk with you?" However, most difficult children do not know how to label their feelings correctly, much less talk about them. Even adults pout, quit talking, and react immaturely when experiencing strong feelings. Many disturbed children simply have not come from backgrounds where people talk things over! They may have witnessed much adult acting out in the form of "punching each other's lights out," or smashing property to release emotional energy. The children must have their feelings verbalized for them, and they must be taught to label them and discuss them in more appropriate ways.

◆ **Children use behavior to control situations.**

Many children feel anxiety and even panic when they are not in charge. This panic and anxiety lies beneath the surface and does not show. What shows is the obnoxious behavior. Sometimes the problems that lead a child to panic about losing control go back to the first and second year of life, to times the child doesn't even remember or has no verbal memory of. He cannot describe it to you or to himself. When abuse and/or neglect have taken place in the first year of life, children feel panicked about losing control and they are unaware of the motivation for their behavior problems.

They just know they don't like taking orders from anyone else! And when they do, they feel frightened and unsafe.

◆ Bored children often become behavior problems.

When a situation is not structured tightly enough, or if there is nothing appropriate for them to do to keep busy, children will insist on making life interesting for themselves and others! Most kids do not lapse into good behavior, they lapse into bad behavior. Many behavior problems can be helped simply by the parents tightening up on the time structure. Parents must make sure that what they are offering is more exciting than what the kids can come up with on their own. And because every chore cannot be exciting, at least be sure it is necessary and consequenced if not carried out.

◆ Children may become rebellious when they perceive their parents as being uncaring or too rigid.

Children must see their parents as basically loving and fair. If parents are loving and fair, then they can usually be fairly strict or structured. All children must know that they are cared for. This is the primary directive for all parenting. Fair does not mean equal. Children can understand a parent who treats each family member fairly but differently, depending on his needs and abilities.

◆ Children have behavior problems because they have neurological damage, immaturity, poor impulse control, or the inability to plan ahead.

Sadly, some children do not become behavior problems because they are bored, or because they need the attention.

Some children simply are "that way." A common reason is prenatal exposure to toxins such as illegal drugs or alcohol, or severe sensory deprivation such as that found in inadequate third world orphanages. Recent research shows genetic factors play a larger role than was once thought.[106] Whatever the reason, psychological testing almost always shows neurological "soft" or "hard" signs that let us know the child's functioning is not normal.[107]

◆ Preteens and teens who act out often confuse *power, control,* and *intimacy.*

Many disturbed adolescents use power and control methods to gain intimacy. They may be seeking negative attention and hope that this leads to touch or holding, as they really need contact but don't dare directly ask for it.

◆ Children adopted at an older age may try to recreate earlier dysfunctional family patterns that they experienced in previous homes.[108]

Many children come from dysfunctional family environments in which parents were in constant disagreement. The children expect this kind of behavior from adults, and may even equate it with love. They know, consciously or unconsciously, how to "fit" in such situations. Any other kind of family interaction is unfamiliar and uncomfortable to them. Almost all difficult children are adept at getting parents to disagree on child management techniques. "Let's you and him fight" is their motto. Disagreeing parents have less energy to direct towards the children. From the children's point of view, it may pay to distract mom and dad from the problem at hand by creating a problem in the adult relationship.

◆ Disturbed kids may cover *sad* with *mad*, leading to oppositional or otherwise difficult behavior.

Depression in children can manifest itself in several ways. One way depression shows may be in aggressive and obnoxious behavior. Mad is easier to handle for some kids than sad. Their sadness is frightening in its intensity. They may feel that to unleash it would be to sink into it so deeply that they could not recover. Loss, abandonment, abuse, and neglect issues can be suppressed and covered up with a tough veneer of anger and acting out. An understanding of the reason behind the behavior often opens us to insight about how to manage it.

7

Foundation Philosophy
and Attitudes

Nancy Thomas, a great adoptive parent from Colorado, said, "I find I'm at my best when I *parent with an attitude*." Parental attitudes are a very important issue in raising children.

Parenting tools and techniques are used within a framework of parenting philosophy and attitudes that allow the right tools to be used in the right ways.

Parents of disturbed children would be wise to cultivate an attitude of curiosity and interest in place of the more usual worry and frustration. In almost every situation where parents might be worried and frustrated, they could substitute curiosity and interest. For example, instead of being angry, frustrated, and worried about the child not completing a homework assignment, the parents could be curious about what the teacher will do when he arrives at school without the homework finished, or how he is going to handle it when his friends move onto the next grade without him. One parent said to a high schooler: "Honey, mom and I have always wondered what will become of you after high school. You don't like to work, and you're not ready for college. I wonder where you will be living, and how you will support yourself." The child, without coaching, decided to join the Army, where she did well. The daily structure and command hierarchy, combined with predictable and fairly applied consequences, were just what she needed. Her basic needs were provided for—in fact imposed upon her. She had to make few decisions for herself, something she had not demonstrated readiness for anyway.

Parents who maintain their sense of humor almost always do better in tough situations. For instance, when Margaret had trouble getting her homework done, her mom said, "It's okay not to learn your spelling words, but you will need to practice saying, "Would you like fries with that burger?" With a glint of amusement another mom noted of her daughter, "Kathy is definitely a piece of work in progress—slow, unsteady progress, but progress nonetheless."

An attitude of caring and fun must accompany such statements to avoid appearing disrespectful or sarcastic to children. The point is not to belittle or condemn, but to lighten the mood and let the children know that they are basically responsible for their own outcomes. It is important that they know that their parents accept them even if they make burger flipping or garbage collecting their career goal. After all, someone has to be happy working behind those fast food counters! This technique is also not effective if the child feels lectured.

When parental attitude is incorrect, techniques and strategies tend to be used in the wrong way, and parents will complain, "I used that method, but it didn't work!" The only correct parental attitude is one of love and mutual respect, often sprinkled with good natured humor.

Major Components of Correct Attitude

Take Good Care of Yourself in a Healthy Way

Parents are the center of a child's universe. When parents forget to take care of themselves, falter and wear out, the family wears out. And the children go nowhere.[109]

Parents should never allow the difficult children to become the center of the family, a vortex that sucks everything in their direction. Married couples and long-term partners should keep their relationship first, presenting a team and a united front.[110] Singles need both respite and a balance of healthy relationships in their lives.

The ability to put oneself first *in a loving way* is a key to successful parenting. Mothers very often set the emotional tone for the family. If mom's burned out, the family is burned out. "If momma ain't happy, ain't nobody happy." Of course, there are as many exceptions to this as there are family styles.

When parents put themselves first in a loving way, they set the correct model for the children to carry with them into adulthood. Naturally, when parents let children know that kids always come first, the children realize that the parents, by default, always come last.

Parents who always put themselves last tend to resent it in time. They may have trouble helping the children develop autonomy and emancipate as adults. When their children do finally leave home, the parents complain, "I gave up my life for that ungrateful child. *Now* where is he?" Conversely, if the parents have put themselves first in a healthy way, all their giving is accepted as love and not as obligation or entitlement. Parents and children then show genuine like and mutual respect for each other as adults.

Helping a frustrated and tired parent understand self-care was the object of the following advice given by one adoptive mom to another:

▌▌ Dear B,

> You wrote that you feel 'trapped.' In a sense you *are* trapped, as we all are, by love, commitment, legal responsibility, and compassion. The kids have all of the control, except in how *we act and treat ourselves.* Maybe you should do what is best for *you* at this point, and think of it as modeling healthy behavior for your child. Don't we all want to teach our kids how to take good care of themselves as adults? What better way to do that than to model that ourselves.
>
> Generally speaking, we should never put more effort into changing a kid that age than he is willing to put into working at it.
>
> In this case, it won't do your child any good if you fall apart or get resentful. Is there some way you can disengage for a while? Let him carry the burden for his decisions and behaviors for a while. It's ultimately *his* choice, regardless.
>
> Thinkin' of you and praying for you,
>
> Carolyn **▌▌**

When parents cry, "I've given up my life for my children," it is very sad. Often society accepts this martyrdom as evidence of caring and dedication, and many adoptive parents buy into this, thinking it is in their children's best interest. It is particularly sad when the children, in spite of all the energy and time invested, still cannot make functional decisions.

It is better to ask the questions, "How much of my life am I willing to give up for this child?" and "How do I balance my life in other meaningful ways as well?" It takes conscious and determined effort not to get sucked into the dark side of a disturbed child's personality and lose sight of one's own healthy needs.

Guard Against Burnout and Compassion Fatigue

Caring for traumatized children is stressful and exhausting work. Caregivers are vulnerable to burnout and "compassion fatigue," an emotional strain that comes from working with traumatized individuals. They may take on the symptoms of the children with whom they work, such as despair, isolation, anger, sadness, and horror. Difficulty sleeping, eating, or concentrating may occur. Awareness of this risk and attention to their own needs can help them act in the best interest of the children in their care.[111]

In the professional literature, the concept of compassion fatigue has emerged only in the last several years. It represents the psychic cost of caring for and about traumatized people. Compassion fatigue is the emotional residue of exposure to working with the suffering, particularly those suffering from the consequences of traumatic events.

Compassion fatigue is *not* the same as burnout. Burnout is associated with the stress and hassles involved in your work; it is cumulative and relatively predictable. Frequently a vacation or change of job helps a great deal. It can be thought of as secondary post-traumatic stress. Eventually it can lead to an overall decline in general health.[112]

Compassion fatigue can have symptoms similar to burnout: exhaustion, short attention span, feelings of anger or depression, apathy, forgetfulness, somatic complaints, irritability, difficulty in concentrating, and sleep disturbance.

There are differences, however between compassion fatigue and burnout. Burnout results from dealing with the difficulties you face in your own life. This can occur in any type of work, usually emerges gradually due to emotional exhaustion, and can take a long time to recover from.

Compassion fatigue, on the other hand, results from your reactions to difficulties that others face. It affects only people in the helping professions, can emerge suddenly with very little warning, and usually involves a quicker recovery. Symptoms seen in compassion fatigue that are usually not seen in burnout include a sense of helplessness, confusion, and isolation from supporters.[113]

Provide Understanding

A first step, before trying to *manage* children's behavior, is to help them *understand* their behavior!

When children show that they feel bad about their actions, sometimes a little loving explanation of the situation will help lock in healthy feelings and responses. These discussions must be on a level the child will understand. Most disturbed children are very concrete thinkers, and diagrams and pictures drawn while they sit beside us can be of benefit:

Mom: So how is it going?

Child: Not too good. All the kids hate me.

Mom: That's too bad. Why is that, do you think?

Child: I don't know, they just don't like me!

Mom: Sweetie, can I give you some of my thoughts about it?

Child: Yeah . . . I guess . . .

Mom beginning to draw on paper: Well, come here and sit down beside me. Look, when you were a little baby . . . I'll draw a baby here . . . I'm not too good at it [drawing a simple baby face] . . . How were you treated before you came here?

Child: Not too good, I guess.

Mom: Right, we've talked about that, right? Well when you were a baby, you got bossed around a lot. Boy, look at that baby's mad face! Well, you didn't like being told what to do when everyone was mad at you. And your life was horrible. Boy were you a mad baby! And right then, that baby—you—made a decision that when times were hard, that you would always be mad, and not ever let anyone else tell you what to do. But are you living in that situation now?

Child: No.

Mom: Do you think you still have those baby feelings of being mad, feeling life's not fair, and never wanting to do it someone else's way somewhere inside of you?

Child: Maybe.

Mom: Well yes, maybe so . . . ! I can understand that. But now you can have more grown-up feelings inside [drawing a happy stick figure of a little child] and you can fight those baby feelings—that baby who always wants to be mad and feels life is always unfair. You are growing up, and every time I see you smile, I think the mad baby is disappearing and the real you is coming out! Right?

Take Time to Give and Receive Support

Living with disturbed children can evoke unfamiliar negative feelings in parents that they didn't realize they were capable of.

I couldn't believe how I acted with the kids. I am not a screaming and shrieking person, but at times with my disturbed kids, that's exactly what I became. Then later I would wonder "Where did that come from?!"

Disturbed children often arouse in parents all the feelings that occurred in the children's own dysfunctional birth homes. They provoke parents to perplexing degrees of anger, the depth of which they may have been previously unaware they could reach. The strength of this rage is frightening to most parents. It can even grow to such an extent that the parent feels an urge to abuse the child.[114]

> *At this point, parents are wise to remember that whatever feeling one finds most difficult to talk over, is the feeling most important to talk over!*

For instance, parents particularly need to talk things over when they are feeling a little ashamed of themselves, guilty, inadequate, jealous, or angry. If they feel hatred or dislike for their child, they most certainly need someone to point out that they do not hate the child, but rather how or she acts, or what she has done to them or the family. They need reassurance that their feelings are typical of most parents in similar situations.[115]

An attachment disordered child may take love and attempt to turn it into something ugly or hateful, since it is only in that frame of reference that they can bring themselves to push it away.[116] In such cases, the harder a parent tries to love the child, the harder life with that child will get. And the extremes that these children will go to avoid intimacy are appalling and can become dangerous.

L. Anne Babb and Rita Laws, authors of *Adopting and Advocating for the Special Needs Child*, offer this wise advice: "We cannot stress enough that adoptive parents of difficult kids need to establish and maintain strong ties to other adoptive parents who will understand. They also need to establish and maintain credibility with professionals, law enforcement, and educators in their community."[117]

Parents of disturbed children can support each other in concrete and specific ways, as well as with understanding and verbal support. Respite care exchange is one way families can contribute to each other's welfare. Sometimes parents need a physical break from dealing with their child on a daily basis. This may be short or long term, depending on the situation and the duration and intensity of the child's difficulties, and the resources available to the family.

Never Try to Control the Uncontrollable

Effective parents are always aware of what they can and cannot control. They realize that they can control only one person's emotions—their own! Disturbed children often hope that their parents will lose control of themselves or their emotions. Then the kids know that *they* are in control.

Parents control their emotional responses in order to:

- Set a good model for showing the kids how they, too, can be in control of themselves.

- Diffuse the situation with rationality and self-control.

- Guard against expressing the child's emotions, especially anger, for him.

Disturbed children who do not know how to express their anger appropriately will often try to force others to express it for them. This makes the children feel better temporarily, but in the long run does nothing to defuse the children's anger or rage. However, expressing the children's anger frequently makes parents feel bad about how they handled the situation.[118]

Four Rules for All Parents to Use All the Time

1. Avoid control battles as often as possible.

2. If you cannot avoid a control battle with your child, *you* must win.

3. Therefore, if you cannot avoid a control battle, pick the issue carefully. (You can't win on the issue of your child using drugs, but you can win on whether or not drugs are used in front of you!)

4. Diligently avoid backing yourself into a corner from which you cannot escape without losing or abusing. Avoid statements like:

   - "That's the last time you are going to pee in your bed."

   - "That's the last time I'm going to put up with . . ."

   - "You are going to stand there and do jumping jacks until you are ready to tell me the truth."

   - "Never let me catch you . . . again."

   - "We'll feed you after you get the dishes done." (A disturbed child might starve himself in order to win.)

Disturbed children are masters at setting up control battles that *they* can win. One mother told us that she told her child, "You can only urinate or defecate in the bathroom." So he went in the bathroom wastebasket, in the bathroom sink, in the corner of the bathroom . . . Parents of disturbed children need to develop the skill of being very specific about the wording of directions.

Wise parents know how to sidestep control battles using the tools described in this chapter. Providing choices, making observations, and skillful use of consequences all help to avoid control battles.

   - The healthier the child, the more control battles can be completely avoided.

   - The more disturbed the child, the more the child must learn that parents really do have control, and that some things must be done the parent's way.

- Severely disturbed children may not allow parents to win a control battle *ever*. They may feel that if they do not maintain control at all times, they will literally die. Such children need professional therapeutic help before any of these strategies will work. Be especially careful, with these children, to make statements you can back up or requests you can really ensure are carried out. Disturbed children are adept at "pushing people's buttons" and arousing extremely angry feelings in those around them. Until the child makes therapeutic progress, parents may have to resign themselves to losing almost all battles. For these children parents must:

  - Draw lines of response behavior for themselves, such as "no spanking" (your anger may prevent you from making good judgments about when to stop) "no restriction of food" (they will starve rather than comply), and so on.

  - Rigidly stick to those rules. Tell their spouse and other family members remind them if they appear to be getting out of control, and offer to do the same for them.

  - Seek professional help. (See the resources at the end of this book for suggestions about finding appropriate, trained professionals who will not make the situation worse.)

- Every time disturbed children win control battles, they become more difficult and lose more respect for the adult authority figures involved.

- *The control battles most easily won are those that involve the adult directly.* This is because it is fairly easy to consequence these issues.

- Parents can usually control how they respond to the child, but not how the child responds to others.

- Parents can often control how the child acts in the parents' presence (the child may be asked to leave), but cannot control how the child acts with others.

Certain issues involve the adult directly, and can therefore be more easily consequenced. These include leaving toys in the parent's area, polluting of the auditory environment with fights and hassles, not doing chores, showing disrespect, and so on.

However, the self destructive issues that involve only the child himself are much more difficult to consequence effectively. The following are examples of issues that involve only the child, and are not in the parent's control: Lying, stealing, and cheating; bathroom issues; what foods are eaten at school; substance abuse outside the home, and so on.

Parents give too much control to their children when

- Parents show frustration. (The child controls the parent's emotion.)

- Parents say, "Am I going to have to . . . ?"

- Parents say, "I don't want to do this, but what I'm going to do is . . . "

Showing Frustration Is Deadly

Disturbed children are often masters at bringing out frustration and anger in their parents. Frustration is often a result of exhaustion, and such children continuously exhaust their families' resources. However, showing frustration to disturbed children is deadly. (Parental frustration increases children's bad behavior far more effectively than any other emotion.)

Both conventional and unconventional parenting techniques, when properly used, decrease parental frustration. In fact, that is perhaps one of the most important reasons for parent training and education!

There is a tendency to think that love is the best reinforcer of children's behavior. And love *does* modify much human behavior under ordinary circumstances. But no other emotion carries the power that frustration does to encourage misbehavior of difficult children. They love frustration! They love to see the show it creates. From a kid's point of view, frustration is an irresistible mix of two wonderful parental emotions, anger and loss of control. Frustration is shown when parents:

- Cry.

- Argue about how to handle the children *in front of* the children.

- Don't get over their anger (or hold grudges).

- Argue with nonsense or respond by saying, "I don't have to answer that," or "I'm not going to argue with you."

- Get into a control battle over who has the last word.

- Get into control battles around smooth muscle issues—eating, toileting, and so on—which parents always lose.

- Give orders as "first line of operation" when speaking to children.

- Confuse acceptance and "giving in" with "giving up" and "losing."

Sometimes parents simply must come to a point where they accept the child's symptoms as more or less unchangeable. Then parents need to find ways to manage them that make things easier and less stressful for the family. (See The Paradigm Shift, page 113.)

▟▟ When our kids were into what we politely referred to as 'inappropriate bathroom habits,' we put washable paneling on their bedroom walls and took out the carpeting, replacing it with easy-to-disinfect tile. After a few intense training sessions, the children were able to clean up their own messes. They could no longer 'punish' us by making *us* clean up nasty messes, and they learned a marketable skill. No one can wash down and disinfect rooms like my kids!

In the beginning, Brian would sit and refuse to clean. He was told very calmly that as soon as his room was clean, he was welcome to come to dinner. Eventually his hunger took over and he did the work to our satisfaction. He was the only one who got angry, and he was the only one who suffered. Missing meals worked for Brian, who dearly loved to eat, but that would never have worked for Carl. Carl would have literally starved to avoid doing it our way. His need to control would override his hunger. We learned the hard way not to make statements like 'Just get it done before your next meal.' But those kinds of consequences work beautifully with less controlling kids who have good causal thinking.

Children who become locked into a "control or die" situation must be protected from themselves or they *will* endanger their own health and safety. Parents of such children must constantly guard against imposing consequences that, if carried to extreme by the child, would be abusive. And if they do find themselves stuck in such a situation, parents must be willing to "lose" rather than abuse. These children are masters at recreating early abusive patterns by backing parents into a corner where they feel they must punish more, or harder, to make a point.

An adoptive mother eloquently summarizes the idea that giving *in* is not giving *up*:

We finally came to the conclusion that if the kids wouldn't change, we'd have to, because something had to. That helped in lots of ways . . . some we couldn't have predicted.

> Some have accused me of 'giving up,' when actually I just
> stopped beating my head against the wall over things that
> probably would never be in my power to change.   ▌▌

The remarkable thing is, that sometimes, by lightening the pressure on children and returning control to them (they really have it anyway), parents change the dynamics of the relationship just enough for positive change to begin to take place.

Don't Take It Personally

Angry disturbed children are internally angry at *any* authority figure. Parents are around more, and make the majority of demands on the child, so they take the brunt of the child's anger. But, as one mother humorously noted, "If Bill and Hillary Clinton, Dr. Spock, Madonna, or Michael Jackson were the parents of these kids, they would have problems behaving. They would be having trouble with *anybody*."

Turn Pathological Behavior into "Personal Style"

A creative way to deal with a child's more outrageous behavior is for the parent to reframe the behavior for the child. Explain it away as "just your personal style." This indicates respect for individuality and acceptance of diversity and difference. Of course, in many cases this is done with parents silently biting their tongues, since the "difference" is certainly not within the so-called "norm." It *cannot* be used when the problem behavior is dangerous to the child or others. It does work well when the behavior is simply bizarre or will be looked at askance by others and peers. Let people outside the family teach the lesson and take the heat for the criticism.

Parents should point out to the child that in some cases diversity is a wonderful thing, and that it takes all kinds of people to make an interesting and functioning society. Even within a family, everyone need not look or act or think just like everyone else. "Not to worry, we love you anyway."

Sometimes there is a need for conformity, and when there is, parents insist that the children comply to the extent that they are able. At other times, it is fine to be different. Even very different. The parents' attitude is that an individual's likes and dislikes, and their unique abilities and handicaps, all contribute to diversity in both the family and the community.

Having a neat or messy (and disturbed children can give new meaning to the term) bedroom may be just a matter of personal style. Being able to keep a room as neat as the occupant would like it, or as health would require, is a matter of personal preference and ability. In a family where all children are expected to take care of the cleaning of their own spaces, one child may be able to handle carpeting, bookshelves full of books and toys, and venetian blinds, and another may be able to handle only surfaces that are easily scrubbed down with minimal effort and few or simple possessions.

A child who insists on expressing his emotions with his rear end, by peeing or pooping in places other than the bathroom, is better off with a simply framed metal platform bed and inflatable mattress of the type that takes regular twin bedding. Each are comfortable and adequate, yet easily disinfected by the child. This relatively spartan bed is *not* a punishment, but rather, an adaptation to "personal style"—he being the type of kid who likes to pee or poop in the bed when he gets mad at mom. Mom wants his life to be easy to manage and fun, so why waste time having to hassle about unpleasant odors or steamcleaning his mattress? When this technique is used, it is important not to add qualifiers such as "when you stop wetting your bed, you can have a pretty bed like Jane's." It is also essential to avoid sarcasm.

Reframing in a positive light removes all of the pressure, and removes the rebellious element from the behavior. "Spitting in your hair sure saves on the family haircare products budget. We used to spend so much on styling gel."

Parents can, in a nonjudgmental way, restrict their children from sleepovers and similar activities until they are able to maintain the standards of the host. Parents should explain such a restriction in a way that expresses as much concern for the child's embarrassment as for the host's family. They might suggest a way for them to decline gracefully, and perhaps suggest an alternative activity, all the while acknowledging and feeling sad about the disability that prevented the original invitation from being accepted.

Appreciating personal style is very effective when a child is using behaviors to shock, disgust, or disrupt the family. His victory depends on parents' negative reaction, no matter how subtle. If there are other, underlying reasons— neurological, medical, or—for the behavior, this method will not necessarily eradicate the behavior, but it preserves the child's integrity and the situation will become easier to manage, generating fewer angry feelings in the caretaker. The opportunity to control is taken away from the child and returned to the adult.

Many emotionally disturbed and cognitively disabled kids have problems with organization, and can become overwhelmed by having too much or too many of anything.

- A little television watching may be okay, but too much sends them off on a day-long binge of out-of-control behavior.

- Some books of their own may be enjoyed and taken care of; too many may be destroyed, lost, or never read.

- A few minutes of play alone in the park may be fun and filled with friendly social experiences; a couple of hours may result in fighting with peers or neighborhood vandalism.

- A few decorations on the bedroom wall may be fine, but too many will be ripped down, broken, or defaced with marker or paint.

- A birthday party with ten friends at a pizza parlor or arcade is an open invitation to disaster. One friend over for pizza and a short video might be just perfect.

In the same vein, too many new things can easily overwhelm a child with organizational deficits, which may be why so many kids freak out at birthday parties and Christmas gift openings. Such children need to recognize their limits, again as a personal style or preference issue. A parent may need to say, "You are the kind of kid who does better with a few new things at a time. Some people just love to savor things and stretch out their celebrations. So we'll open Grandma's gift today, and then in a day or two you can have the one from us. That way your birthday will last and last, and you will have a better chance at enjoying it."

We all have limits to what we can endure and easily manage. Helping children define their limits and develop coping skills for management will significantly improve their lives. Being able to verbalize their limits to others, and suggest alternatives, is also an important skill for social and workplace interaction if they become independent as an adult.

When parents talk to their kids in this way, eventually the children are able to internalize their personal style information and express it in other life situations. We know a cognitively disabled adult whose wonderful adoptive parents taught him how to accept and understand his limitations so well that as an adult he is able to say "I am not a car person. I do better on the bus. I can't remember how to get anywhere in my car, and always end up getting lost."

A mother of an attachment disordered child, who also suffered from organizational problems, made this observation about her own daughter, after many failed attempts to force her into a "regular kid" mold:

// We have to be open to new ways to handle our attachment disordered kids (or "regular" ones for that matter). I was quite squeamish about confiscating all of our daughter's clothes, and then giving her just a couple of outfits, as her therapist recommended. She has to wash out these clothes by hand as well. This puts the ball fully in her court, keeps her room from getting trashed by yucky clothes, and leaves her few choices to make as to what to wear. I finally did it. It has made things easier for the family and for her. She can keep her room clean, which makes her proud, she gets dressed in record time, and I don't have to use rubber gloves to do the laundry.

This has been going on for about three months now and I just inquired about adding new outfits—the answer was no! Why? She's beginning to process a lot right now, spent eight days in respite and is now in summer school—more clothes would just complicate things.[119]

//

Notice the end result: The child recognizes her own limits and says "no" to her mom's inquiry about adding a new outfit to her wardrobe. She is happier, even relieved with things as they are—her own personal style, and a manageable way of living. If she has the ability to generalize, this skill will serve her well in many life situations

This Too Shall Pass

It can be easy to lose perspective when dealing with a disturbed child on a daily basis. Parents spend five times as much time with their children as fellow adults than they do with them as children. As the years pass we have been amazed at the differences that God and time have made as disturbed children grew to adulthood. Many who appeared, truthfully, almost beyond repair, have in their late 20s and early 30s pulled themselves together in a most remarkable way. That is both the good news and the bad news for parents, who may have to delay gratification for 25 to 30 years.[120]

Concerning bedwetting, encopresis, and other obnoxious personal behaviors, we have, for years, tongue in cheek, advised parents to tell their children, "Don't worry, you'll be over this by the time you marry your second spouse." As we grow older, this appears to be true of many tacky behaviors!

Problems of this nature that concern parents greatly at the time of their occurrence can eventually seem to mellow and not seem so difficult in retrospect. And with time the child evolves, so that the only *real* truth is that something *will* eventually change. If a behavior does not disappear, it certainly looks different, has a different effect on life, and can be managed in different ways as the child grows older.

We remember a mother who was absolutely livid when her child stuck a coin in the steering post of their new Jeep. Every time she turned the wheel, the coin rattled and annoyed her. Years later one of the authors happened to see her in a grocery store. She recounted the story of the coin, and said that her son was now off to college. She recalled wistfully that the coin had finally fallen out of the steering post, and that now she actually missed that nostalgic reminder of her boy's antics.

8

Foundation Tools

Provide Structure

Child care workers, parenting experts, and therapists emphasize the need for structure in a child's life. They sometimes tell parents, "You need to provide more structure." What does that really mean?

Providing structure does not necessarily mean making a lot of rules. *Structure is giving a child age-appropriate expectations for a task with the focus on task completion and the resulting feeling of accomplishment.* ✓ Notice there are three basic steps to providing structure:

1. Assign a task.

2. Follow the task through to completion.

3. Accomplishment - self eval

3. Encourage the children to feel proud of their accomplishments by asking them for self-evaluation.

Some people mistakenly feel structure is simply providing children with a list of tasks to accomplish, or scheduling every minute of their day. Others mistakenly equate structure with rigidity, never deviating from the children's painstakingly regimented routine.

Others fail by not providing the proper kind of follow-up. Without follow-through and encouragement to help a child feel proud of himself, job completion by itself can be a little hollow.

An adoptive mom explains:

▌▌ When Taylor first came into our home, we gave him lots of chores to do. As a matter of fact, our son said, "Heck! No wonder you guys adopted me! You have so many chores for me to do!" (Laughing) I told him, "Of course! If kids aren't good for free labor, what else are they good for?" We always felt it important that our children develop a sense of responsibility for things that needed doing in the family. They feel more of a sense of ownership and belonging that way. We also give them their share of the take, by making sure allowances are not withheld as punishment. It is their right as contributing members of the family unit. *▌▌*

Following through takes effort. Many parents fall apart on follow-through. Did the job actually get done? Was it done the right way? In a timely manner? Without extraordinary prodding?

Sometimes a difficult child says the job is done, and it isn't done satisfactorily at all. But it's easier and less hassle to let it go than to check to be sure, and make the child do it again the right way if it is not done correctly. So parents will sometimes let poorly done jobs ride.

In talking about the hassles, one adoptive parent said, "You can get Sandy to do the wrong thing at the right time, or the right thing at the wrong time, but it just takes a too much effort to get her to do the right thing at the right time." But it is definitely worth the effort in the long run, and essential to effecting any real change in the child. It is the only way to effectively teach accountability and responsibility.

The father of nine-year-old Mary told us:

/// ** Mary's job was to make her bed before she went to school. Shortly after she came to our home she began slacking off on her chores. I went into her bedroom one morning and the bed was a mess. It hadn't been touched. So I phoned the school and told them that I'd be coming to get her. They were ready for me when I arrived. I walked into her third grade classroom and called her out into the hall. 'What's the matter?' At first she was surprised. Why I was at school? She thought that maybe a family member had died. You can imagine her shock when I told her the bed wasn't made and she needed to walk home and make it. It was quite a long but manageable walk. I went on to work. After she arrived at home, and made the bed, her mom took pity on her and, going into town anyway, didn't make her walk back to school. But the lesson held well, and the bed was always made after that. **///

Note that Mary's father did not embarrass her in front of her classmates by yelling or talking to her within their range of hearing. That would have given Mary legitimate reason to focus on being mad at her dad instead of at herself for not making her bed.

Keeping Healthy Family Members Healthy

We cannot overemphasize the need for families to consider what physicians and therapists have for years made a code of conduct:

"First Do No Harm!"

This is so important, we have given it center stage on its own line. It probably deserves its own page, but we think you get the idea.

When a disturbed child enters a family, the entire function and dynamics of the family change to accommodate that child's needs and personality.[121] The dark side of a disturbed child's personality can be a very dominating and infectious force. Many clever and deceptive children keep their pathology hidden. We know of children who routinely had sex in the therapist's waiting room while the therapist talked with the parents!

Making an effort to maintain the emotional health of the existing family members, and to guard against being sucked into the child's whirlpool of pathology, will pay dividends worth any amount of time and trouble. Parents must work to make sure that the disturbed child is not allowed to triangulate or pit one against the other. The first step in this process is being aware—and making all family members aware—that triangulation is to be expected!

Parents must give as much time and attention to healthy behaviors in their healthy kids, as they do disturbed behaviors in their disturbed child. Exhausted parents can be understandably eager to take the easy route, or postpone relating to and complimenting a child who seems generally to be doing okay.

One mother told us:

// We decided to homeschool our adopted kids so that they could have the experience of living in one home with a stay-at-home mom for the first time. We were hoping to make up for some of the things they had been deprived of in their first few years. They weren't very sure what a mother did during the day. They had seldom been grocery shopping or watched cooking in progress, much less participated in such activities. They were behind academically, but even more behind in terms of bonding to a family and experiencing the things a family does together around the home. We felt that the added attention and individualization we could give them at home would help them become more securely a part of our family, as well as catching them up in schoolwork areas and filling in a lot of social gaps. Our birth daughter, who was in a gifted and talented program at her school, had been asking to be home schooled for some time, but we had denied her, rationalizing that the school system was providing more for her than we could. After she became sad and upset at the idea of her disturbed siblings getting what she had always wanted, we decided to rethink the situation. Would it be right to send her the message that in order to get her own needs met she would have to become 'disturbed' like her brothers and sister? We decided to include her in home schooling, and it was one of the best decisions we ever made!

Joyce's security was greatly enhanced by this decision. She knew then that her needs were equally important in our eyes, even though they were expressed far more subtly. She also learned, throughout many years of struggle, that we would at times set aside the needs of the others to give her special and individual time and attention; things she had grown to expect, and things that all children need, to remain emotionally healthy and secure. Parental resources must be divided and distributed among all of the children, except in times of genuine crisis. Even then, the healthy children must be sure that you are there for them and will give to them as soon as the crisis is over.

The Real Meaning of Fair

It is entirely possible to find some children more likable than others and still be fair. Nancy Thomas, a professional foster and adoptive parent and parent trainer, says, "When I came into this job, I expected myself to like every kid. Then when I didn't, I hated myself. What a bunch of baggage. Now I realize that we find some children easy to like and some very hard to like. And that's okay. Sometimes we just don't like some kids." Regardless of how well we like a child, being fair to each child is essential. We should consequence equal behavior from all of our children the same way—whether or not we find the child likable.

However, fairness does not mean treating children with different problems exactly the same. Truly there are "different strokes for different folks."

An adoptive mother explained that sometimes one of her kids would say, "You don't pay the same attention to me when I do things right, and if I acted like Joel, you'd be a *lot* madder." And I say, "You're right, honey, and I'm so glad I don't have to go into congratulations every time you do some little thing well. It makes my heart sing that you do great things just 'cause it makes you feel good. How wonderful! Maybe someday Joel will be like that too, and I won't have to overlook little things, and 'have kittens' every single time he does something well."

// Howie used to complain that 'Lisa has all the freedom in the world,' and that was not fair because they were the same age and he suffered many more restrictions than she did. We simply pointed out that when he was able to make good decisions about safety and conduct, and show the same willingness and ability to be responsible, he would have the same privileges as Lisa. He didn't like it, but he accepted it, and I think, in his heart, he knew we were right. **//**

The Healthy Kid Is Boss

John is two years younger than Tracy. Tracy has no neurological problems and is a bright child, but very sneaky and
resistant. When the two brothers are left alone, John is
boss. John assumes the parental role in terms of authority:

> **▮▮** I let Tracy know that she has to do whatever John says. John
> is very responsible, and takes his job of supervision very seri-
> ously. Tracy remains pretty resentful. I tell her that when we
> can start to trust her behavior, and when she shows she is
> being a good boss of herself, John won't call the shots. But
> she is still a long way from being a good boss of herself. **▮▮**

When disturbed children are unwilling to accept and
honor a healthy child being in control, they are not ready
to be left in the care of a sibling. The situation could
become dangerous to one or both children.

Never Lie to Your Child

On the surface, this might appear obvious and self-evident,
but too often parents hedge the truth. If they find a child
difficult to like or live with, they don't tell that to the child,
perhaps out of fear of ruining his self-esteem, or because
they feel guilty about their own negative feelings. The parents may be dishonest about other feelings as well. But the
truth is, *any feeling not talked about is acted out.*

When children are told the absolute truth, with love and
respect, in a way they can understand, without punches being
pulled, they generally accept the facts and grow. Most often
they know the truth anyway, at least subconsciously. When
they know they are being lied to, or that their relationship

with their parents is based on false pretenses, they lose faith in other things their parents say as well. Real trust can not be established this way. Sometimes a child may need to hear the truth:

- "Jake, right now, you are making it difficult for anyone to like being around you."

- "Jean, if you treat your friends the way you treat me, I'm kinda surprised you have any."

- "Do you think you would like me very much if I acted the way you are right now?"

- "John, I have some bad news. We won't be taking you skiing this weekend. Mom and I think the family will probably have more fun without you. So we will be taking the other kids. One thing for sure, you have a lot of neat qualities, and if you ever wanted it to be different, I'm sure you could be a lot more fun. Then we would love to have you with us." (This technique is only used if a child is deliberately and repeatedly spoiling the family fun, not if the problem is something he honestly cannot help, such as a physical condition that prevents him from participating.)

Parents must consider the type of role models they are being in these situations. Our children are far more likely to imitate what we do than what we say.

Most difficult truths should not be discussed in anger. If a parent is angry, it is better to wait for another time to point out truths that might be hard for the child to accept. For instance, a wise parent might ask, "Susan, do you think you want to work this out here with us while you are still young, or do you think it will be better to work it out with your first husband?" While this might sound sarcastic, it is not meant to be, nor should it be said in a sarcastic or belittling tone of voice. It is truthful, and should be said with caring and respect for the child. People either work out their problems with parents or they work through them (sometimes!) with first spouses.

Express Expectations

Anyone can give an order. Children can always be told to "quiet down." Orders are easily given and easily rebelled against. And because orders can always be given, it is better not to rush into them. Try other things first. It is best to begin by making a request or an observation. It is impossible to rebel against an observation, and it is difficult to rebel against a kindly phrased request.

Some parents make life difficult for themselves by asking children if they "can" perform. They ask "Can you bring me my coat?" or "Can you help me out?" This opens the door for the child to answer, "No, I can't." Many children do better when given a polite request: "I would really appreciate your helping me out with this. Thanks a bunch, sweetie."

Using the following six statements, different parents ask their child to settle down in different ways. Which do you think have the best chances of working? How would you like to have the same requests made of you? (Hint: Those are the ones that have the best chance of working!)

1. *"Stop that!"* It will never stay stopped if the child is a difficult child.

2. *"Quit it, you're driving me crazy."* The behavior will almost inevitably get worse. The parent has given all control to the child and the child thinks he has accomplished his goal of driving the parent crazy.

3. *"If this continues, I'll have to ask you to leave."* Two problems here. First, the child is given control of the parent with the statement "I'll *have to*." Secondly, the child now knows that warnings will always be given prior to a consequence, so the child will constantly walk the line of misbehavior. The "three strikes you're out" approach teaches children that they can misbehave twice for free, but that there may be a penalty the third time.

4. *"Honey, I would appreciate it if you would quiet down. Thanks a bunch."* Requests work better for most children most of the time.

5. *"Sweetheart, you are hassling my ears and eyeballs."* No request, no order, nothing to rebel against. Healthy children will be more likely to take the parent's feelings into account and quiet down. A disturbed child may be *trying* to hassle parents and will be rewarded by this statement.

6. *"Honey, will you please take your activities elsewhere? Thank you."* This has the advantage of telling the child what to do, rather than what not to do. It is permissive rather than punitive. Most children learn to obey the first time when rules are clarified and warnings are not given.

When making a request, it is effective to use the "anticipatory thank you." That is, the adoptive parent requests a particular behavior from a child, turns his or her back to the child and, walking away, says "Thank you." Sometimes younger children are fooled into thinking that they are compliant children, even though they haven't completed (or even begun) the task. Airlines use this tactic all the time: As the plane sits at the gate, before even being pushed off, the flight attendant says, "Thank you for not smoking"— before anyone has even had time to light up! Saying thank you before the child has responded also indicates to the child that you are confident he will comply. His subconscious attitude is "If my mom says it's so—it must be so."

Rescue

Parents can sometimes have a tough time knowing when natural consequences are too tough. Parents understandably have a tendency to rescue, even though rescue often makes children weaker. Rescue places all of the concern about a problem squarely on the parent's shoulders instead of on the child's where it belongs. Wise parents allow mistakes and failures, even hope that their child will make many, many mistakes that are not life-threatening, knowing that these are excellent learning opportunities. Children who are unnecessarily sheltered from consequences, grow up to be irresponsible, entitled, and blameful. And yet . . .

There are those times when our children are in a jam of one kind or another, and every fiber in a parent's being says, "for heaven's sake, lend a hand to help them out of this."

There are times that it is safe, effective, and wise—more than that, it's just *nice*—to help children out of jams.

At the time of this writing, the federal government is concerning itself with the rules for rescue. How much assistance, Medicare, Medicaid, SSI, and food stamps is enough, and how much is too much? How much helps people, and how much keeps them dependent on government handouts for the rest of their lives?

Luckily, the rules for rescue apply across the board. They apply for families, for businesses, for neighbors and for government. They apply for special needs children and for the "normal" child. Let's look at some situations where rescue is effective and appropriate, and some where it is ineffective and harmful.

The following is a true-life rescue example involving a common situation:

▌▌ It was a snowy evening outside. My 16-year-old son wanted to drive 30 miles to Denver with a friend, the two of them taking his friend's car. His friend, Bill, wanted to drive. We lived in the mountains at the time, and have only fairly isolated mountain roads. I told Andy I didn't think it was a good idea. It was cold and snowing, and the roads were icy and, if it were me, I wouldn't go. He decided to go anyway. At about midnight, the phone rang . . .

'Dad, Bill and I are in the ditch over by the Henderson House. Will you please come winch us out?'

I rubbed the sleep out of my eyes. I thought about my nice, warm bed, and my nice warm wife beside me. I said, 'In the first place, Andy, I thought Bill was driving. Aren't you phoning the wrong dad?'

"Yeah, I know, Dad, but if Bill's dad came down he'd get mad at Bill and jaw at him about it for days, and I'd really appreciate your doing it.

▮▮

What should this father do?

The Rules for Rescue

There are two basic types of rescue. We will call them *guardian angel rescue, and milk of human kindness rescue.*

Guardian Angel Rescue

- As parents, like it or not, we sometimes must function as our children's saviors. *Guardian angel rescue means doing all one can to save a person when life and limb are in definite danger.*

- Guardian angels perform their functions invisibly.

- Guardian angels are fairly unreliable and no one takes them for granted. ("I'll drive inattentively. My guardian angel will watch over me and see that nothing bad happens.")

Luckily, "life and limb" issues don't come up very often for most of us. When they do, and we must act to save the child's life, it is better to do so unobtrusively and in a way that the child knows he cannot necessarily count on at other times.

Is the child in the above example a candidate for a guardian angel rescue? No! His life and limb are not in danger. He made it to a phone. He wouldn't freeze in the car overnight. He'd live no matter what his dad does.

Milk of Human Kindness Rescue

Most of us would want to help others out of a jam. That desire to help others is one of the special drives of the healthy human soul. However, helping others too much or at the wrong times, can also disable them. Then they become less able to help themselves when they need to. There is a rule that, if followed, will almost always ensure that rescue is helpful, not harmful:

It is usually ill-advised to go more than halfway to help solve a chronic problem that people cause themselves.

- If the problem a person causes herself is *acute* or *new*, it is generally safe to go all out to save the person— even from herself.

- Regardless of whether the problem is acute or chronic, self-inflicted or not, *no one deserves to be helped if they demand it.*

With the rules for rescue in mind, let's look at the situation with Andy and his dad:

- It is not a guardian angel problem.

- It *is* an acute problem. He does not have a history of calling for help and making poor decisions, which would make this situation a chronic problem.

- He did not demand help. He asked nicely and hopefully.

So should dad get out of bed to help Andy out of the snow drift at 12 o'clock in the morning? You bet!

And then comes the hard part for this dad. He must bite his tongue, and not say "I told you so." Doing that will negate the learning for Andy. It will simply make him feel stupid, and might make him resentful and mad, but it will not open his mind to thoughtful reflection on his poor decision. Instead, when Andy's dad said, "Well, this *is* a pretty bad curve. It would be easy to slip into the ditch on this one." Andy said, "Yeah, but we shouldn't have been out in this storm tonight anyway! The roads aren't safe. You were sure right about that, Dad!"

When the rules for rescue are followed, kids can learn from their mistakes!

Special needs children *should* be rescued if they:

- Have causal thinking problems and may not be able to learn from their mistakes.

- Have chronic problems that they did not cause.

- Have immediate or life and death issues.

9

Conventional Parenting Tools and Techniques

This section will briefly describe the conventional parenting tools and techniques that form the foundation of good parenting.

Conventional parenting tools are readily available to parents. For those who want more conventional parenting information than we provide in this book, we highly recommend the following resources:

- The *Love and Logic*® Parenting Materials. A catalog of books, audiotapes, and videos is available by calling the Love and Logic Institute at 1-800-338-4065.

- *Success in Parenting,*® by Foster W. Cline, M.D. and Benjamin Brucker, Ed.D., complete parenting information in audiotape, video, and book form is, available by calling Lon Gibby Productions, Inc. at 1-800-200-1113.

When parenting disturbed children, the conventional techniques should be the first line of response. Unfortunately, as we have emphasized, conventional techniques are often not effective with disturbed children. Still it is essential to be certain that these usual techniques are ineffective before embarking on the specialized techniques we provide in chapter 12. The specialized techniques are controversial and easily misunderstood and misused. Sometimes parents of disturbed children are caught between a rock and a hard spot. Should they continue to use normal parenting techniques that don't work for the children, or use techniques that may be effective for the children but misunderstood by the community? We believe the specialized techniques should be made available but used with all the cautions we emphasize in chapter 12. In the long run this boils down to parental judgment and good sense.

Let's take a common example. In this chapter we talk about the use of the "I" message. An "I" message is expressed when a mother, without anger or frustration, says, "Honey, I feel upset when you interrupt me." The average child, wanting to please the parent thinks, "Gee, I don't want to upset Mom. I think I'll change my behavior." The average disturbed child, wanting only to please himself or to get even, thinks, "Yes! I've got her!" This "I" message is simply used as a map of how to behave to stay in charge of mom's feelings and control the situation.

Effective parenting exists within a framework of techniques and attitudes. The techniques are actions and reactions that are thought out and consciously decided upon beforehand, not simply based on impulse, emotion, or gut reactions. When the correct techniques are used for any length of time, they become habitual and automatic. Each parenting tool is effective or ineffective depending on the underlying attitude of the parent. For instance, ignoring behavior is a common parenting tool. There are many different ways to ignore: Leave without comment; stay and distract; or give alternative behavior without reference to the undesirable behavior.

Effective use of parenting tools depends on three variables:

1. Parental attitude and personality (style or temperament).

2. Child attitude and personality and/or level and type of disturbance.

3. Training.

Unfortunately, many parents use only the techniques their parents knew and used on them. In dealing with their children, some parents are ruled more by heart than by brain, more by reaction than action. Some parents are calm and cool under fire, and others are jumpy and fly off the handle about every little thing. Both may have taken parenting classes and have the proper tools, yet one is more likely to be effective than the other because of attitude. Still, the calmest parent in the world is unlikely to be successful without tools. A parent may have a great attitude, yet lack basic techniques that will put that attitude to its most effective use. To be effective, the two must go hand in hand.

Other influences determine whether some tools will be effective:

- Availability of backup.

- Ego strength of parent.

- Number and ages of other children in the home.

- Available time.

- Appropriate space.

Deciding to leave five-year-old Johnny home from the family outing because he has decided to have a temper tantrum about which movie they are to see, is only practical if there is a readily available baby-sitter. Asking a child to spend time alone in his room until she is willing to be fun to be around could be a punishment for the siblings with whom she shares the room, particularly if she decides on an extended isolation period.

Minimizing Rebellion

Avoid control battles with children to whatever extent possible. Much of the time, kids win control battles. Therefore, when battle lines must be drawn, give thought to where and how they are drawn. Often, the amount of rebelliousness a child exhibits, even a very disturbed child, depends, in large part on the parent's wording and projected attitude. Demanding parents who give orders without affection will almost always have rebellious children.

> Strict parents + unloving parents =
> sneaky and rebellious child.

Ignoring the Behavior

Ignoring the behavior is the first line of defense unless safety issues are involved. Ignoring handles most low-grade childhood misbehavior.

Advantages:

Ignoring behavior is the easiest thing of all to do. It takes no thought and little effort. It can be done immediately. It comes naturally. It is least intrusive and a good starting point unless someone's health or safety is at stake.

Disadvantages:

Disturbed or difficult children often escalate their behavior when it is ignored. Unconsciously or consciously the child thinks, "If you think you can ignore me, try this on for size!"

Ignoring does not work if the child's sole mission at the moment is to get your attention. He or she will simply try something else that is equally annoying or undesirable.

Ignoring behavior does not mean telling a child, "I am not going to answer that question," or "I am not going to pay attention to that kind of talk," or "I'm not listening to you." Ignoring means tuning out, turning off, and walking away. It means leaving the child psychologically and sometimes physically if necessary. It means giving absolutely no attention to the problem behavior.

▌▌ The week after we adopted our daughter, she was in the back seat— a picture of obnoxious inquisitiveness. 'What was the name of that dog?' 'How much further do we have to go?' 'Why is daddy wearing a purple shirt?' 'Is red a prettier color than blue?' 'Can I have some money?' She was just running off at the mouth, asking nonsensical or silly questions, so my husband I just ignored her and talked only to each other. Finally, in the back seat we heard her say, 'No one is talking to me, and I know why. I'm saying stupid things.' We hadn't said a thing about what we thought of what she was saying, but she was right on. Of course, after that last comment, we paid a lot of attention: 'Honey, did you hear a real intelligent remark from the backseat?' ▌▌

Generally, the healthier the child, and the more acute the behavior problem, the better ignoring the problem works. When a behavior problem has been present for many years, or there are emotional or neurological disabilities present, ignoring will generally *not* work.

Distracting and Offering Alternative Behavior

Advantages:

- Can be carried out quickly.

- Does not require a lot of thought.

Disadvantages:

- Angry or controlling children rebel when given redirection.

Redirection means recognizing the children's feelings and giving them something else to do, rather than arguing about the situation. It means saying, for instance, "I know you are angry, Troy, but right now, I don't want to discuss it. I would like you to change clothes, get cleaned up, and get ready to go."

Making Observations about Behavior

Making observations about behavior is simple. It gives children the satisfaction of knowing that we notice their behavior and allows them to make conscious, thoughtful decisions. Observations might include the following:

- "John, I see you're having a bit of trouble handling yourself right now."

- "Sally, I notice you are picking on your scabs again."

- "Troy, you are not being very much fun to be around right now."

Simply making the observation implies that the child will know what to do about the behavior and change it. This is true for many children, and it's certainly worth giving them a chance.

Advantages:

- Making observations is easy to teach and learn.

- It does not invite rebellion.

- It can be extended into a leading question—"What do you think you might do about that?"

Disadvantages:

- Making observations doesn't usually work well for special needs children or children with emotional or behavioral disorders.

- If used with the wrong tone of voice (judgmental, angry, or belittling), it becomes ineffective.

"I" Messages

An "I" message consists of three parts:

I feel _____ (feeling state)

when people _____ (action)

because I _____.

For example, one might say "Guys, I feel *annoyed* when people *make this much noise,* because I *can't concentrate on what I'm doing here.*"

Advantages:

There are many advantages to "I" messages.

- They do not place blame on the child.
- They give the child control.
- They imply that the child will take the feelings of the parents into account.
- They imply that the child is competent.
- They model openness and expression of appropriate feelings.
- They allow the child to figure out what to do.
- They give no order to rebel against.

With all of these advantages, it is no wonder that "I" messages often work well!

Disadvantages:

There are also a number of disadvantages to using "I" messages.

- "I" messages take thought.
- They don't often come naturally to angry people. Parents from dysfunctional families automatically

doubt their effectiveness and shout the "I" message. When said with anger or pleading, they will not work.

- "I" messages never work with children who have no conscience because they really don't care how others feel.

- Children who cannot empathize (a higher-level emotional skill), or who do not have good causal thinking, cannot respond appropriately to "I" messages.

- "I" messages may be too subtle for a cognitively disabled child. (It's about *them*, not *me*.) This kind of child thinks concretely, and needs to be told what you want him to do, not how you feel.

Hugging and Touching a Child

Advantages:

- This is a normal and natural (to healthy adults) parenting technique.

- All human beings need touch.

- Most children like it.

Disadvantages:

- Disturbed children can cry "child abuse" after being hugged by a well-meaning teacher or therapist. Many foster care agencies and some state and county laws prohibit touching foster children!

- Children with attachment disorder or children who have sensory integration problems may be overly sensitive to touch and may react poorly to touch as a means of behavior control.

A touch on the arm or a gentle arm around the shoulder can serve as a reminder of appropriate behavior or a physical redirection of attention or task.

Choices and Consequences vs. Protection and Punishment

Parents should impose consequences when children make unwise choices about their behavior. Sometimes *the emotion the parent shows makes the only difference between a punishment and a consequence.* The difference between a punishment and consequence is simply the attitude and wording of the request.

For instance, two mothers ask their sons to leave the room:

1. When Linda asks her child to go to his room, she is *angry.* She wants her boy to feel bad, and the child feels punished, resentful, and rejected.

2. When Janet asks Skip to "take that behavior and hop off to your room, please" she is matter-of-fact, not angry, and gives the message that she is requiring the removal of the auditory or visual hassles that her son is causing. She is not making her request to make the child feel bad, but does it because the environment is temporarily more pleasant without him. The child feels consequenced, not punished, and learns from the interaction.

Consequences and punishment differ in the following ways:

- Consequences lead to thought; punishment leads to resentment.

- Punishment is done to make children feel bad; consequences are carried out to make the parents feel better or the environment more pleasant.

- If children feel upset with the consequence, that is frosting on the cake. It is *okay* for a child to feel upset about being consequenced, but not *necessary*. For instance, a child might stomp off to his room and scream over his shoulder, "Good! I like going to my room. I have all my favorite things there." The parent might reply with understanding, "Well, John, that's great. We want everybody to be happy. It's just that the way you are acting right now, it's pretty hard for any of us to be happy. We'll be glad to see you again when you are ready to be more thoughtful of others."

- Consequences generally fit the crime; punishment usually fits the parent's feelings. For instance, if a child often comes home late, grounding makes sense. It is a logical consequence for not returning home before curfew. If a child is talking back, grounding does not make sense.

- Punishment is usually applied in an angry state; consequences should be applied in a matter-of-fact fashion. There are two types of consequences: natural and imposed. Using natural consequences, those which occur with no intervention, parents simply do not rescue the child but let the chips fall, hoping he learns from the result. Using imposed consequences, wise parents invent creative responses that "fit" the misbehavior.

Allowing for Natural Consequences without Rescue

Sophie has messed around getting ready in the morning and will be late for school. She wants her mother to write an excuse for her. Mom replies, "Honey, I understand you are late, and I understand the teacher will want a note from me. But if I write it, I'll just have to say, 'Sophie was moving real slow this morning, and so she's late.' That doesn't sound too good, so we have a choice here of no note at all when you walk in late, or a truthful one that doesn't sound too good." Another possibility is simply saying to the child, "Honey, I don't do notes."

Creatively Provide Choices and Consequences

Robert must leave for school when his mother leaves for work. She drives him to school because it's too far to walk. Robert is not ready to go. Mom explains, "I'll be late arriving at work because I waited for you. This hassles my head. It's a big energy drain for me. But, honey, this Saturday, when you wash the outside of all the downstairs windows, it'll put this lost energy right back into me."

Paul can't find his school materials. He pleads with his mom, "This is a test day and I need your help to find my stuff or I'll flunk the test." Mom helps him find them, but reminds Paul, "Unfortunately, I have a lot to get done, and since I used so much time finding your stuff, I won't have time to take you and your friends to the movies tonight."

Typical Consequences

Effective consequencing might involve some sort of isolation. Thus, consequencing a child might be asking him to go to his room, sit in a corner, or stand by the wall. Alternatively, consequences may involve "payback." Thus, if a child steals from another child, her she might have to pay the other child back by giving or selling something valuable of their own. Or, the child may need to write a note of apology, or pay back time lost by doing chores for the other person.

Sometimes "thinking about behavior" can be requested without asking for written work, but often it involves asking the child to write about his behavior and his plans for change. For instance, an adoptive parent might request, "John, I want you to write out, on two pages, at least twenty different ways you could have said 'I'm upset' rather than 'Fuck you.'"

Cautions Regarding Consequences

Consistency is a concept that is often misunderstood. When dealing with problem children, parents can be rigid and overly controlling while believing they are being consistent. Consequences get confused with punishment, and consistency with overpersistence. When this happens, parenting responses move out of the realm of making sense. *Being consistent does not mean carrying out a consequence forever until the child responds.* Consistency requires that there is always some kind of learning opportunity for a misbehaving act. It doesn't always have to be the same response.

It may be beneficial to allow children to be uncertain about exactly what kind of response will follow misbehavior, and when that response will occur. It is not always necessary for consequences to be immediate. This is a commonly held misperception. Only children with limited cognitive ability may need immediate consequences in order to connect the learning experience with the "crime."

Highly controlling children *like* predictable responses as they are more easily manipulated and controlled—so keep these kids guessing with statements like "Gee, this is really sad! In fact, it's such a sad thing, we don't need to talk it over now. I'll let you know tomorrow what I've decided you can do to handle the problem." Telling children that they need to think about how the parent is going to respond can in itself be a consequence. It allows the children time to mull things over and imagine future events. Uncertainty is difficult and worrisome for many disturbed kids. They cannot control someone who is unpredictable or changes tactics frequently.

Misbehavior in public is a common problem. Responses to children's behavior in public may, and often should, be different than responses to misbehavior at home. In public, the children may feel that they can get away with more, and parents feel they are being watched and judged. Some things that occur in public absolutely must be handled immediately; many do not. In public, it is often sufficient to say, "I'm not sure how I'm going to handle this, but it'll come to me later." Or ask the child, "How do you think this needs to be handled when we get home?"

Parents should carefully guard against expressing a low level of glee in providing consequences. If the child picks this up, it negates the learning experience, understandably builds resentment, and models the "get back or get even" response. A few parents we have met feel a crazy mixture of frustration, hope, and power when consequencing. They demonstrate an almost triumphant pride for imposing lengthy or heavy consequences on their kids such as having the children eat nothing but "Nutrameal" for weeks, or having their kids live for days in the garage, or allowing them no personal belongings in their room. When we hear such talk among parents, we find it worrisome. In certain situations with a very disturbed child, such consequences might be imposed with limited duration. However, a healthy parent does not usually feel particularly good about imposing consequences on a child, and certainly is not delighted or proud that the child is not responding to their efforts.

A Word of Warning

Generally, consequences should work fairly quickly to improve or eradicate behavior. If they do not, other strategies should be employed. If nothing seems to work, it may mean that the underlying cause of the behavior needs to be addressed therapeutically or medically before behavioral techniques can be effective. *Duration and intensity are two areas in which a perfectly appropriate consequence can be turned into an abusive act.*

Parents are in trouble when a consequence is carried out:

- Too long.

- Too hard.

- Too intensely.

- Too many times.

When parents find themselves increasing the intensity, frequency, or duration of a consequence as the children increasingly step up behavior problems, watch out! Parents may slip into a dangerous power struggle with a very disturbed child, and abuse could be the result. *Parents must stop the cycle—the children will not.* When parents fear that "backing off" indicates they are "losing," they may already have overstepped the boundaries of healthy parenting. Parents win by being healthier than the child, by having good control over their emotions, and by knowing when to back off and regroup.

Problem Solving

Simple problem solving leads many rebellious children to be more compliant. Therapeutic parents often use problem-solving techniques with very difficult children. The nice thing about a chronic problem is that it will always happen again, so the parent can wait for exactly the right moment to handle it and have a plan in place.

- "Honey, you are a bright kid. Would you like to sit down? Maybe together we can figure out why so much is going wrong for you right now."

- "Troy, there is a lot of mud all over the carpet. There are several ways that it could be cleaned up. Let's discuss how you are going to go about it."

Exploring Feelings and Use of Active Listening Skills

Active listening and exploring of problems calls for rephrasing what the child says. The parent has an attitude of curiosity, interest, and compassion.

Advantages:

- Active listening does not invite rebellion.
- Active listening is generally fun to do.

Disadvantages:

- Good reflective listening and problem exploration often takes practice.
- When poorly done, attempts to listen actively can sound like parroting.
- Active listening and problem solving take time.

Procedures For Active Listening

- Usually the child introduces the topic by describing an experience about which they have feelings.

- Listen to the child and use door openers such as, "Oh," "I see," and "Uh-huh . . ."

- Try to let the child do most of the talking; be slow to give answers, but express real interest and patience.

- Pick out what the child has said and paraphrase back to the child: "Sounds like you are pretty unhappy, right?"

- Avoid giving advice and appearing judgmental.

- Encourage resolution by asking questions such as "So how do you think you will handle this next time?" or "Is there anything I can do to help?"

Younger children and children with neurological thought-processing problems need to have their feelings explored with multiple choice questions rather than open-ended questions. In such cases, wise parents do not ask "How are you feeling, John?" rather "John, are you feeling mad, sad, disappointed, or just totally upset?"

Expressing Parental Feelings of Anger

Disturbed children can bring out an extraordinary amount of anger in parents, even in normally laid-back individuals. Parents often tell us of their feelings of shock at discovering themselves capable of such rage. Parents need to be able to feel and express their angry feelings. Anger, however, can be expressed in a manner that either makes the situation better or worse. When anger is expressed correctly, it lets the child know that anger can be expressed in harmless and productive ways. Children need a model for the expression of feelings. They need to know that parents can't always control how they feel, but they *can* control how they express their feelings!

Effective parents (who want to stay out of jail!) must "know when to hold em; when to fold em; when to walk away and when to run."[122] And when parents feel their anger burning out of control, that's the time to run. It is definitely okay for parents to walk away when they are angry. That does *not* mean they lose and the child wins. Parents can always come back and win later with an angerless plan.

When Expressing Anger Makes the Situation Worse

- Thoughtless explosions always indicate a lack of control on the part of the parent. Such expressions of anger will make the situation worse and give children too much control.

- Anger that has no resolution does not teach the child coping skills.

- Expressing anger when applying a consequence can defeat the importance of the consequence.

- Ineffective expressions of anger can

  - Make the children feel resentful.

  - Shift the focus from learning to the parent's feelings.

  - Prevent children from taking responsibility and change their focus to "my parents are so mean."

  - Give the child control of the situation; when the parent makes statements like "You make me so mad."

  - Let the child off the hook by making hidden negative assumptions. For example, the parent says "Can't you do better than this?!" (Answer: "No."), "Why did you have to do this?" (Answer: "I don't know, but I had to.") or "Do you always have to do this?" (Answer: "Yes.")

  - Reflect on the child's personhood, when the parent says "You are so stupid!," "You will never amount to anything," or "You'll never learn, you always do things the same dumb way."

When Parental Expressions of Anger Can Be Helpful

- When it is a relatively *rare* experience.

- When the expression of anger is a *decision* rather than an impulse. This shows the parent is in control.

- When parents take responsibility for their feelings with statements such as "I am feeling really angry right now because . . ."

- When parents show they are in control of their feelings by ending the scolding on a positive note. (See "The Sixty-Second Scolding," page 251)

Family Dynamics

Examining family dynamics and triangulation issues will help set the stage for the more controversial, nonconventional parenting tools that are examined in chapter 12.

Triangulation—pitting one family member against another—is common in the homes of disturbed children.[123] It usually takes one of these forms:

- Other children in the family feel ignored or unimportant as the parents spend an undue amount of energy on the disturbed child.

- Disturbed children attempt, usually unconsciously, to target their mothers and initiate a game of "let's you and him fight." Disturbed children often present differently to each parent.

- The core rage of severely disturbed children is often directed at the mother, who may overreact, or react appropriately and feel misunderstood by the husband and those outside the family.[124]

- Disturbed people, including children, tend to con and manipulate others to get their way. This sets one family member against another.

- Often the family must deal with community anger over the behavior of the child. Neighbors may express anger at the parents for using unconventional parenting techniques in their attempt to control the child.

Of all the ways disturbed children may be unusual, the degree of skillfulness they display when *triangulating,* or playing one parent against another, is perhaps the most unique.[125]

Living with a Child Who Triangulates

All children may at times attempt to play one parent against another; however, this is not to be confused with the manipulation and pathology shown by disturbed children. Many disturbed children show their rage by scapegoating the mother and manipulating and triangulating relationships with her.[126,127] Fathers are especially vulnerable to this type of manipulation, and need to make every effort to openly support their wives in front of the children. Any questioning or doubting within the couple must go on behind closed doors, not in front of the child. These children are skillful at "pushing buttons" and a day or even a few hours spent with one of them can be a stressful event. Mothers may appear upset and angry, frazzled and exhausted at the end of a day. Imagine then, Dad arriving home to find 13-year-old Jason diligently cleaning the garage.

> "Hi Dad, I thought I'd surprise you by cleaning out the garage!"
>
> "Wow Son, that's really great! I'm so proud of you for doing this without being asked. That is very thoughtful."

"Well, Mom's having a hard day. Think she's kinda losing it, ya know?"

"No, what do you mean?"

"Well, like I was bringing some rags out here to wipe off the shelves, and she started screaming at me about getting fingerprints on the bathroom mirror or some stupid thing like that. She's been so touchy lately, Dad. Be careful what you say or she'll bite your head off."

(Laughing) "Thanks for the warning, Son."

Dad enters the house to be greeted by his wife, who shrieks "Roy, you are going to have to deal with him this time. I've had it. I don't know how much more of this I can take!" It appears to Dad that Jason is trying to do a good deed for his parents, and he is confronted with an apparently hysterical woman screaming about things that don't make sense from his point of view. Who and what should he believe?

He doesn't see what occurred prior to his arrival home. He doesn't know that Jason began his day, when his mother went to wake him for breakfast, by telling her to "get the fuck out of my room and stay out, you bitch!" He doesn't know that when Mom refused to drive Jason to school because he missed the bus due to arguing and glacial-speed movement, he went to the neighbors' house begging a ride, saying, "Mom didn't wake me up on time this morning and now she won't drive me to school either. Could I pay you from my allowance to give me a ride so I don't miss my algebra test? I really want to do well in math so I can go to a good college."

Of course the neighbor drove Jason, and then mentioned it later to Mom who was out in the yard raking leaves—a job Jason was supposed to have done the night before. Mom was livid. First of all, Jason doesn't even take algebra, and secondly the school had just phoned to say he didn't show up for any of his morning classes. He got a free ride into town, and was probably hanging out at the mall again! Then, after arriving home and lying about where he had been all day, he took her favorite lipstick and ruined it by writing "what a bitch!" on her bathroom mirror. She also found he had urinated all over the toilet seat, and onto the floor the way he typically did when he was confronted with bad behavior. When she asked him to clean up the mess, he stormed out of the house yelling "You aren't my real mom, and you can't make me do squat!" So Mom spent the rest of her afternoon scrubbing the bathroom floor, but left the lipstick for her husband to see. It was her only evidence of a day from hell.

Still, Dad has trouble not siding with his son. Maybe his wife *does* act bitchy to the boy. She might be demanding more of him than he is capable of. She can be surprisingly rigid at times, or so it appears. He wonders out loud if perhaps if it is that "time of the month." At this point his usually calm and understanding wife goes ballistic.

Dad goes out to the garage to help Jason clean. Mom sits down on the floor and weeps. As these kinds of interactions become more frequent, and because no one believes that Jason "could be that bad when he seems so eager to please," she feels alone and abandoned, helpless and hopeless. She feels as if her son has stolen her husband's loyalty, and resents her spouse's not believing and supporting her. They had always had such admiration and respect for each other before Jason entered their lives. Has her husband forgotten that? Or is she really losing it and becoming a "bitch"? More and more she doubts her ability to be a good mother.

Her husband, her parents, the school, and the neighbors have accused her of everything from "being too strict and unyielding" to " just not liking boys." Maybe they *should* have adopted a girl. Even her own mother asks her "what is it that you don't like about Jason? He is such a nice, helpful boy." She wonders if maybe she is going crazy.

Over a period of time, and after repeated interactions like the one described above, in which the child appears charming, cooperative, and sincere to others but acts belligerent, defiant, and hateful towards the mother, the balance of trust and power in the family makes subtle and pathological shifts. Mom appears crazy, angry, and unloving, and the child allies with others to make her look even more so. This pattern of destruction must be recognized and stopped if the child is to be helped and the family to remain intact. As Richard Delaney and Frank Kunstal warn in their book *Troubled Transplants*, "A house divided cannot stand."[128]

Fathers caught in this situation must ask themselves if their wives were always so volatile, unstable, and unbelievable. If not, why would she suddenly become so? Was she always prone to exaggeration and impatience? Most importantly, was, or is she this way with all the other children?

Usually, disturbed children are caught in their deception—eventually. Sooner or later someone witnesses or overhears them treating their mothers badly, or catches them in a lie, and begins to question their credibility on other occasions. But amazingly, some kids get by with this kind of thing for years, and by then the damage to the marriage and other family relationships can be irreversible. The emotional toll on the family can be enormous.

Parenting classes are often filled with mothers who have extremely difficult children. Often these mothers have excellent parenting and interpersonal skills. It is the *children* who need help. But the mother's self-esteem has been so shattered by her ineffectiveness with her child, and others' refusal to support her, that she thinks there is something she should be doing better. She arrives at parenting class desperate for help and understanding.

Solutions for Triangulators

Parents can and must avoid being triangulated by their disturbed child. These five agreements can help:

◆ Agree to openly support and believe each other in front of the child.[129]

The rule of thumb is that the more lenient parent in any given situation supports the stricter parent when both are together in the child's presence. If the stricter parent seems too strict, this is talked about later when the couple is alone. If the stricter parent is still thought to be too strict by the other, seek third party consultation.

Ed and Amy, were at odds about handling their eight-year-old adopted daughter, Christina. In the first therapy session, Amy noted wryly, "B.C.—before Christina—Ed and I agreed on everything. And we treated each other with love and respect. A.C.—after Christina—we disagree on everything, and we are not as loving to each other."

Ed felt Amy was too ungiving, cold, and punitive with Christina. Amy thought Christina was seductive toward Ed and had him "conned and wrapped around her little finger."

In discussing the situation with this couple, we found that Amy came from a loving background. She related well with her own parents and siblings. She loved and competently cared for her other children, and they responded well to her. She had always been an excellent mother. Although we found Christina a charming little girl and even wondered if Amy was being too rigid with her, we told Ed to back his wife to the hilt. We encouraged him to back Amy at every turn. When Christina would turn to him for support, instead of saying, with some doubt, "Well, I guess that's what your mother wants," he was to respond more along the lines, of, "Hey, your mother asked you to . . . so I, expect you to jump to it."

In very little time, Ed and Amy reported that they were feeling much better about their relationship. Ed noted, "Boy did I learn a lot. As soon as I started backing Amy, this 'sweet' child turned on me. I haven't been called names like that since I was in grade school! She was a hellion. I understand now what Amy was experiencing. It was the difference between night and day. I thought this was a sweet kid, but she is a real problem. I hope we can handle her!"

◆ **Plan in advance how to deal with attempts by the child to discredit one or the other parent.**

An ounce of discussion about how to handle a problem before it occurs is worth a pound of discussion afterwards. Parents often know their disturbed children will complain about school at home; complain about home at school; complain about dad to mom; and about mom to dad. How are parents going to handle this? What are the responses going to be? Usually the best responses when children attempt to triangulate by tattling on the other parent are variations on

▮▮ Why are you telling *me* this?",

"Whom do you need to take that up with?", or

"I hope you figure out what you can do to help things go better with . . . ▮▮

One adopted daughter told her parents, "Jeez, I hate it when you tell each other all the things I say around here." Although she could not express it well, this little girl was saying that this new home was a lot different than the foster home where she could set parent against parent by bad-mouthing one to the other. Here, instead of one parent blaming the other, they asked what she did to bring on the problem in the first place. And they had no secrets from each other.

Parents must give disturbed children the message that "We talk to each other about everything because we value each other's opinions so much. So anything you tell either of us is gets heard by both of us. We don't keep secrets from each other in this family, and we work together as a team for the good of all."

◆ **Double check with each other about rules, permissions, and so on.**

A good rule of thumb is to tell the child that if one parent says "no" to anything, then the answer is "no" regardless of how the other parent later responds. Often parents don't realize the request is being made for the second time.

◆ **Make it clear to the child that you are on to the game, and that you will be advising others, such as his teacher and the neighbors, as well.**

Difficult people (including adults) manipulate with secrets. This is particularly true of triangulating children: "Don't tell Dad what I said." "Don't tell Mom you helped me with the homework." Such children say to teachers, "Don't tell my parents I told you this, but . . ."

◆ **Be explicit and firm about the fact that both parents support each other.**

Let the children know that there is trust in the marriage, but that children will have to earn and prove themselves worthy of that kind of trust. Say for example, "Troy, Mom and I have known each other for a long time. I love her most of all. If you tell me anything, or her anything, we always tell each other. You can count on that! I always believe Mom, and she always believes me. Perhaps there will be a time when we both believe you. What do you think will make that happen?"

How Parents Can Educate Teachers

Educators are often not familiar with the special problems of adopted or foster children. They, as most adults, know that, if a child has problems, the parents frequently have problems. Perhaps without blaming the parents, most teachers understandably feel that the child's problems are a response to the parents' problems. In the case of adopted and foster children, as we have so often pointed out, this is often not the case. Therefore, parents can help themselves, the children, and the educational system by educating educators, *one teacher at a time*. Parents must be prepared to do this over and over again. Education is a never-ending process well worth undertaking. Every teacher you inform about special needs children and adoption issues will be better equipped to help adoptive families in the future.

We suggest that a meeting with the teacher be scheduled before the child even arrives in the classroom. With disturbed children, an ounce of prevention is worth a pound of cure. At this meeting, *give your child's teachers a copy of the following information*, and ask them to look it over as you tell them about your child's issues, behavior problems, and responses to authority.

Include the children in this meeting. There is a tendency for some educators to feel that it is inappropriate for children to be present at parent–teacher conferences. This lends an air of secrecy to such meetings that is unhealthy in families where triangulation, manipulation, and lies are a problem. Explain this to the teacher at the outset. Even healthy children wonder what secrets are being discussed or what things are being said about them at those mysterious conferences.

As parents, we need to remember that teachers are not always accustomed to having positive interaction with parents. Many teachers report negative experiences when trying to elicit the cooperation of parents. This is unfortunate, for it often predisposes teachers to expect trouble from every encounter with parents. It is helpful to address this at the beginning of the meeting as well. Stating that you hope to open the channels of reciprocal communication and cooperation is essential to starting your meeting with the right attitudes in place.

Including the children in parent–teacher meetings whenever possible:

- May help minimize the children's ability to manipulate the teacher with lies.

- Openly spells out the relevant problems that already exist or have evidenced themselves in the past.

- Models openness and honesty, for the children and for the teacher.

- Models good communication skills.

- Establishes a team effort.

- Lets children know that there will be reciprocal communication and cooperation between home and school.

- Makes it clear to the teacher that the children themselves are aware of their problems.

- Adds immensely to the parents' credibility by making the children available to corroborate the parents' statements about their problems.

In certain cases it might be appropriate to exclude children from a parent–teacher meeting. Common sense and good judgment must be applied in all situations.

Tips for Parent–Teacher Meetings

- Be honest about the problems, if any, that you have in the home. If possible, have the children do some of the talking. For example:

Parent: "Howie, you have had some problems with sneakiness in the past, have you not?"

Howie: "Well, a little . . ."

Parent: "Last year when Mr. Sneider asked you to take a note to the office, what did you do instead?"

Howie: "Well, I went into the back room of the cafeteria and ate some of the rolls that were sitting on the racks."

Parent: "Some of the rolls?"

Howie: "Well, lots of rolls I guess. And lots of water too."

Parent: "Then what happened?"

Howie: "I got pretty sick. I had to go to the doctor and he said what I did was dangerous. That I might have ruptured my stomach."

Parent: "What do you think we could do this year to prevent that from happening again?"

Howie: "I dunno."

Parent: "Mrs. Lisser, do you have any ideas?"

Mrs. Lisser: "Well, perhaps if I need to send Howie on an errand, he could go with a responsible buddy."

Parent: "What a great idea! Howie, what do you think?"

Howie: "Yeah. That'd probably work."

- Share techniques that you have tried that may or may not have been effective. Depending on the situation, this might be best done without the children present. In these cases, tell the teacher in the children's presence that you will be providing this information later. Say, for instance, "I will be talking to you later about some of the things we have done at home to control this behavior and what we found are the best ways to help Jessica understand and correct her behaviors."

- Let the teacher get to know you as a person, not just "John's mother." This is a variation of the "take a teacher to lunch" idea. It is a wonderful way to get to know your children's teachers and for them to see you outside the context of the children's problems.

- It takes time to process and assimilate new information. Expect some resistance at first. Be patient, and express your understanding of this process.

- Make requests and suggestions, not demands.

- Offer to be available to teachers *at their convenience,* to answer questions, consult, or simply lend an ear. If your children are difficult to parent, it is likely that eventually their teachers will find them difficult as well. "We're all together in this and need to support each other" is the ideal spirit you wish to convey. This also may take some time to develop, but is well worth waiting and working for.

- Put the teacher in touch with the children's previous teachers. Give everyone involved permission to communicate openly.

- Write a "nice to meet you" and "thank you" note after the meeting—even if you feel things did not go well. Rarely do teachers receive positive feedback or thanks for the efforts they put forth. We all like to be acknowledged every now and then. Teachers are no exception.

How Teachers Can Help Special Needs Families

- Keep in close communication with the parents. Check and double check the accuracy of children's statements. Avoid making assumptions or inferences based on children's statements.

- When stories conflict, believe the parents. (If abuse or neglect is suspected, try to determine the reliability of the children's reports before involving authorities.)

- Examine how other children in the family look, act, and are treated. If they are doing well, the problem is probably not the parent's fault.

- Communicate to the parents that you think they are capable, worthwhile, responsible, and loving.

- Empathize with and validate parents' feelings of frustration, anger, disappointment, and so on.

- Involve parents in educational and behavior management planning.

- Involve parents in assessment processes.

- As much as possible, coordinate responses with parents so the child experiences consistency.

- Avoid criticism of the parents in the children's presence.

- In front of the child, try to support or at least remain neutral concerning parental decisions about discipline, privileges, and limitations in the home. If you have questions or doubts, express them privately to the parents.

- Avoid answering children's questions with answers that imply permission or express judgment about home issues.

- Offer a shoulder to cry on, a listening ear, an encouraging word. Parenting a disturbed children is a relentless job with few if any rewards.

- Remember that adopted and foster children brought their problems with them when they arrived in their new homes. Poor parenting occurred prior to the adoptive placement, not after.

- By all means have compassion for what the children have suffered, but also realize that they are no longer being abused or neglected. Do not allow their tragic pasts to become excuses for poor behavior or lack of responsibility in the present. Do not remark about "those poor children" within hearing range of the children.

- Avoid making comments to parents such as, "God will surely bless you for taking in these poor children," particularly in front of the children. Imagine how it feels for children to hear that their parents are saints for wanting them. How awful they must be, if that is the case.

- Ask parents how you can help.

- Become familiar with correct adoption terminology. Say

  - *Birth mother*, not *real* mother.

  - *Placed* for adoption, not *given up for* adoption.

  - Brothers and sisters, not *real* brothers and sisters.

  - *Birth children*, not *real* children.

  - "Do you have any other children?," not, "Do you have any children of your own?"

- Find out from parents or adoption literature how to handle sensitive studies like genetics or family tree projects. Advise parents when units on child abuse are coming up. Children who have been abused may need special consideration or may need to be excused entirely. The children's therapist, if they have one, can advise the family.

- Offer to talk to the children's therapist if he or she feels it would be helpful.

- Ask parents how you can help.

- Offer parents this book.

Some Examples of Correct Teacher Responses to Disturbed Children

Example 1:

Child: "Is it okay to ride for kids their bikes to the store after school?"

Teacher: "What does your mom or dad say? Parents usually know best what is right for their children."

Example 2:

Teacher: "Johnny, where is your social studies notebook?"

Child: "My mom won't buy me a notebook."

Teacher: "Did you tell your mom or dad you needed one?"

Child: "Well, no, but . . ."

Teacher: "It's your responsibility to do that."

Example 3:

Child: "My dad made me stay in my room all day on Saturday. I didn't get to go outside to play at all."

Teacher: "Your dad is usually very fair. I'm sure he had a good reason."

Example 4:

Child: "Can I have some mittens out of the 'poor box'? My mom won't give me any and my hands get soooo cold."

Teacher: "Oh, come on Billy, I know your mom and she buys nice things for all of you. What happened to your mittens? Would you like me to give her a call to see what's up in that regard?"

Child: "Nah, forget it."

(Checking later with Billy's mother the teacher was told that he had "lost" three pairs of warm snowmobile gloves in one month. Each pair cost over 20 dollars. She suspected he was throwing them away in order to elicit sympathy from the teachers and mother helpers at school, or possibly to make her look like a neglectful mother. When confronted, he grudgingly admitted that his mother was telling the truth.)

A supportive teacher can make a world of difference in children's lives. In the case of disturbed adopted children, that support must include the parents as well.

10

Cautions and Guidelines for the Use of Nonconventional Techniques

In dealing with children who triangulate, we touched on techniques that will be useful to many parents, not just those living with disturbed children. Likewise, the information in chapter 9 on conventional parenting techniques could be used by many parents with their "normal" children. By themselves, however, *techniques that are useful with normal children may be entirely ineffective in controlling and training disturbed children.*[130]

More often than not, conventional parenting techniques are more than adequate for difficult children. As previously noted, good parenting information is everywhere. The *Love and Logic* Books by Foster Cline and Jim Fay have been helpful to many thousands of parents. *Love and Logic* audiotapes, books, and parenting classes cover all of the common issues of childhood and give parents, individually and in groups, specific advice for parenting children of all ages. *Success in Parenting,* by Foster W. Cline, M.D. and Benjamin Brucker, Ed.D., covers many of the conventional techniques that work with most difficult children most of the time. These materials show parents how to handle situations with consequences, how to be empathetic about the consequences the child suffers, and how to give choices and avoid rescue so parental frustration is much less likely.

> *Most of the specialized parenting techniques and strategies in chapter 12 are designed to be used with children who suffer from emotional illness and behavior disorders—not with emotionally healthy children. To use these techniques with a "normal" child is generally not necessary, and could put both parents and children at risk.*

1. Many of these parenting techniques are last resort strategies for use when conventional parenting techniques do not work. *Always use conventional parenting tools for a reasonable length of time before initiating therapeutic interventions or unconventional strategies.*

   It is always a good idea to consult a mental health professional or counselor if the child exhibits behaviors that fall outside the developmental norm, in order to rule out simple problems that could be easily solved, before resorting to therapeutic parenting strategies. In other words, be sure the child is really suffering from emotional or behavioral disorders before giving them this sort of "medicine."

2. A therapist skilled in the treatment of your children's particular disorder should be aware of, and approve the use, duration, and intensity of these techniques. It may

take some shopping around before parents can find a professional they feel comfortable with and who is able to work effectively with their children and family. Many of these children benefit from unconventional approaches. Traditionally trained therapists may have a tendency to blame the parents for the children's difficulty, particularly if the children are skillful at conning or presenting a falsely cooperative and compliant front to outsiders. Parents should find a therapist who does not isolate children in therapy. Parents must be kept informed and, ideally, should be encouraged to participate in the therapy sessions. Disturbed children can be very skillful at triangulation and a well-trained, experienced therapist will be aware of this and guard against it. *Above all, parents must find a therapist who believes them and not the disturbed child.* (See the Outside Resources section at the end of this book for agencies and support groups that can help parents find well-trained, experienced therapists in their area, as well as a list of professionals we recommended.)

3. None of the unconventional strategies described in this chapter should be implemented impulsively. Thoughtful planning and preparation must accompany their use. Part of this planning *must* include an alternate course of action should the technique fail. Specific time limits and suggestions for back-up measures will be included with the description of each strategy.

   It is imperative that parents heed these limits, no matter how tempted they might be to "try just once more." If parents have even the slightest doubt that they can limit themselves in the prescribed ways, they must not attempt to use these strategies and should instead seek other means of helping their children. Parents needn't feel bad or inadequate in any way if they find themselves unable to use the unconventional techniques with the restrictions we give here. Most parents are not mental health professionals, and do not come equipped, and may not desire, to provide a therapeutic milieu in their home. It was probably not a part of the job description when they adopted. Using these specialized parenting techniques in effect creates a treatment center atmosphere in a family home.[131] This is not for every family!

4. Parents who are extremely angry, resentful, or desperate can sometime suffer impaired judgment when it comes to limiting their discipline of their children. *The Cline/Helding Adoptive Parent Attitude Assessment*, page 203, helps to assess the proper mindset for using non-conventional techniques with severely disturbed children. Because this is so important for the welfare of both children and families, we will continue to reiterate these warnings and run the risk of overstressing them.

5. If parents live in a resource-poor area and do not have access to therapists who are both trained and experienced in the area of their child's disability, or are unable to obtain a professional diagnosis that they feel is accurate, they should contact one of the resources listed at the end of this book to obtain information about professionals who will consult by telephone. Some may be willing to travel to provide services.

6. Always use the traditional parenting interventions first.

7. If the child in question is new to the family, parents should not assume that techniques that were unsuccessful in other situations will not work in the present one. They must start once again with conventional strategies. Children respond differently with different people and in different situations. If a child has experienced a move from one home to another it will also have had an effect (usually negative) on the child's behaviors.[132]

One of our adopted children appeared to have minimal problems in his last foster home placement. When moved to our adoptive home, he displayed extremely disturbed behaviors, including smearing feces, and became very noncompliant and rebellious. He had managed to hold himself together through five moves, and the last one was apparently the last straw.

The Cline/Helding Adoptive Parent Attitude Assessment

The checklist below was designed to be used as a thought-provoking self-examination of attitudes and feelings for parents. If parents spend some time honestly evaluating themselves using this list, they should be well equipped to decide if they are good candidates for success using the unconventional strategies with their child.

Q Are you generally angry at, or do you feel that you hate, your child?

Many parents feel this way momentarily or for brief periods of time when faced with a disturbed child's behaviors. It is often related to a particularly trying situation or a series of difficult things occurring in a short time span. But if this is the *usual* feeling, then it makes consequencing with empathy difficult if not impossible. Consequences and punishment become confused, and consequences easily and swiftly become more punitive than necessary, sometimes without the parents' conscious awareness. In the worst case scenario, this can result in abuse of the child, and at the very least, leaves the punishing parent feeling guilty and out of control.

Q When your child tests or defies your limits, do you feel a need to always control or always "win"?

We have found that "persistent" parents tend to raise "stubborn" and "strong-willed" children. Highly controlling children will up the ante to the point that a parent must be willing to give in or abuse. If you cannot set limits and give in or change tactics when reasonable limits are reached, you are not a good candidate for using these specialized techniques.

Q How important is it to you that every parenting strategy you try result in some "success" in managing behavior or making improvements in your child's condition?

We can promise you, that parents of disturbed children have to be *very* creative, because so many techniques don't work or work only for a limited amount of time, and then parents need to come up with new creative solutions.

Q Can you maintain a sense of humor, even when a situation does not turn out the way you had hoped?

Years ago in a study in Evergreen, we found that parents who worked well with very difficult children had four qualities, one of which was a good sense of humor. The more difficult the situation, the blacker the humor. Though shocking to outsiders not familiar with what it is like to live with disturbed children, this is a *normal* and *healthy* response. Parent support groups are great places to experience and share this sometimes macabre sense of humor with others who will understand and appreciate it.

Q Do you love, or more importantly with disturbed children, do you *want* to love your child?

Many parents say, "I feel like I just don't even *love* this child," and then break into tears of guilt and sorrow. But the real question to consider is, do you wish to love the child? Sometimes even the wish to love the child disappears as the years pass, which may make it impossible to accept him even if his behavior changes for the better. Such parents would be wise to examine their desire to make the commitment of time and effort the parenting strategies require. If they are unable or unwilling to rejoice in and embrace their child's progress, behavior changes will revert back to the negative quite quickly. Parents who have a genuine desire to love their child will usually be able to feel that love growing as the child improves in his relationship with them. They may find that the unconventional techniques will enable that kind of positive and healthy change.

Q Are you proactively prepared to deal with false allegations of child abuse should they occur?

All across the United States, parents of extremely disturbed children who use unconventional techniques to control or teach their child are being accused of child abuse—sometimes by the child, and other times by misunderstanding professionals or outside observers.[133] This is so widespread in many areas that competent, trained and experienced foster parents are leaving the field because of fear of legal repercussions. In such cases, the burden of proof is on the parent. Unlike other types of criminal charges, when the charge is child abuse, you are considered guilty until proven innocent![1] Parents must be prepared and ready to defend themselves and provide investigators with proof of their innocence. We devote the next chapter to this topic.

Q Do you have back-up persons to call on in times of stress, and with whom you can share your parenting ideas and expect honest feedback on your feelings and responses?

Some families find that an agreement with a spouse can serve this purpose. Parents may agree that if they call on the other and say "I've reached my limit, I need your help," the spouse will immediately and without criticism or question, drop everything and take over with the child. For families with flexible jobs this may work, but most people cannot drop everything and leave their jobs in the middle of the day to rush home and take care of a child. For those families, a backup person, and ideally more than one, can literally be a lifesaver! Be open with these persons about the child's disabilities and the techniques you use. Teach them to respond constructively to the child. Ideally the backup persons will be trained in dealing with disturbed children. In a pinch, however, anyone who will simply provide you with a break and keep the child from harming himself and others will do.

Q Are you flexible and creative?

These are essential qualities for success with disturbed children. Most likely you have these qualities if you are reading this book.

Q Do you have a sense of faith and hope that things can change and improve for the better?

It is important to project your sense of faith onto the child, giving her the belief that she can make positive changes.

Q Do you take what your child does and says personally?

Although a disturbed child's behavior toward parents, especially the mother, can sound, look and feel very personally directed, it usually is not. It may stem from subconscious rage against the birth mother or other rejecting or abusive parent figures in the child's past. It can even be helpful to point this out to a child who has the ability to self-reflect.

Q Can you accept regressions as a normal and expected part of improvement?

Disturbed children progress with "two steps forward and three steps back." In each stage, the child reworks many early life issues.[135] This reworking can result in behavioral regression, and is often self-limiting.

It is also true that very often when you are doing the right thing, the child's behavior worsens as he attempts to gain control or force you to revert to earlier, more familiar reactions. This too is usually self-limiting.

Q Can you accept the child's regressions, without wanting to accelerate the behavior management techniques beyond their stated limitations?

Disturbed kids will try to push the limits. Children who have suffered child abuse at the hands of a parent become masters at recreating the abusive situation in the adoptive home. The healthy adult has the responsibility to avoid being caught up in the child's pathology. Often standing firm at the limit line will result in a positive response, once the child discovers that you will not re-abuse him.

Q Can you ask for help when you need it, and back off entirely until backup arrives when things are out of control?

Q Can you accept the fact that you may be strongly criticized for using unconventional techniques?

Q Do you have the patience to delay gratification, perhaps for years?

Q Can you notice and accept even very small changes, and feel a sense of satisfaction from them?

Some disturbed children can make only very small changes, particularly at first. Redefining "success" can help us recognize and support the child when he takes small steps in the right direction. For example, a child who has been urinating in dresser drawers and in the bathtub is now only urinating in the bathtub or toilet. This is success! It is movement toward better functioning.

Q Do you believe that you may be having a positive effect on your child even if you do not see immediate and positive change?

Do you understand that you *are* having a positive effect on your child that may equip him or her for later life? Some children have trouble demonstrating what they have learned. It is as though they need to process it for a while before making use of it. Others will not give their parents the satisfaction of giving in to their wishes, but demonstrate their new abilities when outside the home. Yet others appear to be making no progress at all until they reach their late 20s or early 30s.

Q Prior to finalizing your child's adoption, can you work within the limitations imposed by your agency—even though you may feel that they impede the child's progress?

Q Can you reward yourself for undertaking a most difficult and outwardly unrewarding task?

Most likely you were unprepared for the difficulty of parenting a disturbed child on a daily basis year after year. It is virtually impossible for others to appreciate this enormous task unless they have experienced it firsthand. Congratulate yourself for making it through each day with your child. Give yourself a hug! Find others to do it! Take a break! Give yourself some time off!

11

Coping with False Allegations of Child Abuse

We spoke earlier of the fact that a number of misunderstandings can arise when outsiders observe or hear about parents using nontraditional methods of discipline with their child. Sometimes these misunderstandings are translated into child abuse charges, usually by well-intentioned persons who honestly think they are looking after the child's best interest. Parents need to be aware that this is a possibility that occurs all too frequently and weigh the risks against the possible benefits to their children of using the techniques.

Proactive Preparation Against False Allegations of Abuse

There are some steps parents can take to minimize the risk of false accusations, and if they do occur, to handle them with minimal disruption to the family.

1. Parents must operate as if they are expecting such charges at some stage in their child's life. Parents need to prepare for charges as if they are *certain* to occur. Then they will feel a greater sense of empowerment when using the specialized techniques and an added measure of confidence if questioned about the methods.

2. Proactively retain an attorney knowledgeable about child welfare, adoption, and parental rights. This is almost an essential investment in today's world. Spend an hour or so providing the attorney with background about your child's problems and the unconventional solutions you plan to implement. Take along this book.

3. It is not unusual for child protective services workers to overstep their lawful bounds when investigating child abuse complaints. Know your rights. Ask your attorney to advise you about what to do if you are accused, and be sure you know how to get in touch with him or her in an emergency.

4. If the child has made false accusations against anyone in the past, the placing agency should be asked for a letter certifying that fact. This type of documentation may make the difference between enduring a few questions and being incarcerated or having all the children removed from the home while you are being investigated.

5. The child's medical and dental checkups, immunizations, treatments, and records must be kept up to date. One family paid their pediatrician for a one-hour office

consultation and provided him with extensive history and background on their child and his problems. This paid off for them later, when a neglect accusation was made and the child's abnormally short stature and weight were questioned. The pediatrician provided documents stating that he had seen the child regularly and that his small size was the result of early neglect in the birth home, not negligence by the adoptive parents. Ideally, parents are on a first-name basis with the professionals involved with their children.

6. If a disturbed child threatens to report abuse, it may be advisable for the parents to tell the child, "Oh honey, let's call them right now—together!" This is not what the child expects. Children who are trying to manipulate and scare parents into giving up all control may back down at this point. If not, parents must consider calling protective services and the police department that has jurisdiction in their area. Advise them of the situation and invite them to pay a visit to the home to check things out. Demonstrate an attitude of "we have nothing to hide, we have done nothing wrong."

7. Tape record or have a credible witness to *every single conversation* with abuse investigators. This is essential to ensure that parents not be misunderstood, misquoted, or have their words confused with those made by another accused person. If an abuse investigator asks to speak to a parent, that person should immediately reach for a tape recorder, or inform the investigator that it will be necessary first for a neighbor, friend, or some other witness to be present. This protects everyone and fosters accuracy in the investigation. The recorded tapes should be kept by the parent in a safe place, or the witness should be asked to take live notes, and to later write down what he or she remembers from the conversation. It can be especially helpful for parents to have a professional, such as their

attorney or family therapist accompany them to the interview with officials.[136]

8. It may be helpful for families with disturbed children to be somewhat in the public eye. It's good to have witnesses who have seen the parents interact with the child. If the child says, for instance, "My parents never let me out of the basement," it is helpful to have neighbors who have seen the child playing in the yard.

Five factors contribute to an explosive mixture that leads adults living with disturbed children to be at high risk for charges of child abuse:

1. Disturbed children often have bonding problems.

In order to develop the ability to bond, the individual must re-experience the bonding cycle that ordinarily takes place after birth. The first-year-of-life bonding cycle, like all bonding cycles, involves need, distress, gratification, and resolution. All bonding experiences involve elements of trauma or distress. This is true of the bonding of mother to child that takes place after the pain of birth, as well as the bonding of infant to mother though the child's hunger pains and their relief after birth.

When trauma is referred to in bonding situations, it refers to elements of distress and emotional upheaval, not truly life-threatening trauma. In the case of abused children, reworking early trauma leads the child to experience the same *feelings* but not the same physical danger. In essence, the so-called *trauma* of bonding takes place in both healthy and unhealthy situations.

When a child is reworking the old feelings, the child may act and sound as if he is experiencing the same early physical danger and abuse. It is at this point that parents are at highest risk for being misunderstood and reported for abuse by outsiders. The distress that unattached children must go through to develop the ability to bond and attach may be interpreted as abusive even by professionals.

2. The corrective emotional experience involves the same feelings as in earlier abusive situations.

Unresolved feelings from traumatic situations lead to the child's disturbance. The corrective emotional experience is an undoing that involves the child feeling the same feelings but experiencing a different, healthier outcome in which the feelings are resolved with acceptance and love. Many professionals confuse respecting the symptom with respecting the person and have problems understanding such approaches.

An adoptive father tells of first meeting his six-year-old daughter who had been sexually abused by her birth father:

> ▓▓ We were meeting for the first time and on our way to an amusement park. She knew we were her prospective parents, and when we got into the car, I put my arm on her shoulder. It was the type of warm friendly touch anyone might do with any kid as a gesture of friendship. But she overreacted strongly, insisting, "I don't like *anybody* touching me." Most kids would have thought nothing of it. Most would have liked it. She had an abnormal response based on an abnormal past. ▓▓

Sexually abused children, especially, need touch as much as or more than other children do. They may equate it with past sexual experiences or abuse, but must experience and learn to accept normal touching within healthy boundaries to heal.

Another example of a corrective emotional experience is that of Drew, who at three had been abandoned by his birth mother. Whenever his adoptive family took him on a family outing, he did something to spoil the fun for the entire family.

Drew, prior to the finalization of his adoption, had been making the family miserable fighting with his brothers and being noncompliant for his new parents. They decided not to take him to Disneyland with the other children for a summer vacation, and left him behind in the care of an aunt. Drew was very upset about being left out, but his anger paled compared to that expressed by his placement worker, who threatened to remove him from the adoptive family because she blamed the parents "for adding to all the losses and rejections and feeling of abandonment that this child has already experienced."

After the family returned from the trip, Drew was much more fun to take on family outings. His mother explains, "He knew we wanted to love him and wanted him to share in the family fun, but he needed to get the picture that this family would not tolerate him repeatedly spoiling things for others. We didn't talk about it. We just showed him. I think these kids need to know parents will walk the walk, not just talk the talk." In this case, any feelings of abandonment that he may have had were resolved by the family returning. And *that* is what made experiencing the same feelings a corrective emotional experience.

3. Most disturbed children come from traumatic backgrounds and have learned to act the victim role.

There is a tendency for abused or neglected children to feel "unfaired upon" by others. They feel that everyone else has it better. They complain that they are picked on. They take a disproportionate amount of the parents' time, while still feeling neglected. Any demands placed on the child by the parents are seen by the child as unfair. Consequences are always "mean," and are exaggerated in the "victimized" child's mind. They become masters at telling "poor me" stories to sympathetic persons. Unfortunately, adoptive parents are often the bad guys in these stories, and there seems to be no end to the people who are willing to lend a sympathetic ear to a "poor abused child." We are not lacking in compassion or empathy for the pain and suffering small children endure at the hand of abusive parents or in deprived life situations. It is certainly sad and true that these children were once victims. That needs to be accepted, understood, and worked through—but not used as an excuse. Once children have been placed in a loving adoptive home, it is not healthy for them to continue to view themselves as victims.

One father told us he could not bring himself to say 'no' to his child when he thought of the horror the child had suffered before coming to his family. Thus the child stayed locked in the victim role, unable to learn to handle frustration, delay gratification, or accept responsibility—all the things that are expected of healthy people.

4. Many disturbed children are charming and relate better to strangers than to family members.

Often disturbed children have learned to adapt to almost any environment in order to survive. They may have had to go to extraordinary lengths to please a very inconsistent alcoholic parent, for example. They have learned to be sweet and compliant when they want or need to be. In short, they have a finely honed sense of what other people want them to say or do. They learn to manipulate as a way of staying alive. They blend into their environments like chameleons. When disturbed children complain to the school or others about their parents, they are *extremely* convincing. They may cultivate gullible school personnel for just such occasions by being helpful, polite, and ingratiating during previous encounters. Parents can appear unloving, dishonest, and suspect when they accuse their child of lying in front of someone who has only seen a very honest, trustworthy, charming kid.

5. Individuals on child protective teams *may* come from dysfunctional and abusive backgrounds themselves. The psychological defense mechanism of projection leads people to see parents against the background of their own parenting. If their own parents were abusive, they tend to see all parents as potential abusers. Those who come from healthy backgrounds automatically expect parents to be healthy. People tend to find what they look for.

Unfortunately, it is not necessarily the healthiest children in the senior class that want to become social workers and case workers. Many people go into the profession with a conscious or unconscious desire to work through unresolved issues from their own childhoods. They feel that "no child should have to endure what I went through." Thus they identify with the apparently victimized child rather than the loving but beleaguered parents. These individuals may project their feelings about their own parents onto the parents they are investigating.

One would think that when an allegation of child abuse is made, the child abuse team would investigate a complaint hoping *not* to find abuse. Not necessarily true. Protectionists often investigate with an agenda of their own, seeing the citizen as the enemy.

The past *professional* experiences of the caseworker may also play a role. When a caseworker has made the decision to leave a child in the home, and then the child is abused, injured, or killed, that worker is more likely to remove children from the next home they investigate. No one wants to make such a horrible mistake twice.[137]

In summary, when children who are predisposed to see themselves as victims are treated by their adoptive parents in a manner they don't like, but is in their best interest, they may respond convincingly with allegations of abuse to a worker who is predisposed to believe them.

Families in Need of Protective Services

What would you do if you were faced with this situation? Your 16-year-old adopted son has a history of behavioral and mental health problems. You've had the child in therapy of various types since you adopted him at age three. First play therapy, then attachment therapy, and lots of talk therapy in between. Several times since the age of 12 he has become verbally abusive and violent, threatening to harm family members. There have been incidents that resulted in minor injury, and quite a bit of property damage was incurred during his angry outbursts. Several times you called the police to file damage charges, and they talked you out of it. So far you have managed to restrain him and prevent serious injury.

But lately, he has been working out at the gym in the high school, and you are afraid of his size and increasing rage. You have asked for help in getting him admitted to an inpatient program that specializes in treating anger management problems in adolescents, but the laws in your state protect his rights to the extent that he cannot be forced to enter the program against his will. There is no way to place him outside the home so that you feel safe and he is protected. Unless, that is, he does something so dangerous that the police are called to control him. In that case, he would be taken either to jail, or to a hospital for evaluation. He still would not end up in the anger management program. Such an incident would render him ineligible for safety reasons. Then, in the course of an argument with his older brother, he flies into a rage and breaks his brother's arm.

You know that something must be done to stop this accelerating cycle of violence. The sense of helplessness and fear is more than you can continue to bear. The strain on the family is enormous. Think about it. What would you do?

A child who behaves in this way is effectively holding his family hostage. He has all the control. Parents become so afraid of the child's rage that they begin to feel like they are walking on eggshells around him for fear of setting off an explosion that will result in serious injury. The child's behavior can accelerate at an alarming rate, and none of the professionals families traditionally turn to for help may be able to offer any practical advice. It appears that unless the child murders someone, no one will intervene.

This unfortunate scenario, and others like it, is playing out in homes all over the country. There is presently *no effective system available to families who need help with noncompliant, mentally ill, behaviorally disturbed, or delinquent youth.*

Although there is little protection for parents or families, the children themselves are protected. Our legal process has a definitive term for children who are in danger of being harmed by family members: *children in need of protective services* (CHPS). CHPS hearings are regularly held when there is a possibility that children are endangered. A court order will be issued to ensure their protection. Potentially abusive family members will be kept from seeing the child unless supervision and safety can be guaranteed. Because no such legal protection exists for parents or other family members, a child taken into custody for dangerous or delinquent behavior, if not returned to the home, will be considered a CHPS case. In the scenario described above, the family has only a few legal choices:

- Call the police and have the child arrested.

- Attempt to manage the child at home.

- Keep trying to encourage the child to obtain help.

- Ask the child to leave the home.

- Turn the child over to the county foster care system.

Let's look at likely scenarios for each choice.

Call the Police and Have the Child Arrested

The police arrive. By now the child's rage has diffused, and he is somewhat subdued and apologetic. The police see a troubled child who needs help, and try to discourage you from pressing charges. "We have to do it," you say. "We are at our wits' end, and are afraid if we don't do something drastic, he will kill us. Maybe a judge will order him into the treatment he needs."

The police arrest the child and transport him to the stationhouse where he is charged and booked. Around midnight, you get a call from the arresting officer. "You can come get your son now." he says. "What? Oh no officer, we want him held down there until he goes to court. He can't come back home. We can't control him." The officer hears the rising panic in your voice, and calmly explains that as parents, you have an obligation to pick up your child, and that if you don't he will have no choice but to call social services to come and place the child in a foster home, at which point you may be charged with the crime of child abandonment.

Attempt to Manage the Child at Home

As parents, you wrestle with the choices available at this point. You do not want your child to have a criminal record, or to have his fate placed in the hands of a judge who might order him into a program for juvenile offenders. You have heard about some of the kids who come out of those programs tough and streetwise. Your child is violent, but so far at least he has not turned to drugs or street crime. He won't even go to his therapy sessions anymore, so finding another counselor is out of the question. Punishing him only enrages him further. Turning him over to the county feels like sending him straight back to the place you wanted to rescue him from in the first place. And wouldn't he see that as just another in a series of rejections? You love him, and are committed to helping him. You decide to keep him home and show him true unconditional love. Maybe in the end love will win out. You do wonder how you will handle the next episode, and how the family will deal with the constant tension and fear. Your other son is upset and shares with you the fact that his brother has been sneaking into his room at night and whispering threats in his ear. You decide to sleep in shifts, so that one parent is always awake to prevent such occurrences.

Is protection called for in this situation? Yes indeed! But not for the child. The entire family must be protected from the uncontrollable rage of the child. It is time for the child welfare community to accept that, in some instances, children need to be removed from their homes for the protection of others. Legal provisions must be made for this eventuality as well. We know of a family who successfully argued with a judge at a CHPS hearing and convinced the court to order a change of wording in the documentation and disposition of their case. *He ordered the words "child in need of protective services" stricken from the documents, to be replaced with "family in need of protective services."* This family refused to be stigmatized by the incorrect wording. They refused to accept the blame that the CHPS petition implied. They would not allow their efforts to help their child and to be good parents to result in criminal records for themselves. It was bad enough, they thought, that they would have to voluntarily relinquish guardianship of the child in order to get him into a state-funded program—the only treatment program in their area that would accept a violent child.

Just before this book went to print, our research turned up some excellent additional information from the *Victims of Child Abuse Laws (VOCAL)* website,[138] that we felt was too good not to pass along to our readers. That information makes up the rest of this chapter.

- *Can you afford* legal fees which average $10,000 to fight an accusation of child abuse?

- *Can you afford* up to $17,400 if your child is placed in state-run foster care, after being seized by child care caseworkers?

- *Can you afford* forced counseling, which can cost over $30,000 per year for a family of four?

- *Can you afford* $45,000 a month if your child is placed in a psychiatric hospital?

Too often "system professionals" with unlimited legal resources waste valuable tax dollars and the financial resources of families, while real child abusers and pedophiles often get away with their crimes.

Too often child care caseworkers, who operate under the shield of 11th Amendment Sovereign Immunity Protection, are misguided and overzealous during abuse investigations.

Too often government agencies, who get state and federal grant moneys for conducting "investigations," will cause catastrophic financial devastation for families who have been falsely accused of child abuse.

Too often child care caseworkers will undermine the stability of a family and destroy any possibility of reconciliation between parents and/or their children.

The laws relative to government child care protection agencies are so vague that thousands of innocent people are being convicted of child abuse, and allegations can be for anything a child care caseworker claims is child abuse. If caseworkers can't file criminal charges, they often file charges in civil courtroom proceedings where victims do not have a right to due process, a jury trial, or an attorney if they can't afford one, nor do they have the right to face their accuser in court. Incredible, American citizens have no constitutional rights if they get caught up in civil "kangaroo" courtroom proceedings of the juvenile justice system.

What To Do If You Have Been Falsely Accused

- Do not talk to a police officer, caseworker, or anyone involved in the case without a lawyer, VOCAL representative, or some reliable witness present.

- Get the locks changed on the house. Caseworkers have been known to "steal" what they consider evidence.

- Never let a police officer or caseworker into your home without a search warrant. Do not let them take your children without a warrant from a judge. If you don't want to talk to them, don't answer your door.

- Let everyone in the neighborhood know if your children are taken, and that you have been falsely accused.

- Tell your employer what happened. Chances are it has happened before and will explain your problems at work. You need to keep your job.

- If you have to appear in court and can't afford a lawyer, insist on a public defender before you say anything. Whenever possible, call VOCAL for advice before you make any decisions. Do not totally trust lawyers and/or public defenders. Laws in many states have been manipulated to deny constitutional rights in civil court proceedings. Go to a law library to learn about civil court rules, child abuse laws, their rules, and your rights in the state you're in.

- Clean up your house and be presentable at all times. Get rid of anything in your home that could be used against you and do not put those discarded items in your trash. Caseworkers have been known to go through garbage.

- Contact your church. Meet with your minister or priest and ask for counseling in this time of trial. State your hardships to the minister. He can make notes about the meeting, but does not have to testify under clerical confidentiality.

- Keep a journal in a composition notebook of everything you do—every phone call, every visit, letter, etc., and "tap" your own phone to record relevant conversations (let the caller know you're taping the call).

- Never, never accept a plea bargain if you are innocent, and do not allow anyone to coerce, intimidate, or lead you to believe they are doing what's best for you.

- Never sign anything when you're not absolutely sure of the consequences. You may unknowingly sign away your rights.

- Always contact a VOCAL representative before and after any meeting. Let every "system professional" know that you have notified a VOCAL representative for advice and counseling.

To locate a VOCAL chapter in your state, please call NASVO (National Association of State VOCAL Organizations) at 303-233-5321.

12

Specialized Techniques for Disturbed Children

The unconventional parenting techniques we describe are based on the following truths about working and living with disturbed children:

- To help a child heal and obtain health, it is often necessary to disturb the disturbed.[139]

    We have previously remarked upon the importance of the distress some children need to feel. And we have also written of the corrective emotional experience. Concerning these issues, a wise parent remarked, "The heck of it is, the techniques that work best are the ones you want to use the least!" Healthy parents and therapists would much rather not have to watch a child experience emotional pain. But they know that this is the only way for some children to heal. We wouldn't think of neglecting our infant's immunizations, even though they may scream in fear and pain. Parents know that the momentary agony will be soon forgotten, and that the benefits are well worth the pain.

- Very controlling children control by keeping their parents off balance.

   Often extremely difficult children have severe problems accepting authority. They are children who must be in control of every situation because of their inability to trust the control of others. Disturbed children may need unconventional management techniques to be kept off balance long enough for the parents to regain some control. Controlling children think they are happier when they are in charge, but in reality they do not feel safe and protected. Deep down inside they know that they do not have the maturity or experience to manage things well, and that they need the guidance and authority of parents in order to really be safe.

Unconventional parenting techniques put the parents in control, lower their frustration level, and serve to depersonalize the child's rebellion. Almost all of the unconventional parenting techniques are based on the assumption that the disturbed child is *choosing* to be oppositional and not that he is *unable* to comply or behave correctly. This is an important distinction. Neurologically or cognitively impaired children sometimes cannot behave in the prescribed way. Using the specialized parenting techniques with these children is inappropriate. They do not have the necessary cognitive functioning to learn from them.

Unconventional techniques require training, and the right attitude, to be used most effectively. If used incorrectly, (and sometimes, even when used correctly) they have the potential to make the situation worse.

Unconventional interventions should be a team decision, and the team should consist of the parents, teachers (and sometimes others involved in regular care of the child), and the professionals involved with the child.

This symbol, when placed next to one of the parenting techniques described below, indicates that it has the potential to be misused, or misunderstood. If misused it can be abusive to the child; if misunderstood, parents or the person applying the technique could be erroneously charged with abuse. These techniques are therapeutic and extremely effective and helpful to both child and parent when used correctly. We include conservative limits and explicit guidelines with each technique.

We begin here with the least controversial of the specialized techniques. If parents have decided to attempt these techniques, this is a good starting point.

Interpreting Behavior

Interpreting behavior requires skill and usually improves with practice. Interpreting children's behavior means commenting on the feelings that *probably* underlie the behavior. The hope is, that when parents verbally express, recognize, and accept their children's feelings, there will be less need for the children to act out their feelings through bad behavior. Interpreting behavior is one of the old therapeutic techniques used by traditionally trained therapists, but it is easy and less expensive to use at home.

Advantages:

- Interpreting the behavior lets children know that parents understand and recognize their feelings.

- Children are not given orders they can rebel against.

- If done in a kindly manner, it shows the parent is concerned and caring.

Disadvantages:

- The main disadvantage to interpretation is that it can appear to be mindreading. Judgmental interpretations can stir up resentment. Such interpretations might include:

  - "You're just doing this because you're mad."

  - "You're upset so you decided to take it out on Robert."

- Another problem with interpretations is that they can be outright wrong. When this is the case, children have less respect for the parent giving the interpretation. If the child contradicts the parent, an argument can ensue.

/// I am not feeling mad, I'm sad.

No, you're mad all right, you kicked the cat because you're angry.

No I'm not, I'm sad. I wanted to go to McDonald's.

McDonald's has nothing to do with it. You're mad at me for making you do the dishes.   **///**

Not only is this a no-win situation, one person's word against another's with no way of proving either, but it distracts the parent from the original behavioral goal.

Use of Shocked Surprise When a Job Goes Well

Unconditional praise is hard for many people to hear. When self-image is low, any praise causes cognitive dissonance. This is especially true of disturbed children who have a hard time psychologically accepting praise or rewards for a job well done.[140] Praise does not fit with their self-image. Many parents tell us that they dare not praise their child for anything—even for trying hard. Praise extinguishes the good behavior, and the last thing parents want to do is extinguish good behavior when it may appear infrequently. For these children the use of shocked surprise is ideal. It is carried out in a light, joking way that is not intensely personal and threatening to their fragile self-images. When parents express shocked surprise at a job well done, highly controlling children respond with enjoyment:

// John! We've had microseconds now of super behavior. What's gotten into you? Can this last?!

Wow! Juanita, you really wrote a good paper. Okay, who did you copy this from? You did it yourself? I'm gonna faint! **//**

Springing the Reward

The more disturbed the children, the less able they are to earn or accept a reward. Sometimes their self-images are so damaged that they cannot see themselves as capable of doing anything good, and other times it is a control problem—they simply won't do things someone else's way.

In behavior modification programs, many disturbed children are never quite able to make it to the highest level. Because once they attain the highest level, a reward or congratulations for doing something right will follow. This inability to earn or accept a reward is the childhood equivalent of adult success neurosis. For these children it is better *not* to set up reward criteria. Instead, surprise them by springing the reward on them when they are not expecting it.

This eliminates the possibility of the child setting himself up to fail before the final success. The adults involved feel gratified when they are able to do something positive for a misbehaving child who tends to keep adults at arm's length by refusing to be responsive. The child's behavior and effort are acknowledged and reinforced, and he learns that he can handle positives.

Examples:

// Terry, I've decided I'd like you to go on the amusement park trip with us today. Don't know why—maybe just because I like you, and everybody deserves a good time now and then.

Jason—you've almost finished your math paper. Super! Have a candy bar for your efforts. **//**

Give Only Conditional Positives to a Child with a Poor Self Image

Children with a poor self-image respond poorly to *unconditional* positive remarks about their personhood. Such remarks as "You are such a neat a kid!" and "What a good girl you are!" lead many children to feel very uncomfortable. They may feel that the adult is either lying, trying to manipulate them or trick them, or simply ignorant. They will make every attempt to educate or prove that person wrong, immediately!

◢◢ I don't know what got into Troy. This morning was his best ever. He was an angel. I told him that, too. And this afternoon he had the worst behavior he has ever had. He was horrible. I just don't know what to make of that boy! ◢◢

Troy's message to his mom: "I am definitely not an angel. See!?"

When well-meaning outsiders give children a message that is different from reality and different from the messages they get at home, it can cause problems for the family. Since so many disturbed kids put on very convincing acts in public places, they may appear "good as gold" to others.

◢◢ Lisa sat like a perfect lady in the waiting room at the doctor's office—too perfect if you thought about it. She never moved an inch, but sat with hands and ankles crossed for nearly 45 minutes, smiling at the receptionist whenever she looked her way. Other kids were running around, screaming and misbehaving. The receptionist was obviously annoyed by their behavior. So Lisa stood out as particularly angelic. As we were leaving, the receptionist called to Lisa and handed her a pile of reward stickers for being such a 'good girl.' 'You are so lucky to have such a good little girl' she remarked to me. What could I say? Lisa was hell on wheels at home, and she knew it. Her smug smile said it all. And later at home, she was worse than ever. ◢◢

In addition to being unable to accept the global "good girl" label as either realistic or possible, Lisa is getting mixed messages from the adults in her environment, and reinforcement for manipulating and presenting a false front to others. Paradoxically, she will feel victimized by having been adopted by demanding and mean parents who are unhappy with her "angelic" behavior.

Conditional positive remarks, however, may be accepted if they are specific and merely observational: "You've been behaving like a champ *this afternoon*" or "I appreciate the response you're giving me *right now*." Adding "right now" or "this time" to the statement make it easier for the child to swallow: "Good, she doesn't expect me to be like this all the time." Parents can sometimes diffuse the reaction to globally positive remarks made by outsiders by immediately rewording them as conditional remarks: "Yes, Lisa was very well behaved in the waiting room *today*."

Symptom Prescription

One adoptive parent told us, "The most effective way to approach my kids when they are trying to get to me is to snag them in a double bind by using symptom prescription." Symptom prescription gives the children permission (or even orders them) to do what they were going to do anyway.[139] This technique works especially well for extremely stubborn children.

Advantages:

- Parents always 'win.' If the child *doesn't* do what you have ordered him to do, you are stopping a behavior you don't like. If he *does* do it, he is being obedient.

- It can be a fun, creative way for parents to extinguish some pretty severe and tiring behaviors.

- When it works, it works immediately.

Disadvantage:

- At first, children often respond to the symptom prescription by stopping the behavior. That is, when requested to stomp to his room, the child won't. Sometimes, however, the child catches on and stops responding to this technique.

Examples of system prescription statements include "Please stomp when you go to your room," and "Empty the trash, but please whine and cry first." One mother described her own experience with the technique this way:

▐▐ My son could throw up at will. And he usually landed it right on my feet. I'd never seen a child do this, and the first couple of times I thought he was actually ill. It always happened when I was scolding him or telling him something he didn't want to hear. I'd feel so bad for scolding him when he was not feeling well. Then it dawned on me that a pattern was developing. So the next time I needed to talk to him about bad behavior, I told him, 'I think you probably won't like what I am going to say. In fact, knowing you, I'd bet it will make you pretty mad. And when you get that mad, you usually need to throw up. So why don't you just hold this little barf bag from the airplane, just in case you need to throw up while I am talking. Some kids talk about how they feel, but that's not usually your style and that's okay. I feel so bad for you when you have to clean all that mess off my shoes.' I had my son carry a little bag around with him after that, so he would have it when ever he 'needed' to throw up. He hated carrying his bag. And he completely quit throwing up all over my shoes.

Symptom prescription will not work with all kids or with all behaviors. But our collection of success stories include cases in which it stopped three years of feces smearing, two years of eight-hour tantrums, and the child who vomited every time he was mad. It stopped a little girl who had unraveled hundreds of socks from ever unraveling another, after her mom encouraged her to unravel socks for hours one Saturday.

It is important to not show anger or sarcasm when using this technique. Parents must be matter-of-fact, acting as if they have just had a brilliant insight into their child that now enables them to understand and accept, or even *appreciate*, the child's way of handling things.

Practicing Behaviors

There are two ways to use the technique of practicing behavior to encourage positive behavioral changes in children. One is straightforward, the other paradoxical. Asking children to practice 'fast and snappy getting ready to go to school' is an example of the straightforward method of practicing good behavior. Having a child practice kicking a door in order to perfect her technique is paradoxical practice of bad behavior. Each type is explained more thoroughly below.

Practicing Good Behavior

Practicing good behavior is primarily useful for children who have already developed the skills needed to do the behaviors as desired, but refuse to do them at the proper time, in the desired manner, or use them to inconvenience family members in some way. It should be done in a fun, relaxed manner, with no punitive tone. The more silliness and drama the parents can muster the better.

Practicing good behavior works well for things like

- Dawdling over chores or tasks.

- Hassling parents about doing chores.

- Not doing chores as requested.

- Half-completing chores.

- Annoying others while accomplishing a task or chore.

Lisa, Jason, and Todd always fight over who is going to sit next to the window in the family van. The fun of family outings is often spoiled by their arguing, pushing, and shoving. Their parents often intercede to stop the ruckus, which puts them in a foul mood.

One Saturday, after an hour or so of hard work raking leaves in the yard, Mom suggested they all go out for ice cream. But first, she said, before they could go, they needed to practice getting seated in the van without fighting. In a fun, lighthearted way, she suggested that perhaps ten practices would be enough for a start.

She lined them up inside the back door and said, "Okay kids, let's go get some ice cream!" At first the kids grumbled and did not take her seriously, but when they discovered that she meant it, they scrambled out to the van and, careful not to discuss seating arrangements, climbed in and buckled their seat belts. Mom got into the driver's seat and did the same, all the while giving the kids lots of pizzazz.

"Yes! Amazing! Miraculous! If you can do that nine more times, I'll have to eat at least two banana splits to help me get over the shock!"

Everybody giggled as mom gestured and acted more ridiculously amazed at each successful practice. Once she even pretended to faint and fell on the horn, attracting the attention of a neighbor, who gave them all a strange look.

Soon the family was off to the ice cream parlor in a good mood. The next time a squabble broke out over seating in the van, mom simply mumbled to herself (in earshot of the children) "Hmm, I think it might be time for another practice session."

Practicing good behavior can work well when children regularly do not complete their chores correctly, or use up a lot of parental energy by needing reminders or follow-up, or dawdle getting ready for school, making the parents feel anxious or arrive late at work. When it is convenient for parents, but *not* convenient for the children, a practice session can be held to encourage children to correct the problem. Parents might say to a child:

▌▌ Suzanne, the last few mornings you have been getting up late, and then dawdling over getting dressed and ready for school. I know that you have softball practice in a few minutes, and I will be happy to take you as soon as you show me how "fast and snappy and right the first time" you can brush your teeth, get dressed, and get your bookbag ready for school. *▌▌*

Suzanne is now instructed to get her nightclothes on and hop into bed. Mom, in an easy and fun way, might pretend to be the alarm clock.

▌▌ Rrrrrringgg! Okay Suzanne—GO! *▌▌*

Suzanne might then be cheered through the process of getting ready in an efficient, fast, and cheerful manner. This can be done in a silly way, with mother holding a flag at the finish line, or in some other lighthearted manner. After each successful practice, Suzanne must once again get into her nightclothes and back in bed to start over. She is encouraged to cooperate by her mother's fun manner, as well as by the fact that she wants to get to baseball practice before it is over. Should Suzanne again have trouble with dawdling in the morning, the number and inconvenience of practice sessions could be increased, as long as the number of sessions does not become unreasonable or too much hassle for the mother. If Suzanne balks or dawdles during the practice sessions, her mother might insist on some "hassle-time chores or payback" (see page 248) later for her efforts.

Advantages:

- Gets the point across with children in a way that "saves face."

- Parents have control over the timing of the practice sessions.

- Can be fun for parents and children. Children love to get the parental pizzazz!

- Offers a way to break habitual behaviors.

- Can completely eradicate certain bad behaviors, or at least shorten their duration.

- When dealing with generally compliant children, it is easy to do.

Disadvantages:

- With noncompliant children this can become a control battle.

- It requires planning, supervision, and participation from the parent.

Practicing Bad Behavior

Practicing bad behavior involves asking children to repeat their bad behavior at a prescribed time, in a prescribed way, and for a prescribed period of time or to a prescribed end. This varies slightly from symptom prescription, in that the child is not told it is okay to show his or her symptom, but instead is asked to practice the symptom to the point of satiation. The child practices her symptom until she gets sick of it.

Advantages:

- Practicing bad behavior takes control of the timing of the behavior.

- It places the behavior under parental control, and parents may modify its expression.

- When dealing with generally compliant children, it is easy to do.

- It can completely eradicate certain bad behaviors, or at least shorten their duration.

Disadvantages:

- With noncompliant children, this can become a control battle.

- It may require supervision from the parent.

- Repetitive practice of some bad behaviors can physically harm the child. (For example, a child cannot be required to practice punching his fist through a wall . . .)

- Parents and other family members may have to tolerate a lot of noise or unpleasantness for a short period of time.

Examples:

- Nadine had to spit into a measuring cup until it was full. It cured her of spitting on the coffee table when she got mad.

- Jerry was requested to practice kicking his closet door for half an hour. After 15 minutes he was getting pretty tired of it. He promised he would never do it again. But he was told that he needed more practice so that the next time he wanted to kick doors, he would be an expert!

- Lisa loved to call her mom a bitch. She was asked to stand in the kitchen the entire time mom made supper and loudly call her a bitch. After about one hundred times, it lost much of its appeal.

If You Can't Lick 'Em, Join 'Em

Remember how much fun it was to play "follow the leader" as a child? Joining the children in their misbehavior can be almost as much fun. Parents just need to have the right mindset. Another name for this technique is "Two can play that game." It involves mirroring the child's symptoms on the parents' terms, at a time parents' choose. This technique is only effective if the child is not demonstrating behavior already picked up from the adults in the environment. And it can only be carried out if adults are not sarcastic, angry, or mocking.

Advantages:

- This technique can be quite enjoyable, as parents put themselves in their child's shoes. Some kids will actually laugh at themselves when they see their parents looking or acting like them.

- The whole family can get involved.
- It takes the edge off anger about the behavior.

Disadvantages:

- If done improperly, it can appear that the parent is making fun of the child.
- This is a technique that will lose all effectiveness if it is overdone. It is best used only once or twice.
- It can't be used on behaviors involving aggression or pain.

Examples:

- Tony was a seven-year-old boy who cried at the drop of a hat. This set him up to be made fun of by other first graders. Joyce, his mother, told the following story:

▟▊ My husband, and I planned this out ahead of time. We were eating dinner, and Jim said to me, strongly but not impolitely, 'Don't eat your food with a spoon, use a fork.' I immediately burst into tears, sobbing. Tony had this look of horror on his face. Jim said, 'Honey, what's wrong?' I said that my feelings were hurt and started crying harder. I told him that it was just a family trait, and that lots of people cry when they have their feelings hurt, particularly in our family. I said that we had all better get used to it. That was all that was said. Tony never burst into tears again over small issues. I think the poor kid thought, 'Jeez, this could be catching! I better quit it.' ▟▊

- Wayne stole things. He always denied it, of course. All of a sudden things began to turn up missing. Wayne's stuff, too. His parents were puzzled saying "Holy cow! Now your stuff is showing up missing too?! Things just aren't safe around here. I bet the same gremlins who snuck in and stole my stuff are now starting to take yours! Who knows what will turn up missing next. Of course, if we're lucky, maybe whoever stole them might start sneaking the stuff back."

- When asked by her mother to help around the house, Angie harangues, "Why do I always have to do things your way? It's just not fair. I always have do stuff you tell me." She takes her sweet time completing the task.

  Dinner is late. Angie asks, "Where's dinner?" Mom answers, "Why do I always have to do things your way? It's just not fair. I always have to do stuff for you." Mom walks off and takes her sweet time getting dinner.

- Joining the behavior has also worked for some children who lie. If unsuccessful, the technique should be tried twice at the most. Even if successfully used, it can easily be overdone. Properly used, the technique will look something like this:

// Honey, have I been on your case about lying and not telling the truth?"

"Yeah."

"Thank you! Right. I have. And I want to apologize, and I guess I was just trying to make you like me . . . . always telling the truth and stuff like that . . . and that's probably not fair to you. And I've been doing some deeper thinking and I realize it is hard to tell the truth all the time. Maybe I've been too rigid. Heck, even I should be able to relax and lie sometimes. Sorry for the hassle I've caused you.   **//**

At this point the parent walks away. Hopefully, the child is a bit taken aback and confused. He may even give it some thought.

Then, the parent waits for something to come up that the child expects the parent to do—take him to a party, drive him to soccer, take him to his favorite restaurant.

▮▮ Oh, it's time to go to your soccer game? Oh dear! I know I told you that I'd take you. Sorry, I guess I lied about that. No offense. **▮▮**

We believe in honesty, and in teaching children to be honest. This last example might seem like an abandonment of the value of honesty. If parents have trouble being temporarily dishonest with their children, they should not attempt this. If lying to the child once or twice about something that is important to the child does not bring about an immediate change in the child's chronic lying, it should not be used again.

These techniques of mirroring the child's behavior will not work if the parent is naturally whiny and complaining, and so forth and the child has simply identified with the adult's problem behavior. It won't work because it's not a technique, it's a family lifestyle!

⭐ Their Problem Your Way

Sometimes it is not wise to attempt to completely eradicate a behavior. It simply can't be done! In these cases, it is best to encourage a more acceptable or easier to live with variation of the behavior.

Advantages:

- Is effective as a *first* step towards extinguishing behavior.

- Often serves as a way of reframing "different" behavior into something quite acceptable or a "personal style."

- Provides the child an acceptable way of expressing her behavior when it is neurologically or medically based. For instance, Jane has a box of objects that she is free to pick apart which helps keep her from picking her clothing to pieces.[142]

Disadvantages:

- Parents still have to find a way to live with the objectionable behavior that is continuing.

- Without careful planning, parents may be setting themselves up for charges of abuse or neglect by those who don't understand the theory and necessity of the technique.

Examples

- Nancy tore up flooring and pulled off wallpaper. She was allowed her to do it in her room only, with no consequencing other than the understanding that it would not be fixed or replaced when she decided she didn't like her room to be trashy looking. This might raise questions about why one child's room is "trashy" and all the others are neat, well cared for, and nicely decorated, especially if the child complains about being unloved and "not getting as much as the other kids in the family."

- Jason shouted obscenities. His mother told him that she would listen to his comments and take them under consideration only if he would whisper them. "If you have to do it, let's figure out a way that's not so bothersome." It was still irritating when Jason spoke, but a lot *less* irritating. And he swore less often, since the words lost much of their punch by being whispered.

- Carl spit on the furniture. His need to spit was respected, and he was given permission to spit in the house plants to help them grow.

Minimizing Lying, Stealing, and Cheating

Lying, stealing, and cheating are especially difficult for parents to handle because parents can't control this issue. They become frustrated, and the misbehavior of the children often escalates. It won't work:

- To tell the child he's lying.

- To make the child feel guilty.

- To try to shame the child into telling the truth.

Instead, it is best for the parents to take good care of themselves. They may say, "I don't believe you." That is an unarguable statement. "You're lying" is always arguable.

A typical discussion might go like this:

▲▲ I don't believe you.

"But it's the truth!"

"Did I say it wasn't the truth?"

"No."

"What did I say?"

"You said you don't believe me."

"Right. Thank you."

"But it's still the truth"

"Maybe, but if you are telling me the truth, and I don't believe you, I guess we both lose. But if you are lying about lying, then it's doubly bad for you!

Although not appropriate with "normal" children, "conviction on circumstantial evidence" may be helpful with disturbed children. There is always the chance that another child set up the problem child; however, our experience shows that often the disturbed child is the perpetrator, if chronic lying, stealing, or cheating has been the child's modus operandi. Sometimes parents simply have to play the odds and act as if the child is guilty until proven innocent. The following explanation and consequences are given to the child:

Robert, I heard you say you didn't take Dad's watch. But let me tell you a story. Once there was a man who had robbed several banks. He went to jail. While he was in jail no banks were robbed. Then he moved back into the neighborhood, and a bank was robbed. Who do you think was the person the police suspected?"

"Probably him."

"Right, and you were in the house alone when the watch disappeared, right?"

"Yeah, but I didn't take it."

"That could be true, but do you know what? Just like the bank robber, sometimes people are convicted on circumstantial evidence. That's what is going to happen to you. Somehow you are going to have to pay for that watch, and if it turns out later that we were wrong, we'll do everything we can to make it up to you.   ▟▟

Cheating is handled in the same manner. Not by telling the child he is, or could be cheating, but by simply saying, "I'm sorry, John, but the truth is, because of your past record, I don't trust you."

Hassle Time Chores and Payback

Hassle time chores provide a logical and fair way of consequencing misbehavior. A good consequence relates directly to the crime. That is, if a child is misusing the car, he has his driving privilege revoked. If he can't manage his behavior on the bus, then he can't ride it and has to walk.

However, there are some problem behaviors for which a good consequence is difficult to define. What's the consequence for lying? What's the consequence for being low-grade irritating? One can always isolate the child, but many disturbed children, particularly if they have problems with relationships and closeness, prefer to be isolated and alone. Isolation for this kind of child might actually reinforce the pathology and give them too much control.

All the above examples put a definite drain on a parent's energy, and that can be consequenced. We first learned of hassle-time-payback from a wise foster parent from Denver, Colorado, Laurie Sexton.

▟▟ We had a very disturbed little boy named Kurt in our program. He arrived angry and would pick fights with whomever was in sight. He had been particularly hard on his siblings in his previous Kansas home. His classmates were in danger, too. Constantly in trouble, and constantly picking fights, we knew he would be a handful in his home. He was placed with one of our most experienced foster parents and a number of weeks after his 'internment' there, he was seen in therapy in Evergreen. He came into the clinic, holding his mother's hand. He appeared more relaxed. I asked Kurt how his fighting was going, as that was his forte—that was always what he did best. To my surprise, Kurt looked up at his mom, with blooming love and respect, and said, 'I'm not fighting much anymore.'

'Why not?'

'Cause I hate doing all the chores.'

'Hey, whatever works.' But this surprised me. The consequence did not fit the crime. I did not see how not fighting was related to doing chores. I must have looked puzzled, because Kurt spontaneously explained, 'My mom says when I fight with the other kids, it drains the family's energy. But when I clean behind the refrigerator, I put energy back into the family.'   ▰▰

Stepped-up Supervision

Many children do not need twenty-four-hour supervision; however, most older adopted children will require stepped-up supervision at times. They may be developmentally immature and may have critical thinking and judgment deficits. Parents who use stepped-up supervision can appear over-controlling or overprotective to outsiders, but the fact is the children have few internal controls. They need someone outside of themselves to be the "little internal voice" that tells them how to act and react in appropriate ways. Most kids can be allowed to run in the park, because when they run, they are not necessarily running away. A disturbed child might be. Most older children don't have to hold their parents hands in public places because they need that physical reminder to remain in the area!

> **//** We had a little neighbor boy over to play, and I was talking with his mom. All of a sudden, our kids, Amy and Eric were gone! I immediately starting looking for the kids, and Eric's mom said, 'Don't worry, I think they are just out in the backyard play area, playing house.' I didn't know exactly how to tell this mom about Amy's precocious sexual behavior, so I just said, "My kid doesn't play house like your kid plays house! **//**

Stepped-up supervision often involves altering the physical environment in creative ways to allow children some autonomy and age-appropriate freedom, and to free the parents from need to be in the child's presence at all times.

Sometimes having a child check in with a parent at frequent intervals serves the same purpose. Many children can handle a few minutes of freedom, but could get into serious trouble if left to their own devices for too long. A kitchen timer can be set and given to very small children who cannot tell time. If the child does not return to check in at the appointed time, the parent then goes to look for him and tighter restrictions are applied until the child demonstrates a willingness and ability to check in as planned. Intervals may be as short as two or three minutes at first.

> **//** Twelve-year-old Tom had problems whenever he was left alone in the bathroom. He had been severely sexually abused as a toddler and was a compulsive anal masturba-

tor. He would engage in this behavior for so long and with such intensity that he would make himself bleed internally. Even at school this was a problem, and he had been virtually kicked out of a couple of schools for it. Then we hit on the idea of the timer. When Tom went into the bathroom, he had to tell someone he was going, and we would set a timer for three minutes. If he was not back to us within that time, we would go to check on him.

Line-of-Vision Supervision

Some disturbed children are bent on destruction—of their possessions, of parents, and of themselves. Line-of-vision supervision is required to prevent them from hurting themselves or others and to catch behaviors and consequence them immediately—which for cognitive and neurologically impaired children is essential for their learning.

Line-of-vision supervision is needed by almost all disturbed children at one time or other. It keeps the children close to parents, allows them to witness good decisions and appropriate use of time and environment, and models healthy behavior. If the adults doing the supervision talk or sing to themselves, or to the child, about what they are doing, this may help impaired children process what is happening. Children with attachment difficulties may benefit from the added contact with others that this strategy forces upon them.

An out-of-control child, or a child who is suicidal or self-abusive, needs physical protection in addition to professional counseling and treatment. Other family members and family property often need protection from a disturbed child. Line of vision supervision provides this safety in addition to external control for the child.

▐▐ Before Donald was adopted, at age three he had broken a bathtub in the foster home and thrown himself through a plate glass window in their family room. Windows that he could reach had wood over them and all the mirrors and glass had been removed. This kid had a thing about glass. They told us to take off our french doors, that they would never survive. We never wondered exactly what a three year old would have to do to break a bathtub! But he quickly demonstrated it for us, and it didn't take long at all to put line-of-vision supervision into place with this kid! ▐▐

Line-of-vision supervision can be used in several ways:

• To keep a child physically safe.

• To monitor and correct aberrant thinking and behavior as it happens.

• To instruct a child about social or other interactions.

• To keep other family members safe.

> Martha spends time on many Saturdays supplementing her income by working on the computers of her business customers. Jason goes to work with her. While she works, Jason sits in the corner of the office working on his hooked rugs, or some other project. The most difficult thing for Martha to handle are the comments and criticisms of well-meaning strangers who naturally feel the child should be outside playing, when in fact, if outside, he would not be playing but vandalizing.

Line-of-vision supervision is very draining for the adult doing the supervision, especially if the child is being difficult and overcontrolling in order to force an end to the program. Good respite or backup is often necessary. Video monitors are helpful in some situations. When personal safety or property issues are involved, room alarms such as the type available at Radio Shack can at least allow parents to get some sleep at night. They can be set to shriek if the child opens the door to his room so parents are warned that he is out and about.

The Sixty-Second Scolding

The sixty-second scolding is best carried out as a team (parents and helping professionals) decision. It is *always* preplanned. It *can never be done when the parent is angry* or about to lose control. The sixty-second scolding involves standing over the child and briefly intimidating and surprising the child through words and tone of voice, letting the child know in a loud and forceful way what he has done wrong and, in essence, for about twenty seconds, giving the child "hell and high water." Then, suddenly, dropping to one knee, putting a gentle hand on the child and asking gently, "Why do you think I am talking to you about these things?" Regardless of the child's answer, the parent or professional responds with utmost kindness and understanding, letting the child know that he or she is a bright kid and can behave much differently. Emphasis is placed on the fact that the child is cared for, and that the person giving the scolding wants only good things for them and in their future. The sixty-second scolding ends with a hug and with the statement, "I hope things go better in the future for you." Needless to say, parents cannot show the essential genuine love, affection, and hopefulness at the end of the scolding if they are still seething with anger!

The sixty-second scolding is a brief and intense recreation of the bonding cycle. The child at first feels helpless, hopeless, and angry. He wants and needs relief from the discomfort and unpleasantness of the interchange. Gratification of his need comes when the tone changes to one of gentle and genuine caring, and affirmation. A properly carried out sixty second-scolding gives quick changes in tactile, verbal and visual, and emotional stimulation.

The sixty-second scolding is a very concrete way of saying to a child, "I like you but I don't like your behavior."

The Cline/Fay Institute offers an audio training tape that demonstrates and explains in detail the correct administration and appropriate use of the sixty-second scolding. It is very helpful to hear this technique demonstrated before attempting to use it. We highly recommend this inexpensive tape to parents who would like to use this technique but have not seen it demonstrated by a trained professional. See the Outside Resources section of this book for ordering information.

Summary of Issues Around Scolding a Child

- A sixty-second scolding cannot be carried out when the adult is angry.

- A sixty-second scolding is always part of a planned intervention, not an impulsive response, "because John drove me to yelling at him," or "because I lost my temper."

- The most important part of the scolding is the immediate caring and understanding that follows.

- The sixty-second scolding should only be carried out as part of a team decision.

- A sixty second scolding is not effective when used by parents who rage and yell as a general rule. It is most impressive to the child when used by someone who ordinarily handles things quietly and without a lot of overt anger.

- The sixty-second scolding will not work unless negative emotions—guilt, shame, and/or fear of furthur parental anger or consequences—are *momentarily* evoked in the child.

Unfortunately, these negative feelings must be present for uncaring and rejecting children to find the parent's positive expressions meaningful at the end of the scolding.

Reward and Point Systems

It has been said that all of productive America works on a great behavior modification plan with points awarded or earned for good productive behavior. In the world of work, the "points" are called salary! Boy Scouts, 4-H, Awana Bible clubs, and many other youth programs all work successfully on point systems. Reward is based on effort and productivity. Communism, with its emphasis on individual reward regardless of productivity, has been proven to fail. Capitalism, for all its faults, is the world's most constant and reliable behavior modification system when high levels of production are the goal. Capitalist societies have produced most of the world's inventions and the highest sustained gross national products.

Many disturbed children have not learned to take satisfaction from their own accomplishments, or have no internalized values, a reward system can help them develop both. Provided, that is, that the rewards are something *they* care to work for.

In the home, there are several variations on reward systems:

- It is possible to have the child earn the reward directly: "If you finish cleaning the garage by this weekend, you'll be free to go skiing with us."

- A reward may be earned in stages: "Troy, for every week that you control your temper, you'll earn a major piece of your motorcycle—first the wheels, then the seat, then the frame, then the handlebars, and so on."

- Children may earn points toward rewards of their own choosing, in agreement with the parent, of course. "I'd really like to have a pair of rollerblades like Shawn's."

Advantages:

- A reward program forces consistency.

- A well thought-out program forces parents to be logical and consequential, and encourages nonemotional responses to the children's misbehavior. Rather than becoming angry about a job being forgotten, a parent becomes empathetic and understanding: "What a bummer! I know you were looking forward to going skiing with us this weekend. But if this job gets done this weekend, we'll sure enjoy your company next weekend."

- Reward systems encourage parents to be consistent.

- Reward systems are generally concrete and immediate, and many disturbed children have a difficult time conceptualizing long-term and abstract goals. Most disturbed children have a hard time understanding statements like "grades are important so you can grow up to be a productive person."

- When children are encouraged to help design the reward system, they take ownership and are more likely to become invested in doing well.

Disadvantages:

- The children may become dependent on the system. Some children never seem to internalize the controls they need to manage their behavior without earning rewards or points.

- Parents cannot make the child buy into the system.

- Some children become extremely adept at manipulating this kind of system.

- Some disturbed children will sabotage themselves by never allowing themselves to achieve the reward. They may come very close, and then deliberately or subconsciously blow it.

- This system is used most successfully in institutions where the children have constant supervision and consistency and can't opt out of the program during part of the day. They do not leave to attend school, etc. Everyone they are involved with is also involved with the point system. This is not true in most home situations, which can make this kind of system less effective there.

- It is a lot of work for parents. Parents must keep track of the points, monitor the children's performance, follow up, and so on.

- The system depends on a certain amount of motivation on the child's part.

Many institutions, even those where children live in cottage settings that closely imitate traditional family life, successfully use a system of tight rewards.

▪▪ After dinner the children move to the den, where they record on index cards the number of points they've accumulated throughout the day. Every day is parent–teacher conference and report card day at Boy's Town. Point cards from school are carried home and compared with home cards so that everyone who works with a child knows how that child is doing.[144]
▪▪

Most institutionalized kids can tell you exactly how many points they have accumulated at any given time, just as accurately as some adults know to the penny how much money they have in the bank.

The key to a good point system is the ability to both lose and earn large numbers of points rapidly *for precisely defined behavior* that the parents want to encourage. Joe may have been awarded 10,000 points for saying "please" and "thank you" throughout dinner, but he may also be docked thousands of points for leaving the table without being excused. At Boy's Town, the director noted, "Behavioral points are a lot like Catholic indulgences. We've got little sins, big sins, confessions, and plenary indulgences."[145]

Points are awarded as flamboyantly as praise, but removed with matter-of-fact courtesy, emotional flatness, or low-grade concern. Points often translate into privileges and purchasing power. Thirty thousand points may entitle a child to watch a movie. Another 20,000 earns a bowl of popcorn to share with friends who have also earned the movie privilege. A ticket to a concert may cost 500,000 points. Adding and subtracting high numbers adds drama to the game and hones mathematical skills. (What pinball machine would be exciting if counted up by tens?)

Well-designed point systems never allow children to dig themselves into a hole so deep they cannot climb out. A child who has just stabbed a hole in a sofa, and cursed at his parents the will be docked 50,000 points for the damage and bad language. If he follows his bad behavior by sitting down calmly on that same sofa, he will immediately be awarded 15,000 points for regaining control. "Hey, you've just earned back 15,000 points. You'll be out of the hole in no time."

Children with limited ability to connect cause and effect need immediate tangible rewards. A reward system can still be used successfully with these children. However, a point system that requires saving up for a reward will be meaningless to them. Stickers, M&Ms or small snack items, a baseball card—whatever trinkets the children enjoy will provide greater motivation for these children. A visible award such as a star or sticker chart is a step closer to the "save up for it" reward system and serves the dual purpose of teaching the children to delay gratification.

Therapeutic Parenting Techniques

When the goal of parents is to change children's behavior, to train them to behave in acceptable or appropriate ways, it is often wise to examine the root cause of the undesirable behavior before deciding upon a strategy to encourage change. The majority of disturbed children, to varying degrees, have experienced early trauma or deprivation of some sort. Children who have missed out on normal kinds of experiences, or have been deprived of affection and nurture, can sometimes benefit greatly from corrective or substitute experiences. Parents can easily learn to provide experiences that may, to some degree, fill in the gaps in their children's early development, allowing them to move closer to emotional and behavioral health. The techniques that are used for this purpose are called *therapeutic parenting techniques*. This distinguishes them from parenting techniques that concentrate on training issues and are based on consequencing bad behavior or rewarding good behavior. Although both kinds of techniques can bring about behavioral change, the changes seen when therapeutic techniques are applied result from psychological and developmental gains, rather than from behavior training or modification.

Many children who have lived in neglectful or deprived environments, or a series of short-term homes, have missed out on the normal experiences of early childhood. They have large gaps in social and emotional functioning as well as pieces missing from their knowledge of the world. Some of our children have never been taken into stores, or allowed to tag along with parents on errands to the bank or post office. School-aged children who are deprived of such ordinary early experiences lack the ability to make sense of the world in the way that is expected of children their age. Simply providing such children with those experiences can help them tremendously. Parents should talk about the things they observe in the environment, describing people and places, using descriptive words and lots of explanation, as they would do with a very small child who is just beginning to talk.

Family relationships may have to be explained as well. For example, parents should not assume that an eleven-year-old adopted child understands that her aunt is her father's sister, or that her grandmother is her mother's mother. If her early family situation was dysfunctional, relationships may have gone unexplained, or have been mislabeled. Some children may have been told that their mother's boyfriends were "uncles." In the adoptive home, "uncle" does not have the same meaning.

Filling in the gaps in the children's early environment can be fun and is generally easy to do. For many adoptive parents, it is a way to experience some of the joys of giving that they missed out on because they were not part of their children's early life.

Holding and Rocking Techniques

There are a variety of ways in which holding and rocking therapy can be used to help disturbed children. Some are easier and safer to use than others. Some are easily and effectively done by knowledgeable parents at home, and some require one or more skilled and highly trained therapists to facilitate. In this section, we will describe each in brief, and encourage the interested reader to look further into these techniques by making use of the many holding therapy resources listed in the back of this book.

Normal development occurs in a social context, which for a newborn is the mother–child relationship. The child's optimal development is most likely to take place if there is a secure bond or attachment between mother and child. The formation of this bond normally includes holding and rocking of the child during infancy and toddlerhood—and thereafter. The bond develops when the mother responds with sensitivity to the child's needs and the child finds that its own attempts at communication succeed in eliciting a satisfying response. Without this responsiveness, the bond will be impaired and problems may develop.[146]

More precise and "insistent" holding and rocking techniques can sometimes resolve or improve problems associated with failure to develop healthy attachments, or those caused by a break in the normal bonding routine.[147]

Parents can utilize various holding techniques to facilitate positive therapeutic outcomes for children in their care. Parents are not therapists, although they *are* therapeutic.[148]

Dr. Martha Welch, a physician well known for her success with autistic children, recommends a therapeutic technique called *holding time*, which many parents can use to encourage attachment. Her book of the same name is an excellent and comprehensive guide to using therapeutic holding, and we strongly recommend that any parent who wishes to try this method read Dr. Welch's book in addition to the material we provide here. (See the resources section at the end of this book for information on obtaining book *Holding Time*.)

Holding and rocking therapy, when used correctly, has many potential benefits for both child and family.

- Holding therapy ends positively for the children. The children are brought through the angry, difficult feelings, and then hugged and gently rewarded for their efforts. Just as we cuddle and comfort the infant after immunizations are done, we cuddle and comfort children after a difficult holding session. And the children feel loving and loved, sometimes for the first time in their lives.[149]

- As severely disturbed children move toward health, they can understand and accept that it was necessary for the adult to force them to accept closeness because they were not strong enough to accept it themselves. Many children eventually feel great affection and gratitude for the persons who rescued them from their prisons of isolation.[150]

The goals of holding treatment help the children:

- Validate their feelings.

- Identify, appropriately express, and regulate feelings.

- Resolve early trauma.

- Work through grief and loss issues.

- Cognitively restructure faulty thinking patterns.

- Learn to see the world and their place in it in more realistic terms.

- Develop a positive sense of identity.

- Reshape their behavior to more appropriate and socially acceptable levels.

- Relate to others in a respectful, responsible, and reciprocal way.

- Develop thoughtful decision-making skills.

- Experience and accept loving, nurturing care.

- Increase self-control abilities.[151]

The Correct Body Positions for Holding

Therapists and proponents of holding therapy vary slightly in their preferences regarding the child's body position during holding sessions. The Attachment Center at Evergreen, uses a cradling, across the lap hold, much the same way you would hold an infant in your arms.[152] Gregory Keck, founder of the Attachment and Bonding Center of Ohio, and coauthor with Regina Kupecky, of the book *Adopting the Hurt Child*, tells about the holding position he uses in therapy:

> Holding the child or adolescent is accomplished by having him lie across the laps of two therapists and/or his parents. His right arm is behind the back of the lead therapist, who is sitting closest to the child's head. His left arm is free, or may be restrained if he uses it to try to hit the therapist or to engage in self-stimulation such as scratching or fidgeting.

Another adaptation of holding is to have the child lie on a couch or floor with the therapist sitting at his head.[153]

Daniel Hughes, clinical psychologist and author of *Facilitating Developmental Attachment,* expands upon Keck's description of the process:

▟▎ The standard therapeutic position is for the child to be lying across my lap with his head and sometimes his legs supported by pillows. One of his arms is behind my back; I hold his free hand.

The child is held by the therapist or parent in other ways also. He may sit in his parent's lap as she reads him a story. He may sit in his parent's lap with his back to her as they chat with the therapist. His parent may hold him in various ways as they sing or play hand or finger games. His parent may rock him or whisper in his ear as he 'sleeps.'[154] ▟▎

Dr. Martha Welch, in her book *Holding Time*, talks about her preferred holding position, "The mother sits in a comfortable place with her child straddling her lap, face-to-face, maximizing their awareness of each other. The child's legs are wrapped around her waist. His arms, under hers, are around her back."[155]

Holding position is a matter of personal style and preference combined with practicalities such as the age and size of the children and person(s) doing the holding, facilities available, and so on. Correct holding positions all have some things in common:

- The child is held comfortably, so no pain or discomfort is involved.

- The child is held in a position that encourages direct eye contact with the person talking to him.

- The therapist or parent holding the child maintains control over the child's attempts to protest, struggle, hurt himself or others, or escape.

- Outside means of restraint, such as wrapping the child in blankets or tying him are not used.

- Holding is done in a manner that safely controls the child's ability to hurt himself or others.

- Older, bigger children are held by two or more people (therapists or parents).

Holding is used to:

- Direct attention.

- Nurture.

- Physically contain the child.

- Promote exploration of feelings.

- Confront behavior.

- Resolve internal conflict.

- Enhance attachment relationships.[156]

- Direct interaction.

- Encourage acceptance of the therapist's or parent's reality.

- Encourage compliance.

- Encourage a reciprocal loving response.

Holding techniques can be used for two separate and distinct reasons They may be used for bonding, either to enhance an existing bond, or to treat attachment disorders; they may also be used for restraint, to temporarily prevent children from hurting themselves or others.

The Holding Session Sequence

Regardless of the reason for doing holdings, they should always follow the same sequence. According to Dr. Welch, during a holding session, the therapist or parent attempts to guide the child through a three-part sequence. Other therapists use this same sequence, although they may use different words to describe it. Dr. Welch calls the three phases:

1. Confrontation

2. Rejection

3. Resolution[157]

She describes the confrontation phase of a session with a child who exhibits moderate behavior problems:

> In holding time, you physically embrace your child whether or not either of you feels, at that moment, the usual emotions that lead to an embrace. It does not necessarily begin with—but should never end without reaching—a happy phase of closeness. . . . A holding session evolves differently depending on the circumstances and upon the individuals involved.

The goal of the confrontation phase of the session is to focus the children on the issues and arouse them to respond honestly. Dr. Welch cites an example:

> On the rare occasion when Amy does not express her feelings soon after the start, her mother searches for subjects of distress: 'Are you angry that I had to go to work today?' 'Why can't you cooperate when we have to leave the playground?' 'It makes me angry when you run away every time I try to help you dress to go out!' 'That makes me yell and I don't want to yell at you.' Something will eventually strike a chord, and the child will respond by turning away, fighting, telling her mother not to say that, or indicating in some other way that it is a sensitive subject. Thus the next phase, rejection, will begin.[158]

Some children have more serious and deeply disturbing issues to work through. They may need help to recognize and talk about repressed rage concerning past abuse or abandonment issues. They may go through all three phases of holding over the simple issue of making eye contact with the therapist.

The second phase, rejection, begins as the child tries to escape the embrace, perhaps by kicking, spitting, holding her breath, yelling, insisting that she has to go to the bathroom, and so on. Children can become very creative during this phase. They may try to provoke the therapist's rage, or to change the subject. They may accuse the therapist of not caring or not loving them.

During this phase, it is important that the therapist remain willing to hear what the child says, and accepting of the child's feelings. It is appropriate to respond to such statements as "You don't love me" by saying, "I love you very much and I am sorry that you don't feel my love right now."

Sometimes the child will scream or sob in anger or sadness. It is helpful to remember that this is the child's way of working through unexpressed feelings. It is not a personal attack, no matter what the child says, although it might feel that way. The message to the child is "I can handle anything you say or feel."

Eventually the therapist encourages the child to define the source of their feelings with statements like "Are you angry because I didn't take you to the park today?" or "Did it make you sad when Jason told you he didn't want to be your best friend anymore?"

The most important part of the rejection phase, according to Dr. Welch, is for mother (or therapist) and child to communicate their deepest feelings of distress to each other. This requires reciprocal interaction. Whoever is confronting the child must model healthy expression of emotions and feelings, enabling comments like "I feel so sad when you won't look at me," "I hate it when you call me that," and "I feel like you hate me and don't want me for a mother when you spit at me and refuse to look at me in the morning."

During this phase, therapists often ask the children leading questions, designed to provoke them into revealing previously repressed or denied feelings. "How do you think you felt as a little baby, being left outside a strange place in a cardboard box? Did that little baby feel loved by his birth mother?"

The resolution phase takes place when the children have successfully tapped into their deepest feelings, struggled through their resistance and negative emotionism and surrendered control of the situation to the therapist. At this point an often dramatic transformation occurs whereby the children demonstrate joyful relief by initiating warm and loving interactions on their own or at the request of the therapist. They often express genuine empathy and concern for the feelings of others. Some children become so exausted by the physical and emotional battle of the holding session and the ensuing feelings of relief and trust that they fall asleep in their parents arms.

The goal of each holding session is to come to at least partial resolution. This is not always possible, particularly if time constraints are imposed on the session. Resolution locks in the therapeutic value of holding and is essential to the achievement of long-term positive results.

Simple Holding

Simple holding can be done with *any* child to enhance bonding, open the doors to better communication, improve behaviors, increase appropriateness of emotional responses, relieve stress, and achieve closeness. Even healthy and well-adjusted children can benefit from simple holding.[159]

Simple holding is done by the parent, usually the mother, or the children's primary caretaker. It is not done to resolve deeply rooted psychological issues related to past maltreatment or abandonment. It is best used with children who exhibit moderate behavior problems or show moderate signs of stress and suppressed anger.

Simple holding sessions may last for an hour or two the first few times and gradually diminish to less than an hour. With a little experience, some issues can be resolved in a few minutes through simple holding.

Simple holding is most effective when it is done with all of the children in the home. Each of the children can look forward to their own holding time and know that they will receive the same intense attention and individual time as the others.

Advantages:

- Simple holding is easy to learn.

- It can be done at home.

- It produces immediate results.

Disadvantages:

- Seriously disturbed children may need stronger intervention.

- Sessions may drag on without resolution, making it difficult for parents to know how and when to end the session.

- Children may not respond quickly or as expected.

- Can be time intensive, particularly if there are several children in the home.

- Even simple holding can be seen as too intrusive by those who believe that a child should only be held with the child's permission.

A child who needs holding will not always ask for it or willingly participate at first. Most children do not ask to be immunized against childhood diseases, yet we know it is in their best interest to insist upon it.

Simple holding can produce some remarkable results in a very short time, particularly if the children are not severely disturbed or attachment disordered.

- A clinging child will be less demanding or anxious.

- Your child will have more self-confidence, curiosity, and motivation.

- Your child will show an interest in your feelings about accomplishing the family's work and will help by playing independently alongside you or, if older, by helping directly.

- Your child will show more affection for you.

- Sibling rivalries will diminish, and you will spend less time resolving battles.[158]

Holding for Bonding

Holding for bonding is carried out when parents are caring for a child with poor ability to form healthy attachments.[159] Aside from being extremely noncompliant, rageful, and controlling, these children do not like physical contact and are generally "tactile defensive." They don't appreciate touch. Most lack reciprocity; that is, they don't smile back.[160] They don't respond, and because reciprocity is poor, it is difficult for the parents to attach to the child as well. Holding may help both the parents and the child.[161]

The holding session may last several hours, ending when the child easily and naturally snuggles into the parent, accepting the parent's loving control of the situation. The holding is carried out with one or two parents—and often with a therapist—who sit together on a couch, holding the child in a face-up position and lovingly, face to face, work through the child's need to escape affectionate contact.

Advantages:

- Holding for bonding is perhaps one of the fastest and most effective ways to reach severely disturbed children with attachment disorder problems.

- Parents are actively involved in creating a positive change in the child.

- When done correctly, both parents and children feel a sense of accomplishment and closeness.[162]

Disadvantages:

- Holding for bonding is one of the most controversial of all parenting techniques.

- The child moves, by his behavior, from *needing* to be held, to *demanding* to be held. This is a difficult transition. At first the child needs holding but resists it. As the child moves toward health, he comes to demand it through misbehavior because he likes and wants it. At this point, the child needs to be consequenced for behavior, not held. This is a difficult transition and it is difficult to determine when the line has been crossed.

- Occasionally children may hurt themselves or others during holding.

- It usually requires the involvement of trained attachment therapists, which may be expensive and may mean traveling long distances to obtain services.

- The children may become even more rebellious and difficult to handle if good resolution cannot be obtained during the end phases of a holding session.

- Occasionally very disturbed children are brought to the rejection phase and are unable to reach healthy resolution. Previously repressed emotions are now accessible to the children, and a formerly passive child may become angry and act out. Behaviors can worsen or new undesirable behaviors develop.

- Usually requires follow-up "tune-ups," sometimes for years.

- Children can become harder to manage between sessions as they work through problems.

The primary therapeutic goal of holding for bonding is to facilitate secure attachment in the parent–child relationship. To achieve this goal, it is necessary to recreate the elements of secure attachment that were unavailable in the child's early developmental stages. In the context of the Holding Nurturing Process (HNP), children are provided with structure, attunement, empathy, positive affect, support, reciprocity, and love. The HNP is a therapeutic relationship and milieu that promotes secure attachment via social releasers, safe containment, corrective touch, access to "old brain" functions that control attachment behavior, and the development of a secure base in which positive developmental changes occur.[163]

The calming effect of loving, tender holding is demonstrated in many mammals, not just in humans. Roger Payne, Ph.D., writes about containment holding in whales:

The mother whale simply endures the hijinks of an infant as if her peaceful good nature were an endless resource from which she, and the calf, can draw. I have watched many a calf boisterously playing about its resting mother for hours at a time, sliding off her flukes, wriggling up onto her back, covering her blowhole with its tail, breaching against her repeatedly, butting into her flank, all without perceptible reaction from the mother. When finally she does respond to the torment, it may be only to roll onto her back and embrace the infant in her arm-like flippers, holding it until it calms down. It is hard to think of comparable equanimity among any other mammals, including man.[164]

Holding for bonding has dangers when done by untrained and/or unsupervised parents:

- Parents may be overly controlling, overly forceful, or inappropriately angry, all of which can be very damaging.

- Parents may get into control battles that they can't win.

- Parents may not know how to verbally and emotionally help the children work though their rage at such intimate contact.

- Parents may be unprepared for both the time commitment needed and the depth of the children's rage.

- Parents may have difficulty managing angry children afterwards.

- Parents' own issues and psychological weak spots may be tapped into which may cause difficulty for both parents and children. Without a professional present to help them recognize this and work it through, parents may be left with more problems than they started with.

See the Outside Resources section at the end of this book for a list of attachment professionals who use holding techniques.

Holding and Rocking during Times of Vulnerabilty

As we have noted elsewhere, disturbed children, because of their anxiety and difficulty in feeling basic trust, are controlling and oppositional. They attempt to take care of themselves, meet all of their own needs, and absolutely show and feel no dependence on others. Their war cry is, "I don't need you, I don't want you, and I won't ever need *anybody!*" (They will, however, *use* others if it serves their purpose. This can be deceptive, particularly to outsiders. "He has no trouble asking *me* for what he needs." This is not a demonstration of healthy dependence. The child is merely using others as objects or tools to get what he or she wants.)

Therefore, times when the child is vulnerable and open for nurturing are valuable and must be mined as golden opportunities to reach the child. Children with severe attachment disorder must be in *very* difficult situations before they can easily accept attention, relief, and rescue from the adult caretaking individual. *The most valuable times are when the child is scared, anxious, or sick.* These are golden opportunities to say, "Honey, I know things are going badly, and this is how I can help out. . . ."

When parents are there for their children in these times of stress:

- The child experiences high levels of tension, and the relief provided by the parents' love is more readily appreciated, making the relaxing at the end of the bonding cycle much more profound.

- The child learns (and gratefully accepts) that others can be helpful, caring, and loving, and that accepting their love makes them feel better. Basic trust is built.

Some situations that create vulnerability make the child more willing to be nurtured:

- The child is frightened of a situation he or she cannot control, such as going to the doctor.

- The child is bedridden and needs special care.

- The child is having nightmares and/or fears.

- When the child is ill with vomiting or fever, or has a serious injury that causes pain and fear:

⫽⫽ The closest we ever came to making a real connection with Evan was when he came home from the hospital after eating spoiled food out of a dumpster at school and getting a raging case of salmonella food poisoning. The whole hospital experience was painful, unpleasant, and frightening. He must have thought he was going to die. We brought him home, and laid him on the couch, and he looked right in our eyes and said, 'It's so good to be home!' He *had never* said anything like that before, much less made eye contact. Too bad it took a bout with life-threatening illness to make it come about.   **⫽⫽**

Back in the 1970s, a social worker in Denver adopted a native American child who had severe attachment problems. At age seven, her little daughter was entirely out of control. After a short time in her new home, the child took a bad accidental fall, fracturing her back, and was placed in a body cast for six months. During this time, for the first time in her life, she was completely dependent on someone else for absolutely everything. She couldn't even move without help. And she could not use her typical resistance techniques to maintain distance from her mother. When the cast was cracked after six months, a new and loving child emerged. The accident had forced a tension/release/relaxation/trust cycle that ultimately resulted in the child's bonding to the mother.

This mother was so impressed by the transformation that she used the story as a part of her master's thesis in social work.

Holding and Rocking Tips

- Do additional rocking and holding during times of vulnerability, such as when the child is frightened, anxious, or sick.

- Power struggles should be avoided if at all possible.

- The initial interactions should be short. It is better to have a short *good* time, than a long time of holding hassle. As the child comes to accept holding, the times may be lengthened.

- Play baby games and make the noises that a mother would with an infant. The children who need therapeutic rocking and holding need the normal mother/infant ambience. Therefore, sing songs, play "eensy-weensy" and peek-a-boo, and play with the child's lips and eyebrows as mothers of infants will do. Maintain good eye contact and give lots of big smiles.

- Give children the opportunity to bottle feed or lick honey off a fingertip *if the child feels good about these techniques* and can easily be talked into them. Say, for instance, "You know what, I think you like being held like this because you didn't get a lot of this when you were a little baby. And I didn't get to hold you like this because I wasn't there, so I missed it too. That's why I like it so much now. And little ones often enjoy other experiences . . . would you like to try some of them?"

- Generally, if a child needs holding and rocking, it must be done for at least a few minutes almost every day. This is a big commitment, but one well worth making in terms of the changes you will see in the child. The children will eventually come to ask, "When do I get my rocking and holding time today?"

- Use the holding time as a time for teaching reciprocity. Many adopted and foster children have come from such deprived environments that they do not know how to express feelings with the appropriate intonation, or to say things that "give back" good feelings to others. Teach by example. Give the child the exact words and responses that children his or her age normally give. Have the child practice them *in a fun way* with you:

▐▐ And when someone says something nice to you, what are you supposed to say?"

"Oh, say it happier than that . . . Like this. . . ." (Parent demonstrates proper tone of happiness and excitement.) "Gee, thanks Grandma!"

(Child convincingly mimics parent's tone of voice.) "Great! Now I know you're really happy. You sound happy! ▐▐

Or ask the child to imagine how another person would feel hearing what they have to say.

▐▐ And how would Grandma feel if you said 'thank you' like that?"

"Good."

"Right. She would feel happy right along with you. You would make *Grandma* happy too. ▐▐

Because of their backgrounds, many of our children have not had the positive experience of making another person happy. They must be taught to think of others and realize that their words and actions impact others' feelings as well as their own.

- If a holding is carried out twice in a row, and a positive outcome is not obtained, therapeutic consultation with a therapist trained in bonding techniques is strongly recommended.

- Children who are extremely resistant to all touch and holding need to see a therapist, and the parents need expert coaching.

- Underneath the rage of many children lies grief, pain, and loss. Following the initial responses, these important issues need to be resolved.

Danger of Holding as Treatment for Attachment Problems

In many ways severe attachment disorders are like severe forms of cancer. The prognosis is always guarded and treatments are intrusive and not always successful. The alternative to treatment is to do nothing, and hope that a miraculous cure will be spontaneously effected. As with cancer, this is very unlikely.

Few people would question a parent who permitted their child to have a liver transplant, though this is a very invasive, painful treatment with a protracted course. Those who oppose holding for the same reason usually do so because they believe there are less intrusive alternatives that are equally effective. For severely disturbed, attachment disordered children, however, many professionals believe there is no alternative to holding.[165] These professionals know that Reactive Attachment Disordered children have a severely disabling condition that cannot be loved away or reached by many of the usual techniques.

Why Do Traditional Therapeutic Methods Fail With Some Children?

According to the Attachment Center at Evergreen, "Most traditional therapy involves talk therapy, and is based upon the development of a therapeutic relationship between therapist and client. This relationship requires mutual trust, respect, reciprocity, emotional honesty and the ability to formulate thoughts and feelings into words."

Children with attachment disorder are unable to make use of such methods for a variety of reasons:

- They do not trust.

- They are not emotionally honest, and in fact are frequently not able to identify their feelings or what is behind those feelings.

- They do not respect anyone, including themselves.

- They are not capable of reciprocal give-and-take relationships.

- Their backgrounds of abuse, neglect, unresolved trauma or pain, loss and abandonment often were formed during the first year or two of life, prior to conscious memory of events.

- They do not know why they feel and act as they do.

- They are operating in the only way they know how to survive.[166]

The highest rates of success are achieved when children are empowered by being a part of the decision-making process and agree to treatment, by a process therapists refer to as *contracting*. Contracting with these children is worth considerable effort.[167] However, the most severely affected children, the ones who need treatment the most, are the most difficult to contract with. They are also the ones who have the most to gain if treatment is successful. In the relatively rare instance that children refuse holding, some therapists advise using holding therapy without the children's cooperation. Others, such as Greg Keck of the Attachment and Bonding Center of Ohio, refuse to conduct a holding session with a child unless they are able to obtain at least a grudging contract.[168]

The Dangers of Using Holding Techniques Without the Child's Permission

Some very disturbed children do not respond and benefit from holding in the desired way. They are too damaged or too resistant to heal. These children may retain a strong anger against the parents for any attempts they have made to draw them closer, such as holding. They may retaliate aggressively. Some children have reported parents as abusive or even sought legal representation and initiated lawsuits against the parents as young adults. If this is a concern, obtaining the children's permission is essential and holding should be done under the supervision of a trained professional who should document each session on audio or videotape.

We are often asked about the wisdom of imposing treatment on children against their wills, particularly older children. There are answers:

- Children, especially disturbed children, do not always have the maturity or ability to determine what is in their best interests. Under some circumstances, they need a responsible and caring adult to make that determination.

- Children with attachment disorders are mentally ill. They have a diagnosable and treatable illness as defined in the *DSM IV*.[169] Persons whose judgment is impaired by a psychiatric disorder may not be in the best position to determine what is in their best interests. Their resistance to necessary treatment is part of their disorder.

- It is difficult, even for healthy, mature adults, to agree to even temporarily unpleasant treatment. No one looks forward to chemotherapy, for example, and some people refuse to accept it, often to the extent that it shortens their lives. The closeness of a holding session is very unpleasant and frightening for an unattached child, but may be the only way to reach the child. The alternative is that the child remains unable to form close attachments for life.

- We routinely do things to our children (and ourselves, for that matter) that are temporarily painful or uncomfortable, when those things are necessary to ensure long-term health and safety: immunizations, medical treatments and tests for severe illness, surgeries, spinal taps, chemotherapy, kidney dialysis, etc. Yet few children would happily agree to these procedures and many would opt out of them if given half a chance.

- These children, who are so adept at keeping people at a distance and being in control at all times, need touch to work through their problems.[170]

- Confrontation, such as that often used in holding therapy, is sometimes necessary to break through a child's defenses and reach the hurting child within. Confrontation of faulty thinking patterns and destructive behavior patterns is essential if change is to occur.[171]

Holding for Restraint

When children are held for restraint, they are held for their own protection or to protect others in the environment. It should be used as a safety measure only.

Advantages:

- The children know that adults in the environment are capable of taking care of, and will provide safety for, themselves and others.

- Handled correctly, the children have the advantage of touch and affection *as they gain control of themselves.*

- When parents are trained properly in this technique—which is essential—they feel a sense of mastery and can more easily relax around the children.

- Training and certification is easily available to parents in most geographic areas. (Parents might inquire with local therapists, residential treatment centers, psychiatric facilities, nursing homes, emergency room personnel, or law enforcement personnel for information about safe restraint classes that might be offered in their area. Many people who work in these fields must have this type of certification.)

Disadvantages:

- There is a good deal of secondary gain when children are held for restraint. They get the benefits of touch and they control aspects of the situation, especially when adults make statements such as, "When you are ready to be more calm, we'll let you up." Naturally, the children then think, "Good! I'll struggle for at least another hour or so." It is very difficult—at times impossible—for parents to spend such intense time and energy on one child.

- Occasionally children hurt themselves or others during holding for restraint.

- Used incorrectly, the child becomes more resentful and more rebellious.

- If done in the presence of others, or in earshot of neighbors, it can be easily misinterpreted as abusive. Many children scream "Ow! Ow! Ow!" even when not being hurt. They may put up a convincing show of unnecessary struggle and fight. They are expressing *emotional* pain—not physical pain. But to outsiders, it can look and sound like the parent is deliberately hurting the child.[172]

Additional Bonding Techniques

Adults or children with bonding and attachment disorders need to re-experience the trauma of the need/rage/gratification cycle to learn to bond. All bonding involves elements of trauma. We wish it were otherwise, but there is no way around this fact. It is around needs that an infant perceives as traumatic, such as hunger, that healthy early bonds begin to form.

The bonding routines that are used with disturbed adoptive children involve, in one way or another, a traumatic ordeal followed by feelings of relief, achievement, or gratification. The trauma that rejecting and rage-filled children must go through to develop the ability to attach may appear abusive or unnecessarily harsh to untrained professionals.[173]

Evergreen Consultants in Human Behavior, specialists in treating children with Reactive Attachment Disorder, recommend and use this approach:

// Revisit, Revise, Revitalize: Treatment is developmental, requiring the successful completion of each stage building upon the next. Attachment trauma is first *revisited* to address core issues. Next, *revisions* are facilitated in belief systems, choices, relationship patterns, and coping skills. Lastly, *revitalization* includes celebrating achievements, cementing positive changes, and enhancing hope for the future.[174] (italics ours)   *//*

Outward Bound and similar wilderness survival programs are based on a phenomenon called *trauma bonding*. Trauma bonding takes place when a frightening situation takes place in the presence of one or more people on whom the fearful subject must rely for survival or support. Trauma bonds sometimes develop in hostage situations, stuck elevators, airplane disasters, and so forth. In wilderness survival programs, children may take a challenging and harrowing whitewater rafting trip, or climb a mountain, using ropes and relying on team effort to keep from falling. They are forced to relinquish individual control and depend on others for their very life. Only in such strenuous and stressful situations, situations that feel like 'life or death' to the children, could these severely disturbed children develop reciprocity and begin to trust and bond. One counselor relates:

On the first day, there is nothing but trouble from the kids. They don't want to get up; they need to be poured from their sleeping bags. They moan about the food and won't help fix it. They refuse to follow orders from the counselors. They do not cooperate with anyone*!*

One day on the river changes all that! After they've gotten themselves in trouble with the river a few times, and I've yelled 'back paddle,' 'paddle right,' and 'paddle left' for a day, they honestly believe I've saved their asses from every hole on the river. And [he chuckles] maybe I have. But the next morning it's 'How can I help you with breakfast, Gene?' It's a complete transformation. Suddenly we're a team!

Following the lead and hoping to repeat the many successes of wilderness survival courses, many psychiatric hospitals now have a ropes course to teach cooperation and mutual trust. Many of these high- and low-challenge courses are open to adoptive parent groups who may reserve them for special occasions. They can be of significant help for children who need to develop a closer relationship with their parents.

There are ways that parents can use similar bonding techniques. One parent purposely allowed a child to become lost in a mall, but kept an eye on her as her distress level increased before being "found." Her traumatic realization of dependency followed by her "rescue" from distress by her mother was a recreation of the early distress/relief bonding cycle. Distress followed by relief is the key. If that relief is provided by a parent or helping professional, it can be the beginning of a therapeutic, life-altering bond. It is crucial to note that correct use of this technique requires careful planning and no real danger to the children. Safety *must* be built into the plan. The children *perceive* danger, but are not actually *in* danger. That perception is never carried to the point of panic for the children. The children are always rescued or helped out before real terror can set in.

Bonding techniques, particularly the holding techniques, are often the final attempt to reach the child before the family resorts to enforcing the tightest limit of all—that the child can no longer be maintained in the home.

Reparenting

Reparenting helps many children who have missed out on ordinary experiences early in life, or who have not had their needs met appropriately in infancy. Some of these early experiences can be had by using special techniques at a later time in life.

Reparenting treats children as they should have been treated at the age when earlier deprivation occurred. For instance, an eleven-year-old who spent early years in a neglectful and non-nurturing home might be sat on the parent's lap and taught finger-plays and nursery rhymes, just as one might do with a three-year-old. A nine-year-old might be allowed to choose rattles and chew toys to play with, and be encouraged to use them as is usually done in infancy.

Advantages:

- Reparenting is fun for both parents and children.

- It enhances chances for bonding and attachment.

- It's easy for most families to do.

- Parents feel a great deal of joy and satisfaction at being able to make up for some of the deprivation their children have suffered and see them respond with unencumbered glee.

- Reparenting may lessen the need for professional guidance or help.

- The child's need for this is usually understood and accepted by both the children and outsiders.

Disadvantages:

- Children may not wish to participate.

- It may open the children up to ridicule if not done privately.

- Unmotivated children may use regressive behavior to avoid doing things they dislike.

- The technique occasionally may be disapproved of by outsiders who do not understand the children's special needs.

- It occasionally may be misinterpreted and discouraged by caseworkers who want children to be taught independence and advanced skills to boost self-esteem.

Some children seem locked in a developmental stage until the business of that age and stage is completed. The therapists of old called this "fixation." Reparenting helps such children work through the locked stage and progress into another, one more appropriate to their chronological age. Many children are able to integrate several stages at once. They may attend school in their appropriate grade, behaving much like the others in their class. After school on the same day, they may spend an hour or two doing things as if they were a two-year-old, and another hour or two being age-appropriate. Perhaps they end the day as infants, cuddled on mom's lap drinking juice from baby bottles and gazing into their mother's eyes as she sings them a lullaby.

A Few Guidelines for the Use of Reparenting Techniques

- Children direct this process by telling parents (sometimes through their behaviors) what they need or have missed out on.

- Children who do not eagerly participate after showing only slight incredulity or resistance should not be forced or cajoled into participation.

- An explanation of the reasons for reparenting should be given to the children.[175] This explanation should include these elements:

  - "When you were little, you missed out on a lot of important things."

  - "Those things are necessary for us all to grow and feel good about ourselves."

  - "We want you to have those things, because we love you and care about your welfare."

  - It is okay to have them now, even though you are a little older than most kids are when they get them."

- "This is not a punishment, you have done nothing wrong, and you need not feel ashamed or embarrassed."

- "We are happy to be able to share these things with you—we missed out on them too because we didn't even know you then."

- Children should not be embarrassed by the process. Respect must be shown to the child, and the techniques should not be used in public unless there is no danger of ridicule and then only if the children want to carry them over into their public life.

- Reparenting techniques should never be used as punishment, nor are they intended to ridicule or belittle children.[176] They can be thought of in terms of giving iron supplements to children who have iron deficiencies. It is not their fault they have too little iron, nor is the vitamin elixir a way to get even with them for misusing their supply of iron.

- As soon as children show a readiness or desire to give up the process, they should be allowed and encouraged to do so. A nighttime lullaby can be replaced by a more grown-up ritual, baby toys can be given up for Legos, and so on.

Parents are free to find creative ways to integrate reparenting techniques into daily life, and many special needs parents talk about the satisfaction this technique brings them and their children.

Our little girl was two-and-a-half when she came to live with us. She had never really been cherished in any of her previous homes. Her last placement was with a foster family who preferred older, more self-reliant children, so they did not enjoy having to 'do for' a little girl her age. She had not experienced many of the nurturing things that help kids grow and attach.

One of her behaviors drove us all a little batty. She was very 'oral.' She had her mouth on everything in the house—toys, doorknobs, the arms of the furniture— everything was wet. And she bit! Us, other kids, the pets. She also arrived with an upper respiratory infection that was stubbornly resisting treatment. So all that wet was germy as well. We were all sick all the time and saw no end in sight. Finally it occurred to us that perhaps she had never gotten enough sucking as an infant. We knew she was neglected by her birth mom. So maybe she needed to be oral in order to fill a need that was never met. We decided to try to meet her needs in a way that was more acceptable to the family and easier to live with. We didn't know if we were doing the right thing or not, but our instincts told us to try it. We went to the grocery store and bought a bright pink infant pacifier. When we got home, we brought it out and simply said, 'Honey, look what we bought for you.' We half expected her to complain that she was '*not* a baby!' But she didn't. Instead, she got the most delighted look on her face. We can still picture how she looked up at us with such love in her eyes. It was as if she were saying, 'You understand!' It brought tears to my eyes, it was so intense. And she loved the pacifier. It was in her mouth all the time for several weeks. And then one day we noticed that it was being left laying around the house at times. Just like an infant, she gradually left it behind, and the 'oral' behaviors right along with it. We know we did the right thing by doing this. And her bond to us got stronger because of it. She found out that she could count on us to accept her as she is and try to meet her needs. I still get tears when I remember the joy this gave us.

Reparenting makes up for experiences children missed out on while living in dysfunctional birth homes, or while being moved about from one temporary home to another. Children who come from other countries or from institutional environments also have many gaps in their experiential knowledge of the world, and particularly of family life. We have met children who, at age five or six, had never been taken to the grocery store. Others had no idea what a stay-at-home mom might be doing all day while they were at school. These gaps in knowledge and experience may cause difficulty for children at school, in relating to friends, and in academic testing of general knowledge. Some common things that many special needs children miss out on include the following:

- Family outings of any kind

- Being included in family chores

- Holding hands while walking

- Being helped with dressing and hair care routines

- Helping prepare a meal, licking the leftover frosting out of the bowl, setting the table, and so on

- Shopping for ordinary items

- Starting seedlings, planting a garden, or watering plants

- Making a list, replacing used-up paper towels, toilet paper, knowing where items are kept in a typical home, and so on

- Watching or helping with laundry

- Attending museums, zoos, movies

- Eating out at anything but fast food restaurants

- Going to church

- Going to the library

- Having sights pointed out while driving in the car

- Playing games with family members

- Baby games such as "peek-a-boo," "got your nose"

- Rhymes and finger-play such as "this little piggy," "here's the church," or "eeny-meeny-miney-moe"

- Going on picnics

- Carving pumpkins, decorating the Christmas tree, and wrapping presents

The list above can be modified to suit the children's needs. After a few months with their children, parents usually have a pretty good handle on where their developmental gaps might be. With younger children, many of these things come intuitively to parents. But, how many parents would think to play peek-a-boo with a twelve-year-old? Or let their nine-year-old ride the kiddie car rides at the carnival or the fifty cent merry-go-round at the mall? Yet many delight in just such experiences. (See chapter 2: How Old is the Child Really?) Unless the children's friends are around to poke fun at them, why not let them enjoy being a normal three-year-old once in a while?

Sensory Integration Therapy

Most of us know and are fully aware of our senses of taste, sight, smell, hearing, and touch. We delight in eating a scrumptious dessert, ooh and aah at a beautifully colored sunset, listen to our favorite music, smell the familiar aroma of hot buttered popcorn, and recognize full well when we stub our toe. Different parts of our bodies contain sensors, or receptors, that pick up important information and pass it on to our brain. We are familiar with the effects of light, pain, temperature, volume, and pressure on our skin, eyes, ears, and other parts of our bodies.[177]

Children with sensory integrative dysfunction, however, have problems organizing, utilizing, or interpreting this input. For most children, sensory integration develops in infancy as a result of adequate and appropriate environmental stimulation. Motor planning ability is a natural outcome of the sensory integration process, as is the ability to adapt to incoming sensations. But for some children, sensory integration does not develop as efficiently as it should. When the process is disordered, a number of problems in learning, development, or behavior may become evident.[178]

Children who have been deprived of normal environmental stimulation in infancy, or who have suffered damage to the brain stem, often develop problems interpreting and tolerating ordinary sensory input. This is frequently seen in children who are adopted out of third world orphanages where they have been left to languish in cribs with little attention from caretakers. It is a major factor in what is known as the *post-institutionalized child syndrome.*

What Are Some Signs of Sensory Integrative Dysfunction?

- Overly sensitive to touch, movement, sights, smells, or sounds

- Underreactive to touch, movement, sights, smells, or sounds

- Easily distracted

- Social and/or emotional problems

- Unusually high or low activity level

- Physical clumsiness or apparent carelessness

- Impulsiveness and lack of self-control

- Difficulty making transitions from one situation to another

- Inability to unwind or calm self

- Poor self-concept

- Delays in speech, language, or motor skills

- Delays in academic achievement[179]

Many of these symptoms overlap those of other disorders. If children are suspected of having a sensory integrative disorder, an evaluation can be conducted by a qualified occupational or physical therapist. Evaluation usually consists of both standardized testing and structured observations of responses to sensory stimulation, posture, balance, coordination, and eye movements.[180] The Outside Resources section at the end of this volume contains contact information about sensory integration organizations and post-institutionalized child support groups.

In recent years, large numbers of these children from Romania and the former Soviet Union have been adopted by American families. Many of these families have become strong advocates for their children, and dozens of professionals have become specialists in diagnosing and treating the post-institutionalized child.

Sensory integration therapy involves both work with a professional therapist or physician and a great deal of effort on the part of the parents in the home. It is not as much a parenting technique as a coordinated treatment effort involving the child, parents, and a specially trained therapist. For this reason we do not go into detail about these methods in this book. We do feel it deserves mention, since sensory deprivation problems can tie so closely into attachment, learning, and behavior problems. This treatment can be very successful and is well worth investigating if you have children whose background and behaviors indicate problems in this area.

Physical Safety and Practical Management Tools

Sometimes very disturbed children will act out in ways that make it nearly impossible for an ordinary family to keep them safe or to protect family property or other family members. For example, many families have described to us situations in which a child does not seem to need as much sleep as the average person, and uses the night to terrorize siblings or engage in destructive or dangerous behavior. In this case, the parents may be quickly worn down from lack of sleep. Emotionally they become vulnerable to anger and perhaps poor judgment in terms of child discipline. In their desperation to resolve the situation, they may try to "make" the child stop disrupting in the night. In reality, these children need caretakers who work in shifts, such as residential treatment facilities provide. But, since the present system mandates that they be placed in traditional homes, and does not offer practical and affordable group living situations for the many kids who need them, families are forced to find creative ways to cope with the situation.

Some suggestions we have gathered over the years can help return control to the parents while at the same time providing them with some peace of mind over the safety of their home and family.

Radio Shack and other electronics outlets offer inexpensive room alarms that can be fixed to the child's door or the doors of siblings. These alarms can be set to beep or screech if the door to the room is opened. Some children are extremely clever about disabling these alarms, and in some families the alarms give the homes a prison-like feeling. But for some children, alarms offer security and external control that is easily accepted. The child can be told that "We will do everything we can to ensure that our family members are kept healthy and safe. That means you as well as all of us. Until you demonstrate that you will not do dangerous or destructive things while we are asleep, we will have to put a beeper on your room so we can help you control your harmful behavior until you are able to control it yourself."

Baby monitors, either audio or video, can provide an unintrusive way to keep an eye on children while they are asleep or at play. Sooner or later all children need to develop internal voices that tell them to behave. Until then, these monitors can provide a measure of safety and security during a transition period, giving the child some autonomy when he is not yet entirely trustworthy.

   // Steve's bed was often wet in the morning. It was only after we installed the video monitor that we saw that Henry, who was our bed wetter, went over in the middle of the night and wet on Steve! What kind of kid allows another to wet on them night after night? Probably a terrorized kid. We suspected something was going on but we had no idea of the extent of the situation until we installed the video monitor. **//**

Frankly, it is not a bad idea for some children to think that someone is watching them at all times! In such cases, it adds immeasurably to their security—and yours!

Cabinet locks to fit almost any kind of cabinet door are available at most hardware stores. Liberal use of them can save a lot of hassles and make the atmosphere of your home more pleasant. The fewer small things you have to pick on your child about, the more you can concentrate on fun activities and larger training issues.

Families who live with aggressive, combative kids should learn ways to safely restrain an out-of-control child. Personnel in agencies and organizations working with mentally ill or aggressive individuals must take training courses in the proper use of safety restraint. These courses teach means of restraining children without hurting them or being hurt by them. We consider it essential for parents to complete a course like this before using restraining holds on their child. Should questions arise later about the wisdom of such use, a course completion certificate from a reputable organization will be invaluable and could prevent or be used to defend against criminal charges or litigation.

Some children are so violent and dangerous to the entire family that it might be wise for all family members to take a self-defense course of some type. It is not a good idea to include the disturbed child in this activity. Allowing most disturbed children to take karate is akin to offering them another choice of weapon. Every so often we have found a family that can successfully use karate instruction to instill self-control; however, this takes a *very* special type of instructor who understands the child's pathology and impulse control problems. Many disturbed children learn the combative skills, but don't quite catch on to the self-defense-only philosophy.

Adoptive families become very innovative and creative when it comes to finding ways of living with, disciplining, and training their disturbed children. Many parents have told us that they enjoy sharing their hard-found successes with others who struggle with the same issues. We plan, in the future, to offer a revised edition of this book including additional ideas and suggestions from experienced adoptive and foster families. If any reader would like to contribute to this effort, an address is available in the back of this book where you can send us your ideas and stories for inclusion in this volume.

Providing the Tightest Limit of All: Out-of-Home Placement

Healthier children need fewer limits. The more irresponsible, impulsive, difficult, or disturbed the child, the tighter the limits must be. Because many children resist limits, they must be firm, clear, concrete, consistent and, if the child is disturbed, restrictive. Setting clear limits for children old enough to understand them is not harsh or overly strict parenting. It is common sense protection of individual and family rights. For instance, "You can't speak to Jenny" may seem too restrictive; however, it may be the only way to protect Jenny from verbal abuse.

The tightest limit of all is telling a child "You may not be able to live here." Many adoptive families have trouble with this ultimate limit; however once disturbed children are able to control their behavior, some kinds of behavior should not be tolerated. When behaviors become dangerous to the child or intolerable to other family members, the disturbed children need to know they may not be able to remain in the home. Every family has to draw their own limits in this respect, and certainly safety should play a major role in defining those limits.

Having Your Child Arrested

One way of imposing limits on children is through the law. Parents can report children to the police if they have violated a state, local, or federal law. In situations where the family is in imminent danger, this may be the only way to get the child out of the home safely and quickly. Calling the police may or may not result in an arrest, with the child being taken into custody. Often, even after an arrest is made, juveniles are released quite quickly into the custody of parents. When this happens, parents have only two choices:

- Go get the child.

- Refuse to pick up the child.

In the first case, parents may be left to deal with a very angry child, for whom little has been done other than being put through the arrest procedure. Very disturbed children may not be fazed much by this, and may interpret it as "cool." They may even have succeeded in conning the arresting officers into thinking their parents are the "bad guys." They may return home angry, or filled with a sense of empowerment and control.

▌▌ Our biological kids never did these type of activities, and we kept hearing from our adopted child that we never would have pressed charges for J— or R— (our biological kids). We never could get it through his head that *they* did-n't steal cars or money or checks or hurt people or start fires and on and on and on. . . . ▌▌

When parents refuse to pick up their children, they are usually warned, threatened and cajoled for a time, and then the children are turned over to the social services depart-ment as children in need of protective services (CHPS). Parents may be formally charged with abandonment at this point, or that may come later. In most cases, parents are ordered to appear at a CHPS or, depending on the state they reside in, a child in need of supervision (CHNS) hear-ing, within 48 hours. The children are placed in a tempo-rary foster home. At the hearing, it is not uncommon for families to be ordered to take their children home and to take part in a mandatory counseling program of some type. (See chapter 11, Families in Need of Protective Services page 217.)

Only in cases where children are clearly dangerous to themselves or others, or have behaved in such a way as to indicate that a serious psychiatric disturbance is present, are children taken by the police to a psychiatric facility for evaluation.

In June 1998 a Wisconsin couple, at the end of their rope with their adopted teenage son, expressed baffle-ment over the intense public interest in their decision to file charges against the boy, who threatened to imitate an Oregon youth who had recently shot and killed both his parents and a number of schoolmates. The couple has been highly criticized for having their child arrested. On the other hand, they have been thwarted in their attempt to get help for the child. He would not cooperate with any attempts they made to obtain professional help, and the law does not allow them to have him admitted to a treatment facility against his will. They were frightened that he would carry through on his threats and innocent people would die, and felt powerless to do anything to prevent it from happening. In the June 6 edition of the *Milwaukee Journal Sentinel,* the childs mother expressed her concern:

▌▌ Suddenly it feels like everything is just out of control," the mom said, after a court commissioner refused to release her son from jail without bail to enter treatment. A full week after their son's violent outburst and under the glare of the local and national media, the parents have yet to accomplish what they set out to do . . . get their son in an inpatient treatment facility before allowing him to return home. 'It has backfired' the youth's mother said. "We're afraid of things just going back to how they were and that would defeat the purpose of what this is all about—getting treatment.[181]   **▌▌**

Child or adult, we are all subject to limits of one kind or another. It is our duty as parents to do all we can to help our children understand and accept this while they are still young and the consequences are not life threatening.

Parents who decide to draw these lines are at extreme risk for being misunderstood. If parents keep straight the abandonment/safety issues, they can easily avoid falling into an emotional trap if the child (or any one else) protests that the parents are "giving him away just like everyone else has."

Acting to protect parental limits and provide for the safety and health of the family is not abandonment in any sense of the word—nor is it abandoning our commitment to our children. That commitment centers around doing what is in the best interest of the children. Mom and Dad are still their parents, and can support them while they heal and work on their behavior in a place where they cannot hurt others.

It is never in children's best interest to be allowed to create an unsafe environment in their home. It is a very frightening thing for children to have control of a family, while knowing they do not have the skills or ability to use such power appropriately. By showing children that we will protect ourselves and the rest of the family from outrageous or abusive behaviors, we show them that they too will be protected from abuse while under our care.

Clear guidelines about expectations when they return home empowers children to make the choice of where they live. When children clearly want to *leave* home, or threaten others in the home, the children are in charge. But when children want to *return* home, and the parents set limits on behavior, the parents are in charge!

Advantages:

- It removes the child who is acting out from the home.
- It creates a paper trail of documentation about the child's problem behavior.
- It may provide support for the parents.
- It allows for a cooling-off period.
- It lets the child know you mean business.
- It sets clear limits on behavior.

Disadvantages:

- Parents may be harshly judged or unfairly blamed by authorities.
- Police can sometimes be manipulated by a clever child.

- Police may not detain child for more than a few hours.

- Authorities may have little training or knowledge of the issues and may handle the situation poorly.

- Child may end up a ward of the county.

- Child may return home angry or empowered.

Acting in the Children's Best Interest and Showing Unconditional Love

Most of us would readily agree that as parents, our duty to our children is twofold: to act in their best interests, and to love them unconditionally.

Acting in children's best interest is a matter of common sense coupled with good judgment. Acting in their best interest often involves elements of uncertainty. Parents intent to do good—to do what is right and best for their children does not always provide the parents with the perfect wisdom and insight needed to do the job correctly. Parents can only do their best, ask for help from others when they need it, and hope that the love shown to the children cancels out any mistakes they might make along the way.

The truth is, what is in anyone's best interest can often only be known in retrospect. Life is therefore a series of decisions based on enlightened choices, many of which go wrong. The acceptance of this, without feeling guilty about what goes wrong, is one of the things that gives some people a sense of inner peace that eludes others.

Unconditional love is a concept that is ripe for misapplication when it comes to disturbed or difficult children. Parents love their children, but they do not give in to their every wish and command. Most parents understand that this would not be good for the child. Quite the contrary. Saying "no" to children's unhealthy or unreasonable demands is not showing a lack of love, even though the children may say, "If you loved me you'd let me. . . . " However, we have found that some adoptive parents have difficulty saying "no" to disturbed behaviors and questions arising from the child's disturbed thinking. Parents may confuse "unconditional love" with "commitment," or even with desires to make the children "happy." This can lead to serious problems in setting limits and protecting the family.

For this reason, we include this section on the definition and application of the concept of unconditional love.

Unconditional Love Means

- Acting in the best interests of the children to the best of your ability.

- Modeling healthy relationships and setting limits.

- Maintaining your commitment to the children, *even if the children can no longer reside in the home.*

- Acting in a fair (but not necessarily equal) and loving way.

- Expressing parental feelings for both the children and their behaviors. Saying, for example, "I love you sweetheart, but I cannot allow you to hurt your sister. It's my job as a parent to keep everyone in the family safe. I wouldn't let *her* hurt *you* either."

Unconditional Love Does *Not* Mean

- Allowing the family to be victimized by abusive children.

- That any and all behavior will be accepted and tolerated.

- Parents must take responsibility for the children's problems.

- Parents must rescue the children from the results of their behavior. (See The Rules for Rescue, page 162)

- Permitting an abusive or dangerous child to remain in the home.

- Allowing children who have been victimized in the past to use that fact as an excuse or reason avoid responsibility. (We empathize and show compassion for past hurt, but realize the children's situations have changed, and they are no longer being abused. We should try to help them move on and leave the victim role behind.)

Unconditional love, when misunderstood, can have serious and long lasting consequences on the family, as this therapist/adoptive mother describes:

My birth daughter has been living with a complete loser for years. She told me recently, with some pride, 'Mom, I'm so glad you adopted all the kids. You taught us the meaning of unconditional love.' Suddenly I realized why so many of our kids grow up and live with losers! Another parent was talking to me about the same problem with her children. They hooked up with losers too. It was our modeling! Modeling is the most powerful force in parenting. In this case, it backfired. There should be some limits to unconditional love, shouldn't there? Now my kids put up with abuse from their spouses and think that is the healthy way to love. By not drawing the line with these kids, do we teach them all—birth and adopted—the script of living with folks who abuse us?[182]

13

Conclusion: Can This Child Be Saved?

We began this book by asking an urgent and timely question: "Can this child be saved?" The journey we have taken you on in search of the answer has been uncomfortable and exhausting. The scenes we have shown you have not always been "Kodak moments." Many, we're sure, you'd like to forget entirely. Those of us who had the most to gain by this journey, also had the most to lose by not making it. Yet we had to go. It was time—time to seek answers; time to seek truth.

We have stood for honesty thus far, even when it was tempting to sacrifice the truth for the sake of popularity or political correctness. It would have been unethical and immoral to do otherwise, or to end any other way. Much of our journey has led us to the conclusion that "No, we cannot save these children." We most certainly cannot rescue them from neurological damage, fragile genetics, or physical disabilities. Nor can we spare them, or cure them, of the effects of early abuse and neglect, many of which have been shown to result in lifelong psychological scarring.

We have discovered that the most important question prospective adoptive parents must ask themselves about many of these children is this: "Can we live with them the way they are—even if they never change appreciably? The answer to this one question can make the difference between parental success and satisfaction, and another disruption for the children and disaster for the family. It merits much soul-searching and a realistic and objective evaluation of family resources, energy, commitment, and motivation. Many of these children cannot or will not change, beyond growing chronologically older and physically larger. That single factor is critical to consider. Behaviors that are quite easily managed at age three might threaten the safety of the family at age twelve or thirteen.

Most of us adopt expecting that, with effort and love, some changes for the better are not only possible but likely. But, as we have reluctantly pointed out throughout this volume, this is not the case with many special needs children.

Yet, many of us who have parented these children come away from the experience with a firm belief that we *have* been able to make a positive difference in their lives—that their chances and choices in life have been improved by our intervention. In many cases, we have saved their lives.

And in these respects—"yes, we *have* saved our children!"

We have saved them from some of the pain they might have had to experience had they never come into our lives. Many of them will have a chance to live a functional life because of us. We have given them a taste of love, a look at real family life, a place to call home, and the opportunity to claim all of those things as their own. They know what it is like to have a family meal together, to make conversation, to share in family chores and outings, to ask "How was your day?"—things that most of us take for granted but are sorely lacking in many children's lives. Should they grow up to have children of their own, which for many of our kids is very likely, they will have a healthy parental role model to remember and fall back on. They will have seen relationships based on acceptance and mutual respect, and our children who have lived with domestic violence will now have the opportunity and knowledge they need to stop the generational cycle of abuse.

Sadly, this salvation often comes at great cost to us as parents and to our other children. That cost is impossible to estimate in advance, and impossible to weigh against the odds of success. It is only in retrospect that we know if we have made the right choices and found the right answers. In many cases, the scales are tipped too far in one direction for the average family to restore them to balance. Yet without our intervention, our children would most likely slip deeper into mental illness, substance abuse, violence, or crime. Some would not survive their teen years. Nontraditional therapies and unconventional parenting techniques offer parents a chance to weigh in heavily on the side of health. This added weight might be just enough to help the child hold on, to help the family stay together, and to increase parental feelings of success and satisfaction.

Over and over again, as we talk with families who have adopted special needs children, they express the same hopes, the same desires to help, the same searching for answers they all feel sure must be there. Often there is a pleading hope in their voices as they look to us for answers. "There must be a way to save these children." "We won't accept anything less." "Certainly it is society's obligation to do something." And we agree.

We cannot simply give up on the horrifying numbers of children who need our help. If families are not the answer for many of them, then we must search for other means of offering them help and hope. If their lives and their relationships are such that they cannot live in a family, we must find ways to reach them and teach them with acceptable alternatives. It would be criminal to stop trying, simply because along the way we *might* make mistakes, or because we *might* fail. Unconventional problems sometimes require unconventional solutions. When we have unsuccessfully tried everything that makes sense, then anything else we try will, at first, seem not to make sense.

As parents, we have run the gamut of situations described in this book. We have parented children with normal needs, and children with very serious neurological and behavioral problems. We know what it is like to dream the dream, and to watch it turn slowly into a nightmare of helplessness and hopelessness. We know what it is like to search for answers and find none. We know the sorrows of standing by helplessly and watching children make choices that we know will hurt them. We know of the exhaustion, the fear, and the resentment, as well as the joys, satisfactions, and blessings. And we know well the feeling of not wanting to give up on our children, even when they are threatening.

As consultants, visiting with families around the country in person, by telephone, and on the Internet, we have learned how much alike we all are—those of us who try to save children. We discovered a common ground of caring, compassion, empathy, love, selfless commitment, energy, and enthusiasm. Most of us share a stubborn refusal to give up, although more and more of us are finding support for setting healthy limits.

We have worked with the system, and we have locked horns with the system. We have been both friend and foe. We might be referred to as "saints" or we might be labeled "sinners," depending on whom you ask and the particular situation. We have been lauded for our efforts, and accused of lack of commitment or being "anti-child," or "anti-adoption." We have felt the stabbing pain that accompanies those accusations, knowing that we have done all we could humanly do to "save" our children, and still in some instances have failed. We are well aware of our limitations, our inability to repair the damage done to our children by their early environments and genetics. We know that damage is often exacerbated by the child welfare system's refusal to make the changes necessary to meet the children's needs.

One of the most difficult questions for adoptive parents to answer is "Would you do it again?" One father called that a "killer question." We agree, it *is* a killer question, and perhaps there is no honest way to determine the answer. We would all make different decisions about life in retrospect. Would knowing in advance help or hurt? Would we make wiser choices, better decisions, fewer mistakes? Who knows? One adoptive mother was able to describe this ambivalence quite eloquently:

▌▌ Parenting was not fun with my set of kids. I am not sorry it is over and the kids are grown—well, it is never *really* over with these kids, is it? A friend asked me, 'Didn't you have to be a little crazy to do that?' 'Heck no,' I said, 'you have to be a *lot* crazy.' She asked, 'Are you glad you did it?' And I said, 'For sure!' But it was not easy. I think Ted would be dead of parasites if I hadn't adopted him. I saved his life. By the way, I have parasite stories that you wouldn't believe. But somebody has to adopt these kids.[183]   **▌▌**

For now, we have no better alternative than to offer most of these damaged youngsters a chance for life in a family. Perhaps, in the not too distant future, we would be wise to look at the changing needs of children and families and find alternative ways to "save this child."

But for now, for today's kids, the clock is ticking. The windows of opportunity to make a difference in their lives are closing fast as they fly through their childhoods. We must adopt them, and cope in the best way we can. How can we do otherwise?

This book is our way of trying to effect positive differences in children's lives by helping families decide about adoption and cope with adopted children. It is our way of offering practical hope and means of survival until better alternatives are found and implemented.

In writing this book we have raised many questions as well as provided a few answers. May those questions help define the problem, and lay the groundwork for future research and reform.

We are not alone in our efforts to "save" our damaged children, nor are we finished with our work on their behalf. We invite you, the reader, to join us in our search for solutions and hope that one day we can honestly answer "yes" to the question "Can this child be saved?"

May God richly bless all of our efforts.

You Can Help!

We intend to continue publishing the results of our research and work in the field of special needs adoption and parenting disturbed kids. And of course, we are always looking to improve our services to families.

Send us your comments, suggestions and experiences. Please indicate if we have permission to use them in future revisions of this book or other published materials authored by Foster W. Cline, M.D and/or Cathy Helding.

If you are aware of or involved in a research project, professional resource, or reference work that would be helpful to our families, please let us know.

Write to us at this address:

Can This Child Be Saved?
Solutions for Adoptive and Foster Families
c/o World Enterprises
P.O. Box 396
Franksville, WI, 53126-0396

Or use our e-mail link on the Internet at:
www.cathyhelding.com

Part III

Outside Resources

This section offers a listing of resources for further help and information. We do not necessarily endorse the work or philosophy of these individuals and groups. Instead we offer as many sources of help as space allows, and urge our readers to select those that seem most suited to the needs of their children and family. We have tried to ensure that only persons and organizations with a long-standing history of quality service are mentioned.

Books

A Child's Journey Through Placement. Vera I. Fahlberg, M.D. Perspectives Press, 1991.

Accessing Federal Adoption Subsidies After Finalization. Tim O'Hanlon, Ph.D. Washington, DC: Child Welfare League of America, 1997.

Accessing Federal Subsidies After Legalization. Tim O'Hanlon, Ph.D. Washington, DC: Child Welfare League of America, 1995.

Adopting and Advocating for the Special Needs Child. L. Anne Babb & Rita Laws. Westport, CT: Bergin and Garvey, 1997.

Adopting the Hurt Child: Hope for Families with Special-Needs Kids. Gregory C. Keck, Ph.D. & Regina M. Kupecky, LSW. Colorado Springs, CO: Pinon Press, 1995.

Adopting the Older Child, Claudia Jewett. Cambridge, MA: Harvard Common Press, 1978.

Adoption & Disruption. Richard P. Barth & Marianne Berry. New York: Aldine, de Gruyter, 1988.

Adoption Crisis. Carole McKelvey & Dr. JoEllen Stevens. Fulcrum Publishing, 1994.

Adoption: Opposing Viewpoints. David Bender & Bruno Leone, eds. San Diego, CA: Greenhaven Press, 1995.

Attachment, Trauma and Healing, Understanding and Treating Attachment Disorder in Children and Families. Washington D.C.: Terry M. Levy & Michael Orlans, 1998.

Before It's Too Late. Stanton E. Samenow, Ph.D. New York: Times Books, 1989.

Born That Way, Genes/Behavior/Personality. William Wright. New York: Alfred A. Knopf, 1998.

Children Who Shock and Surprise: A Guide to Attachment Disorders. Elizabeth Randolph, RN, Ph.D. RFR Publications, 1994.

Concepts in Adoption. Pat Holmes. Wayne, PA: Our Child Press, 1984.

Conscienceless Acts, Societal Mayhem, Uncontrollable, Unreachable Youth and Today's Desensitized World. Foster W. Cline, MD. Golden, CO: Love & Logic Press, 1995.

Dangerous Legacy: The Babies of Drug-Taking Parents. Ben Sonder. New York: Franklin Watts, 1994.

Don't Let Your Kids Kill You: A Guide for Parents of Drug and Alcohol Addicted Children. Charles Rubin. Rockport, MA: Element, 1996.

Don't Touch My Heart. Lynda Gianforte Mansfield & Christopher H. Waldmann, MA, LPC. Colorado Springs, CO: Pinon Press, 1994.

Facilitating Developmental Attachment. Daniel Hughes. North Bergen, NJ: Jason Aronson, 1997.

Families at Risk. Jodie Kulp. Minneapolis, MN: Better Endings New Beginnings, 1993

Fantastic Antone Succeeds! Experiences in Educating Children with Fetal Alcohol Syndrome. Judith Kleinfeld and Siobhan Wescott, eds. University of Alaska Press, 1993.

For Children Who Were Broken. Elia Wise. New York: Berkeley Books, 1989

Forever Parents: Adopting Older Children. James E. Kloeppel & Darlene A. Kloeppel. Union City, GA: Adele Enterprises, 1995.

Fostering Changes: Treating Attachment Disordered Foster Children. Richard Delaney, Ph.D. Walter J. Corbett Publishing, 1995.

Ghosts From the Nursery: Tracing the Roots of Violence. Robin Karr-Morse & Meredith S. Wiley. New York: Atlantic Monthly Press, 1997.

Give Them Roots, Then Let Them Fly. The Attachment Center at Evergreen & Carole A. McKelvey. Morris Publishing, 1995.

Growing Up Again: Parenting Ourselves, Parenting Our Children. Jean Illsley Clarke & Connie Dawson. First Harper & Row Edition, 1989.

High Risk: Children Without A Conscience. Dr. Ken Magid & Carole McKelvey. Bantam Books, 1988.

Holding Time. Dr. Martha Welch. New York: Simon and Schuster, 1988.

Hope for High Risk & Rage Filled Children, Foster W. Cline, M.D. Evergreen, CO: EC Publications, 1992.

Inside the Criminal Mind. Stanton E. Samenow, Ph.D. New York: Times Books, 1984.

Nothing Good Ever Happens To Me: An Adoption Love Story. Caroline Hassinger Lindsay. Washington, DC: Child and Family Press, 1996.

Parenting Teens with Love and Logic. Foster W. Cline, M.D. & Jim Fay. Colorado Springs, CO: Pinon Press, 1992.

Parenting with Love and Logic. Foster W. Cline, M.D. & Jim Fay. Colorado Springs, CO: Pinon Press, 1990.

Profane Justice: A Comprehensive Guide to Asserting Your Parental Rights. Suzanne Shell. Sage Wisdom Press, P.O. Box 75863, Colorado Springs, CO 75863. 800-447-3081 ext. 7794. For families dealing with accusations of abuse.

Raising Cain: Caring for Troubled Youngsters/Repairing Our Troubled System of Care. Richard Delaney. Oklahoma City, OK: Woo & Barnes Publishing, 1998.

Supporting an Adoption. Patricia Lynn Holmes. Wayne, PA: Our Child Press, 1982.

The Broken Cord. Michael Dorris. New York: Harper & Row, 1989. About raising children with fetal alcohol syndrome. The author tells his story as an adoptive parent along with much educational information about FAS.

The Clinical Prediction of Violent Behavior. John Monahan. Northvale, NJ: Jason Aronson, 1995.

The Limits of Hope: An Adoptive Mother's Story. Ann Kimble Loux. Charlottesville: University Press of Virginia, 1997.

The Long Journey Home. Richard J. Delaney & Terry McNerney. Journey Press, 1994. A book written for children about attachment and separation.

The Out-of-Sync Child: Recognizing and Coping with Sensory Integrative Dysfunction. Carol Stock Kranowitz, M.A. New York: Berkeley Publishing Group, 1998.

The Parent Education Text. Foster W. Cline, M.D. Evergreen, CO: Evergreen Consultants in Human Behavior, 1979.

The Primal Wound—Understanding the Adopted Child. Nancy Newton Verrier. Gateway Press, 1994.

The Secret Life of the Unborn Child. Thomas Verny, M.D. & John Kelly. New York: Dell Publishing, 1981.

The Whole Parent: How To Become a Terrific Parents Even If You Didn't Have One. Debra Wesselmann. New York: Plenum Publishing, 1998.

Think About Adopting or Foster Parenting Special Needs Children: A Self Assessment Tool for Prospective Adoptive or Foster Parents. Laura Adame Trickey & Bill Trickey. The Adoptive Family Treatment Center, P.O. Box 25434, Kansas City, MO 64119. 816-453-9792. 1998.

Troubled Transplants. Richard Delaney, Ph.D. & Frank R. Kunstal, Ed.D. National Child Welfare Resource Center for Management & Administration, 1993.

Turning Stones, My Days and Nights with Children at Risk. Marc Parent. Orlando, FL: Harcourt Brace, 1996.

Understanding and Treating the Severely Disturbed Child. Foster W. Cline, M.D. Evergreen, CO: Evergreen Consultants in Human Behavior, 1979.

Wounded Innocents—The Real Victims of the War Against Child Abuse. Richard Wexler. Prometheus Books. 700 East Amherst St., Buffalo, NY 14215. For families falsely accused of abuse.

Periodicals, Newsletters, and Products

Adoptalk Magazine
North American Council on Adoptable Children
970 Raymond Ave., Suite 106
St. Paul, MN 55114-1149
Voice: 612-644-3036

Adopted Child
P.O. Box 9362
Moscow, ID 83843
Voice: 208-882-1794

The Adoption Post
RAP—Resources for Adoptive Parents
P.O. Box 27373
Minneapolis, MN 55427
Toll-free: 1-800-944-5230

Adoptive Families of America (AFA)
Toll-free: 1-800-372-3300
website: www.adoptivefam.org/
    Catalog of multicultural resources, adoption books, videos, dolls, and tapes.

Adoptive Families Magazine
Toll free: 1-800-372-3300

An important publication that covers all facets of adoption issues, and is also a good source for agency advertisements and adoption products. Catalog available.

Attachments Newsletter
The Attachment Center at Evergreen
P.O. Box 2764
Evergreen, CO 80437-2764
Voice: 303-674-1910

Attachment Disorder Parents Network
ADPN
P.O. Box 18475
Boulder, CO 80308
Quarterly newsletter.

Connections Newsletter
Association for Treatment & Training in the Attachment of Children
   (ATTACh)
P.O. Box 665
Annandale, VA 22003-0665
Voice: 703-914-3928
Fax: 703-914-3929
website: www.ATTACh.org

Decree Magazine
American Adoption Congress
1000 Connecticut Ave., NW, Suite 9
Washington, DC 20036

The FEN Pen
Family Empowerment Network
610 Langdon Street, Room 517
Madison, WI 53703
Voice: 608-262-6590
Toll-free: 800-462-5254
e-mail: fen@mail.dcs.wisc.edu
    A newsletter for parents of children with fetal alcohol syndrome.

KC Connections Newsletter
KC ATTACh
(A regional chapter of the national organization ATTACh)
6500 W 183rd St.
Stilwell, KS 66085
Voice: 913-897-4774
Fax: 913-897-4477
e-mail: saanda@aol.com

Love and Logic Institute, Inc.
2207 Jackson Street
Golden, CO 80401
Toll-free 1-800-338-4065
    Audiotape on sixty-second scolding available, as well as numer-
ous parenting tapes, books, and training materials. "Love and Logic"
parenting materials and books by Foster W. Cline, M.D. are also
available here. Free catalog.

Love & Logic Journal (quarterly, parenting the "Love & Logic" way)
Love and Logic Institute, Inc.
2207 Jackson Street
Golden, CO 80401
Toll-free: 1-800-338-4065
Free catalog.
    Catalogs and training materials.

National Adoption Center
1500 Walnut Street, Suite 701
Philadelphia, PA 19102
Voice: 215-735-9988
Toll-free: 1-800-TO ADOPT
website: www.adoptnet.org

Private, non-profit organization offering support for adoptive families.

Parents Network for the Post Institutionalized Child (PNPIC)
P.O. Box 613
Meadow Land, PA 15347
Free newsletter.

Roots and Wings Magazine
P.O. Box 577
Hackettstown, NJ 07840
Voice: 908-813-8252
Fax: 908-813-8201
e-mail: adoption@interactive.net
website: www.adopting.org/rw.html

Success in Parenting, A Practical Guide to Parenting
Lon Gibby Productions
E. 113 Magnesium
Spokane, WA 99208
Toll-free: 800-200-1113
fax: 509-467-4763

Foster W. Cline, M.D. and Benjamin W. Brucker, Ed.D. produced this package of parenting materials consisting of a one-hour videotape, ten audiocassette tapes with 20 lessons, and a 125-page manual packaged in an attractive vinyl binder.

Tapestry Book Catalog
P.O. Box 359
Ringoes, NJ 08551-059
Toll-free: 800-765-2367
website: www.tapestrybooks.com/

Free catalog. Most comprehensive listing of adoption books that we have found.

Think About Adopting or Foster Parenting Special Needs Children: A Self Assessment Tool for Prospective Adoptive or Foster Parents
Laura Adame Trickey and Bill Trickey
The Adoptive Family Treatment Center
P.O. Box 25434
Kansas City, MO 64119
Voice: 816-453-9792

This workbook style course is a self-examination tool for families considering adoption or foster care. It is designed to be thought-provoking and to stimulate discussion. It covers many areas of critical importance to success in parenting special needs children. Excellent for use by individuals or agencies as part of orientation or preplacement training.

Organizations

American Adoption Congress
1000 Connecticut Ave., NW, Suite 9
Washington, DC 20036

ARCH National Respite Locator Service
National Resource Center for Respite and Crisis Care Services
Toll free: 1-800-733-5433

Association for Treatment & Training in the Attachment of Children
   (ATTACh)
P.O. Box 665
Annandale, VA 22003-0665
Voice: 703-914-3928
Fax: 703-914-3929
website: www.ATTACh.org

The Attachment Center at Evergreen (ACE)
P.O. Box 2764
Evergreen, CO 80437-2764
Voice: 303-674-1910

Attachment Disorder Parents Network (ADPN)
P.O. Box 18475
Boulder, CO 80308
303-443-1446
   List of parent contacts and local chapters state by state. Please
send self-addressed stamped envelope.

Evan B. Donaldson Adoption Institute
120 Wall Street, 20th Floor
New York, NY 10005-3902
Voice: 212-269-5080
Fax: 212-269-1962

Families for Russian and Ukrainian Adoption
P.O. Box 2944
Merrifield, VA 22116
Voice: 703-560-6184

Family Empowerment Network
610 Langdon Street, Room 517
Madison, WI 53703
Voice: 608-262-6590
Toll-free: 800-462-5254
e-mail: fen@mail.dcs.wisc.edu
Information about parenting children with Fetal Alcohol Syndrome.

Cathy Helding
P.O. Box 396
Franksville, WI 53126
Voice: 1-414-835-2223
Fax: 1-800-932-3686
e-mail: cathychat@aol.com
website: www.cathyhelding.com
Consultant services and seminars for adoptive parents and professionals: parenting children with emotional or behavioral problems, disruption prevention and out-of-home placement decisions, reform issues, family support and advocacy. Educational materials and training for teachers, juvenile justice workers, foster parents, and child care agencies.

KC ATTACh
6500 W. 183rd Street
Stilwell, KS 66085
Voice: 913-897-4774
Fax: 913-897-4477
e-mail: saanda@aol.com
A regional chapter of the national organization ATTACh.

Kinship Center
30 Ragsdale Drive, Suite 210
Monterey, CA 93940

National Adoption Center
1500 Walnut Street, Suite 701
Philadelphia, PA 19102
215-735-9988
Toll-free: 1-800-TO-ADOPT
http://www.adoptnet.org
Private, nonprofit organization offering support for adoptive families.

National Adoption Information Clearinghouse
Voice: 301-231-6512

National Association of Therapeutic Wilderness Camps
4270 Hambrick Way
Stone Mountain, GA 30083
Voice: 405-508-1036
Fax: 404-508-1514
e-mail: info@natwc.org
website: www.natwc.org/

National Council For Adoption, Inc.
1930 17th Street NW
Washington, DC 20009
Voice: 202-328-1200

New Roots
P.O. Box 14953
Columbus, OH 43214
Voice: 614-470-0846
Book: *Adoption Subsidy: A Guide for Adoptive Parents*

North American Council on Adoptable Children (NACAC)
    National Headquarters
970 Raymond Avenue, Suite 106
St. Paul, MN 55114-1149
Toll free: 1-800-470-6665

Parents Network for the Post Institutionalized Child (PNPIC)
P.O. Box 613
Meadow Land, PA 15347

Information on international adoption. Excellent source of information about sensory integration and post institutionalized children's issues. Free newsletter.

Victims of Child Abuse Laws, National Organization (VOCAL)
7485 E. Kenyon Avenue
Denver, CO 80237
To locate a chapter in your state:
Voice: 303-233-5321
website: www.vocal.org

Victims of Child Abuse Laws (VOCAL)
4854 Appleton Avenue
Jacksonville, FL 32210
Fax: 904-381-7097
website: www.vocal.org

Contains an excellent article about what to do if you have been falsely accused of child abuse that should be read by *all* parents of disturbed children.

Professionals

Many of the organizations listed in the previous section offer listings of helping professionals by mail or on their websites. We list below only those with which we are directly associated or personally familiar.

The Adoptive Family Treatment Center
P.O. Box 25434
Kansas City, Missouri 64119
Voice: 816-453-9792

Treatment for children with attachment disorder. Comprehensive services for parents.

Association for Treatment & Training in the Attachment of Children
  (ATTACh)
P.O. Box 665
Annandale, VA 22003-0665
Voice: 703-914-3928
Fax: 703-914-3929
e-mail: kgmoss@aol.com
website: www.ATTACh.org
  For referral to a professional willing to train parents or thera-
pists on the use of holding techniques, or to qualified attachment
therapists by geographic area.

The Attachment and Bonding Center of Ohio
Gregory C. Keck, Ph.D.
12608 State Road
Cleveland, OH 44133
Voice: 216-230-1960
  Treatment for children with attachment disorder.

Attachment and Bonding Center of Nebraska
Lisa Blunt, MS, NCC and Debra Combs, LCSW
7447 Farnam
Omaha, NE 68114-4628
Voice: 402-392-8949
  Treatment for children with attachment disorder.

The Attachment Center at Evergreen (ACE)
P.O. Box 2764
Evergreen, CO 80437-2764
Voice: 303-674-1910
  Treatment for children with attachment disorder.

Attachment Center Northwest
Beverly Cuevas, MSW, ACSW or Rebecca Perbix Mallos, MSW
8011 118th Avenue NE
Kirkland, WA 98033
Voice: 425-889-8524, #3
Fax: 206-230-9187
e-mail: Attachnw@aol.com
    Treatment for children with attachment disorder.

Beech Brook
3737 Lander Road
Cleveland, OH 44124
Voice: 216-831-2255
    Treatment for children with attachment disorder.

Evergreen Consultants in Human Behavior
28000 Meadow Drive, Suite 206
Evergreen, CO 80439-8345
Voice: 303-674-5503
Fax: 303-674-7665
e-mail: evcons@aol.com
website: www.attachmenttherapy.com
    Treatment for children with attachment disorder.

Family Attachment Institute International
Lani Tolman, Director
P.O. Box 1731
Evergreen, CO 80437-1731
Voice: 303-674-0738

Forest Heights Lodge
P.O. Box 789
Evergreen, CO 80439
Voice: 303-674-6681
    Treatment for children with attachment disorder.

Daniel Hughes, Ph.D.
67 Silver St.
Waterville, ME 04901
Voice: 207-872-2121
Fax (Wed. only): 207-395-2560
e-mail: dhughes@pivot.net
    Treatment for children with attachment disorder.

Human Passages
777 South Wadsworth Blvd. Bldg 1 #105
Lakewood, CO 80226
Voice: 303-914-9729
    Treatment for children with attachment disorder.

Todd Nichols, M.S, M.P., M.P. Aff.
Eden Prairie Psychological Resources
5500 Lincoln Drive #160
Edina, MN 55436
Voice: 612-939-0167 ext. 3180
Fax: 612-939-0168 or 612-939-3255
e-mail: atn@sihope.com

Michael Pines, Ph.D., P.C.
124 Hebron Avenue
Glastonbury, CT 06033
Voice: 860-659-0579
Fax: 860-659-0570
    Treatment for children with attachment disorder.

Tulsa Developmental Pediatrics & Center for Family Psychology
4520 South Harvard, Suite 200
Tulsa, OK 74135-2900
Voice: 918-743-9623
Fax: 918-743-9623
    Multidisciplinary services, neurodevelopmental, pediatric devel-
opmental, psychological and attachment services.

The Martha G. Welch Centers
P.O. Box 362
COS COB, CT 06807
Toll-free: 888-447-6872
    Books, tapes, seminars and lectures, training and consultation, videos.

Websites

Adopted Child Newsletter
http://www.moscow.com/Resources/Adoption/Adoption.html
    This site is run by Lois Melina, author of *Raising Adopted Children, Making Sense of Adoption,* coauthor of *The Open Adoption Experience* and, since 1981, the author of the *Adopted Child Newsletter.* This site is for prospective adoptive parents as well as adoption professionals.

AdoptINFO—University of Minnesota Children, Youth, and Family Consortium
http://www.cyfc.umn.edu/adoptinfo.html
Research-based adoption information.

Adoption Information & Support
http://www.adopting.org/

Adoption Information Exchange
http://www.halcyon.com/adoption/exchange.html
    The Adoption Information Exchange includes information regarding adoption education and resources available in Washington.

Adoption Policy Resource Center
http://www.fpsol.com/adoption/advocates.html

A service provided by Adoption Advocates. Here you will find links to all the most important information sites that contain legislative news, subsidy information, legal resources, and how to locate adoption advocates.

AdoptioNetwork
http://www.adoption.org/

Adoptive Families of America (AFA)
http://www.adoptivefam.org/

Established in 1966, Adoptive Families of America is the largest nonprofit adoption organization in the United States.

American Adoption Congress
http://pages.prodigy.com/adoptreform/aacorg.htm

AAC is an international network of individuals and organizations committed to truth in adoption and to reform that protects all of those involved from abuse or exploitation. They publish *Decree Magazine.*

Attachment Center at Evergreen
http://www.attachmentcenter.org/

Cathy Helding's Website
http://www.cathyhelding.com

Biographical information about the author, contact information, descriptions of seminars and workshops, ordering information for the *Cline/Helding Adopted and Foster Child Assessment (CHAFCA),* reproducible articles, and links to resources.

Effects of institutionalization on Behavior
http://www.rainbowkids.com/europattach.html

Families with Children from China (F.C.C.)
http://www.fwcc.org/

Families with Children from VietNam
http://www.primenet.com/~tbarron/fcv/
A support and education site.

Foster Parent Home Page
http://worldaccess.com/FPHP/

Latin America Parents Association
http://www.lapa.com/

Love & Logic Institute
http://www.loveandlogic.com

Maintaining Commitment When a Child Can't Live at Home,
http://www.nysccc.org/articles/maintcommit.html
By Diane L. Hillmann

National Adoption Center
1500 Walnut Street, Suite 701
Philadelphia, PA 19102
Voice: 215-735-9988
toll-free: 1-800-TO ADOPT
website: www.adoptnet.org
    Books, audio and videotapes, and encyclopedia.

National Adoption Information Clearinghouse (NAIC)
http://www.calib.com/naic/
    The NAIC was established by Congress to provide profession-
als and the general public with easily accessible information on all
aspects of adoption.

Parent Network for the Post-Institutionalized Child (PNPIC)
http://weber.u.washington.edu/~dpreston/kellie.htm

Perspectives Press
http://www.PerspectivesPress.com/
An adoption and infertility publisher.

Psychshop
http://www.psychshop.com
Sponsored by Foster W. Cline, M.D. Biographical and contact information for the author, information on seminars and workshops, links to resources and Dr. Cline's materials, and on-line psychological tests. Recommended consultants and professionals list their services on this site.

RainbowKids.com
http://rainbowkids.com
Martha Osborne is the editor of this on-line publication on international adoption.

Roots and Wings
http://www.adopting.org/rw.html
This is an excellent magazine for adoptive parents. At the site you will find some sample stories from the current issue, and instructions for subscribing.

Tapestry Books
http://www.tapestrybooks/com/
Catalog. Adoption and related topics—most of the books listed above can be purchased through Tapestry books.

Miscellaneous

America Online's Adoption Forum

Part of the "Families" area on America Online; offers interactive message boards, chat room discussions and guests on a variety of adoption-related topics, an excellent resource area that is constantly being updated, a bimonthly e-mail newsletter, and more. Many professionals frequent the areas and participate in discussion groups and on the message boards. Some areas are designated for particular topics as well as for particular members of the triad, although anyone is welcome to participate. A rich resource for computer users.

To use: AOL members go to keyword:<ADOPTION> Or enter through the "FAMILIES" area. Subscribe to the e-mail newsletter by sending e-mail to: adptnews@aol.com (You do not have to be an AOL member to subscribe.)

Contributors

Our special thanks to Carole Huxel, Paula Blake, and Beth Meadows, America Online Adoption Forum Community Leaders, for their help in locating, screening, and verifying many of the resources listed here.

Endnotes

1. The White House, Office of the Press Secretary. (1996, December 14). "Steps to increase adoptions and alternate permanent placement for waiting children in the public child welfare system," Press release.

2. Carlson, Susan. (Attorney, Hennepin County District Court). (1998). *November column on adoption, Governor Ame H. Carlson, MN, website*, [On-line]. Available: http://www.governor.state.mn.us/new/firstlad/adoptcol.htm

3. Bowlby, John. (1953), *Child care and the growth of love*, (p. 55). Baltimore, MD: Penguin Press.

National Center on Child Abuse and Neglect, (NCCAN), (1995), *National child abuse and neglect data systems*. [On-line] Available: http://www.hai-net.com/nccan/nccan/htm

Schneider-Rosen, K. & Rothbaum, F. (1985). Quality of parental caregiving and security of attachment, *Developmental Psychology, 29,* 358–67.

Schneider-Rosen, K., Braunwald, K. G., Carlson, V. & Cicchetti, D. (1985). Current perspectives in attachment theory: illustration from the study of maltreated infants, In I. Bretherton & E. Waters (Eds.), *Monographs of the Society for Research in Child Development, 50*(1-2), 194–210.

Crittenden, P. (1988). *Relationships at risk.* In J. Belsky & T. Nezworski (Eds.), *Clinical implications of attachment.* Hillsdale, NJ; Erlbaum.

Fishman, Katherine Davis. (1995). Special needs adoptions should be reevaluated. In David Bender & Bruce Leone (Eds.), *Adoption opposing viewpoints.* (p. 214), San Diego, CA: Greenhaven Press.

4. Carlson, Susan. (Attorney, Hennepin County District Court). (1998). *November column on adoption, Governor Ame H. Carlson, MN, website,* [On-line]. Available: http://www.governor. state.mn.us/new/firstlad/adoptcol.htm

5. Weisman, Mary-Lou. (1994, July). When parents are not in the best interests of the child. *Atlantic Monthly.*

6. Ibid.

7. Delaney, Richard J. & Kunstal, Frank R. (1993). *Troubled transplants* (p. 157). University of Southern Maine.

8. Weisman, Mary-Lou. (1994, July). When parents are not in the best interests of the child. *Atlantic Monthly.*

9. Cline, Foster W., M.D. (1992). *Hope for high risk and rage filled children.* Evergreen, CO: EC Publications.

Spitz, Renee & Cobliner, W. G. (1965). *The first year of life* (p. 53). New York: International Universities Press.

Ainsworth, Salter, M.D. (1969). The development of infant-mother attachment. In B. M Caldwell & H. N. Ricciuti (Eds.), *review of child development research.* New York: Russell Sage Foundation.

10. Nash, Madeline J. (1997, February 3). *Special report: fertile minds. Time. 149,* 5.

11. Sumner, Calvin R., M.D. (1995, September 19). personal communication.

12. Spitz, Renee & Cobliner, W. G. (1965). The first year of life. New York: International Universities Press.

    Harlow, H. F. & Harlow, M. K. (1966). Learning to love, *American Scientist, 54.*

13. Kephart, Newell C. *Children with learning problems,* (p. 318). New York: Brunner/Mazel.

    Sumner, Calvin R., M.D. (1995, September 19). personal communication.

14. Nash, Madeline J. (1997, February 3) Special report: Fertile minds. *Time, 149,* 5.

15. Manthe, Karen M. (1998, April). personal communication.

16. Fishman, Katherine Davis. (1995), Special needs adoptions should be reevaluated. In David Bender & Bruce Leone (Eds.), Adoption opposing viewpoints (p. 224), San Diego, CA: Greenhaven Press.

    Bowlby, John. (1953), *Child care and the growth of love* (p. 55). Baltimore, MD: Penguin Press.

17. Bowlby, John. (1980). *Attachment and loss, volume III: Sadness and depression.* New York: Basic Books.

    Spitz, Renee & Cobliner, W. G. (1965), *The first year of life.* New York: International Universities Press.

    Ainsworth, Salter, M.D. (1969). The development of infant-mother attachment. In B. M. Caldwell & H. N. Ricciuti (Eds.), *Review of child development research.* New York; Russell Sage Foundation.

Karen, Robert. (1990, February). Becoming attached, *Atlantic Monthly*, 35–70.

18. Nash, Madeline J. (1997, February 3). Special report: Fertile minds, *Time*, *149*, 5.

19. Special report: What parents can do. (1997, February 3). *Time*, *149*, 5.

20. Cline, Foster W., M.D. (1995). *Conscienceless acts societal mayhem*. Golden, CO: Love & Logic Press.

21. Erickson, Erik. (1950). The eight stages of man. 1993 reissue. New York: Norton.

22. Nash, Madeline J., (1997, February 3). *Special report: Fertile minds*, *Time*. *149*, 5.

23. Ibid.

24. Preston, James. (1996). Personal communication.

25. Perry, Bruce, M.D. (1996, December 9). Can an entire nation become mentally ill? *Talk of the nation*, National Public Radio broadcast.

26. Carlson, Susan. (Attorney, Hennepin County District Court). (1998). *November column on adoption, Governor Ame H. Carlson, MN, website*. [On-line]. Available: http://www.governor.state.mn.us/new/firstlad/adoptcol.htm

27. Action Alliance for Children, (1997, July–August). FACT SHEET, *The children's advocate*, [On-line]. Available: http://www.4children.org/

28. Perry, Bruce, M.D. (1996, December 9). Can an entire nation become mentally ill? *Talk of the nation*, National Public Radio broadcast.

29. Attachment Center at Evergreen. (1998). *Symptoms of attachment disorder*. [On-line]. Available: www.attachmentcenter.org/

30. Hughes, Daniel A. (1997). *Facilitating developmental attachment* (p. 226). Northvale, NJ: Jason Aronson.

31. Ibid. pp. 226–27.

32. Fay, Jim & Cline, Foster W., M.D. *Discipline with love and logic study guide* (p. vii) Golden CO. Love & Logic Press.

33. Anonymous adoption caseworker. (1997). personal communication.

34. McRoy, Ruth & Grotevant, Harold. (1998). Emotional disorders in adopted children and youth.

35. Delaney, Richard J. & Kunstal, Frank R. (1993). *Troubled transplants* (p. 4). University of Southern Maine.

36. Goldstein, Joseph, Solnit, Albert J. & Freud, Anna. (1973), Beyond the best interests of the child. *Adoption: Opposing viewpoints,* 1995 reprints, Greenhaven Press.

37. V.O.C.A.L. (1998). The Family Tree, Inc. [On-line]. Available: http://www.vocal.org

38. Barth, Richard P. and Berry, Marianne. (1988). *Adoption and disruption: Rates and responses* (p. 37). New York: Aldine de Gruyter.

39. Weisman, Mary-Lou. (1994, July). When parents are not in the best interests of the child. *Atlantic Monthly.*

40. Ibid.

41. Fishman, Katherine. (1992, September). Problem adoptions. *Atlantic Monthly.*

42. Kotsopolulos, S. (1993). A psychiatric follow-up study of adoptees. *Canadian Journal of Psychiatry, 38,* 6, 391–96.

43. Wender, P. H. (1986). Psychiatric disorders in biological and adoptive families of adopted individuals with affective disorders. *Archives of General Psychiatry, 43,* 10, 923–29.

Kendler, K. S. & Gardner, C. O. (1997, March). The risk for psychiatric disorder in relatives of schizophrenic and control probands: A comparison of three independent studies. *Psychological Medicine 27,* 2, 411–19.

Cadoret, R. J. (1995). Familial transmission of psychiatric disorders associated with alcoholism. In H. Begleiter (Ed.), *Alcohol and Alcoholism* (pp. 70–81). New York; Oxford University Press.

44. Dinwiddie, S. H. (1994). Psychiatric genetics and forensic psychiatry: A review. *Bulletin of the American Academy of Psychiatry and the Law, 22,* 3, 327–42.

45. Herrnstein, Richard J. & Murray, Charles. (1995). *The bell curve.* New York: First Free Press.

46. Lombroso, P. J., Pauls, D. L. & Leckman, J. F. (1994, September). Genetic mechanisms in childhood psychiatric disorders. *Journal of the American Academy of Child and Adolescent Psychiatry, 33,* 7, 921–38.

47. Kirschner, David & Nagel, Linda. (1996). Catathymic violence, dissociation, and adoption pathology: implications for the mental status defense. *International Journal of Offender Therapy and Comparative Criminology. 40*(3), 204–11. Sage Publications.

48. Roth, Wendy E. & Finley, Gordon E. (1998, April). Adoption and antisocial personality: Genetic and environmental factors associated with antisocial outcomes. *Child and Adolescent Social-work Journal, 15,* 2.

49. Genetic/Environment: Behavior disorder studies: Literature reviews/Criticisms. *(*1994*) Bulletin of the American Academy of Psychiatry and the Law, 22,* 3, 327–42.

50. Special report: What parents can do: Wiring feelings. (1997, February 3). *Time, 149,* S.

51. Goleman, Daniel. (1996, July 16). Forget money: Nothing can buy happiness, some researchers say. *New York Times.*

52. Ibid.

53. V.O.C.A.L. (1998). *Loving a chaotic or mentally ill adult: When problem children become problem adults.* [On-line]. The Family Tree, Inc. Available: http://www.vocal.org

54. Adoption Studies Institute. (1998). [On-line]. In Renee Garfinkel, President's message, "In This Issue." Newsletter Vol 5, Spring 1997. The Evelyn B. Donaldson Adoption Institute. Available: http://www.adoption-studies.org/

55. Lieberman, James E., M. D. & Whipple, Katherine, Ph.D. (1997). *Newsletters: Adoption and mental health.* The Evelyn B. Donaldson Adoption Institute.

56. Courtney, Mark & Piliavan, Irving. (1995). *The Wisconsin study of youth aging out of out-of-home care.*

57. Lipman, E. L. et al. (1995). Follow-up of psychiatric and educational morbidity among adopted children. *Journal of American Academy Of Child and Adolescent Psychiatry, 32, 5,* 10007–10012.

58. Rhodes, J. Lynn, (1998). *Dysfunctional behavior in adopted children.* Pathways publication.

59. Lipman, E. L. et. al. (1995). Follow-up of psychiatric and educational morbidity among adopted children. *Journal of American Academy Of Child and Adolescent Psychiatry, 32, 5,* 10007–10012.

60. Lipman, E. L. Offord, D. R. Racine, Y. A. & Boyle, M. H. (1992, November). Psychiatric disorders in adopted children: A profile from the Ontario child health study. *Canadian Journal of Psychiatry, 37,* 627–33.

61. Kotsopoulos, S., Cote, A. & Josepf, L., et al. (1988). Psychiatric disorders in adopted children, a controlled study. *American Journal of Orthopsychiatry, 58,* 4, 608–12.

62. Goldberg, D. & Wolkind, S. N., (1992). Patterns of psychiatric disorder in adopted girls: a research note. *Journal of Child Psychology and Psychiatry and Allied Disciplines, 33,* 5 935–40.

Kotsopoulos, S., Cote, A. & Josepf, L., et al. (1988). Psychiatric disorders in adopted children, a controlled study. *American Journal of Orthopsychiatry*, 58, 4. 608–12.

63. Gentry, Jacqueline. *Violence and family project*. American Psychological Association.

64. Carlson, Susan. (Attorney, Hennepin County District Court). (1998), *November column on adoption, Governor Ame H. Carlson,*
MN, website, [On-line]. Available:
http//www.governor.state.mn.us/new/firstlad/adoptcol.htm

65. Ibid.

66. Courtney, Mark & Piliavan, Irving. (1995). The Wisconsin study of youth aging out of out-of-home care.

67. Rhodes, J. Lynn. (1998). *Dysfunctional behavior in adopted children*. Pathways publication.

68. Ibid.

69. Action Alliance for Children. (1997, July-August). *FACT SHEET, The children's advocate*. [On-line]. Available: http://www.
4children.org/

70. U.S. Department of Health and Social Services. (1998). Executive summary. [On-line]. Available: http://www.acf.dhhs.gov/

71. Kirschner, David & Nagel, Linda. (1996). Catathymic violence, dissociation, and adoption pathology: implications for the mental status defense. *International Journal of Offender Therapy and Comparative Criminology.* 40 (3), 204-21-1. Sage Publications.

72. Wright, Kevin N. & Wright, Karen E., MSW. (1994, May). *Report on family life, delinquency and crime: a policymaker's guide,* Oneonta, NY: Office of Juvenile Justice and Delinquency Prevention Delaware and Otsego Counties.

73. Anonymous personal communication. (1997).

74. Feinberg, Neil, LCSW. (1995). *Bonding and attachment therapy training tape.*

75. Kirschner, David, & Nagel, Linda. (1996). Catathymic violence, dissociation, and adoption pathology: Implications for the mental status defense. *International Journal of Offender Therapy and Comparative Criminology. 40* (3), 204-21-1. Sage Publications.

76. Delaney, Richard J. & Kunstal, Frank R. (1993). *Troubled transplants.* University of Southern Maine.

    Delaney, Richard J. (1991). *Fostering changes* (p. 35–40). Ft. Collins, CO: Walter J. Corbett Publishing.

    Attachment Center at Evergreen. (1998). E. C. website. [Online]. Available: www.attachmentcenter.org/

    Mansfield, Lynda G. & Waldmann, Christopher H. (1994). *Don't touch my heart.* Colorado Springs. CO: Pinon Press.

    Keck, Gregory C. & Kupecky, Regina M. (1995). *Adopting the hurt child.* Colorado Springs, CO: Pinon Press.

    Levy, Terry M., Ph.D. & Orlans, Michael, M.A. (1998). *Attachment, trauma and healing.* Pre-publication manuscript.

77. Fishman, Katherine Davis. (1992, September). Problem Adoptions, Atlantic Monthly.

78. Fishman, Katherine Davis. (1995). *Special needs adoptions should be reevaluated.* In Bender, David & Leone, Bruce (Eds.), *Adoption opposing viewpoints,* p. 220, San Diego, CA: Greenhaven Press.

79. Ibid., pp. 214–24.

80. Anonymous [On-line] personal communication. (1997).

81. Child and Family Resources. [Brochure]. Dallas, TX.

    Delaney, Richard J. & Kunstal, Frank R. (1993). *Troubled transplants.* University of Southern Maine.

82. Frievald-Williams, Susan. (1996). personal communication.

83. National Clearinghouse on Child Abuse and Neglect Information. (1998). [On-line]. Available: http://www.calib.com/nccanch/

84. Anonymous personal communication. (1997, March 26). [On-line].

85. Anonymous personal communication. (1997, March 23). [On-line].

86. Fishman, Katherine Davis. (1992, September). Problem adoptions. *Atlantic Monthly.*

87. Mahoney, James. (1992, August 7). Disruption: When to hold and when to fold. [Speech before the National Council on Adoptable Children, Audiotaped transcript.] Golden Valley, MN: Von Ende Communications.

88. Anonymous personal communication. (1996, January 4).

89. Ibid.

90. Anonymous personal communication. (1997, March 23). [On-line].

91. Anonymous, personal communication. (1997, March 24). [On-line].

92. Ibid.

93. Anonymous, personal communication. (1997, March 23). [On-line].

94. Anonymous, personal communication. (1997, March 24). [On-line].

95. Anonymous, personal communication. (1997, April 5). [On-line].

96. Anonymous personal communication. (1997).

97. Katz, Michael. (1995). Address to North American Council on Adoptable Children.

98. Thomas, Dave. (1996, December 1). Every child deserves a home. *Parade.*

99. Child and Family Resources. [Brochure]. Dallas, TX.

100. Warner, Sherrie. (1997) Personal communication.

101. Anonymous personal communication. (1998, February).

√ 102. Attachment theory: The ultimate experiment. (1998, May 24). *New York Times.*

103. Ibid.

104. Weisman, Mary-Lou. (1994, July). When parents are not in the best interests of the child. *Atlantic Monthly.*

105. Bodie, Cindy. (1997, July–September). Hey y'all, Mama's home! *Roots and Wings.*

106. Wender, P. H. (1986). Psychiatric disorders in biological and adoptive families of adopted individuals with affective disorders. *Archives of General Psychiatry, 43*, 10, 923–29.

Kendler, K. S. & Gardner, C. O. (1997, March). The risk for psychiatric disorder in relatives of schizophrenic and control probands: a comparison of three independent studies. *Psychological Medicine 27*, 2, 411–19.

Cadoret, R. J. (1995). Familial transmission of psychiatric disorders associated with alcoholism. In H. Begleiter (Ed.), *Alcohol and Alcoholism.* (pp.70–81). New York: Oxford University Press.

Lombroso, P. J., Pauls, D. L. & Leckman, J. F. (1994, September). Genetic mechanisms in childhood psychiatric disorders. *Journal of the American Academy of Child and Adolescent Psychiatry, 33*, 7, 921–38.

Genetic/Environment: Behavior disorder studies: Literature reviews/Criticisms. (1994) *Bulletin of the American Academy of Psychiatry and the Law, 22*, 3, 327–42.

107. Attachment theory: The ultimate experiment.(1998, May 24). *New York Times.*

108. Child and Family Resources. *Common family dynamics in special needs adoption.* [Brochure]. Dallas, TX.

109. Cline, Foster W., M.D. & Brucker, Benjamin W., Ed.D. (1996). *Success in parenting.* Spokane, WA; Lon Gibby Productions.

110. The Family Tree. (1998) Loving a chaotic or mentally ill adult; living with chronic chaos. [On–line].

111. Action Alliance for Children, (1997, July-August). [On-line]. FACT SHEET, The children's advocate. Available: http://www.4children.org/

112. The ACE Network. (1998). The stress of caring too much. [On-line]. Available: http://www.ace-network.com/

113. Child Protection Connection. (1998). CPS Training Institute, Center for Social Work Research, School of Social Work, The University of Texas at Austin. [On-line]. Available: http://128.83.80.192/

114. Delaney, Richard J. (1991). Fostering changes. (p. 37). Ft. Collins, CO: Walter J. Corbett Publishing.

115. Ibid.

116. Ibid., pp. 44–45.

117. Babb, L. Anne & Louis, Rita. (1997). Adopting and advocating for the special needs child: A guide for parents and professionals. Westport, CT: Bergin & Garvey.

118. Ibid., p. 37.

119. Anonymous personal communication. (1997). [On-line].

120. V.O.C.A.L. (1998). The Family Tree, Inc. *Loving a chaotic or mentally ill adult: when problem children become problem adults.* [On-line]. Available: http://www.vocal.org

121. Watson, Ken. (1994, March 9). Adoption: Finding your piece of the puzzle. [Conference for adoptive parents and mental health professionals.] Milwaukee, WI.

122. Mahoney, James. (1992, August 7). Disruption, when to hold and when to fold. [Speech before the National Council on Adoptable Children. Audiotaped transcript.] Golden Valley, MN. Von Ende Communications.

123. Delaney, Richard J. & Kunstal, Frank R. (1993). *Troubled transplants* (p. 197). University of Southern Maine.

124. Child and Family Resources. *Common family dynamics in special needs adoption.* [Brochure]. Dallas, TX.

    Delaney, Richard J. & Kunstal, Frank R. (1993). *Troubled transplants* (p. 38). University of Southern Maine.

125. Delaney, Richard J. & Kunstal, Frank R. (1993). *Troubled transplants* (p. 67, 149). University of Southern Maine.

    Delaney, Richard J. (1991). *Fostering changes* (pp. 35–40, 49). Ft. Collins, CO: Walter J. Corbett Publishing.

126. Delaney, Richard J. (1991). *Fostering changes* (pp. 35–40). Ft. Collins, CO: Walter J. Corbett Publishing.

127. Goldstein, Joseph, Solnit, Albert J. & Freud, Anna (1973). Beyond the best interests of the child. In David Bender & Bruno Leone (Eds.). *Adoption: Opposing viewpoints,* 1995 Reprint, San Diego, CA: Greenhaven Press.

128. Delaney, Richard J. & Kunstal, Frank R. (1993). *Troubled transplants* (p. 149). University of Southern Maine.

129. Ibid.

130. Attachment Center at Evergreen. (1998). E.C. materials [Online]. Available: www.attachmentcenter.org

131. Delaney, Richard J. & Kunstal, Frank R. (1993). *Troubled transplants* (p. 7). University of Southern Maine.

132. Barth, Richard P. & Berry, Marianne. (1988). Adoption and disruption rates risks and responses (p. 90–93). Hawthorne, NY: Aldine de Gruyter.

133. Kulp, Jodie. (1993). Families at risk (p. 79–80). Minneapolis, MN: Better Endings New Beginnings.

134. Anonymous personal communication. (1995, January).

135. Attachment Center at Evergreen. (1998). E.C. website. [On-line]. www.attachmentcenter.org

136. V.O.C.A.L. (1997). The Family Tree (permission granted). [On-line].

137. Anonymous personal communication. (1995, January).

138. V.O.C.A.L. (1998). [On-line]. Available: http://vocal.org/what2do

139. Zaslow, Robert W., Ph.D. (1975). *The psychology of the Z process: Attachment and activation.* San Jose, CA: San Jose State University.

140. Malm, Peggy E. (1997). Personal communication.

141. Cline, Foster W., M.D. (1992). Hope for high risk and rage filled children. Evergreen, CO: EC Publications.

142. Malm, Peggy E. (1998). Personal communication.

143. Malm, Peggy E. (1998). Personal communication.

144. Mary-Lou Weisman. (1994, July). When parents are not in the best interests of the child. *Atlantic Monthly.*

145. Ibid.

146. Welch, Martha G., M.D. (1988). *Holding time* (p. 27). New York: Simon and Schuster.

147. Ibid., p. 28.

148. Attachment Center at Evergreen. (1998). [On-line]. Available: www.attachmentcenter.org/

149. Ibid.

Mansfield, Lynda G. & Waldmann, Christopher H. (1994). *Don't touch my heart*. Colorado Springs, CO: Pinon Press.

150. Mansfield, Lynda G. & Waldmann, Christopher H. (1994). Don't touch my heart. Colorado Springs, CO: Pinon Press.

151. Attachment Center at Evergreen, (1998). [On-line]. Available: www.attachmentcenter.org/

152. Ibid.

153. Keck, Gregory C. & Kupecky, Regina M. (1995). *Adopting the hurt child* (pp. 155–161). Colorado Springs, CO: Pinon Press.

154. Hughes, Daniel A. (1997). *Facilitating developmental attachment* (pp. 105–107). Northvale, NJ: Jason Aronson.

155. Welch, Martha G., M.D. (1988). *Holding time* (p. 25). New York: Simon and Schuster.

156. Attachment Center at Evergreen. (1998). [On-line]. Available: www.attachmentcenter.org/

157. Welch, Martha G., M.D. (1988). Holding time (p. 25). New York: Simon and Schuster.

158. Ibid., p. 49–50.

159. Attachment Center at Evergreen. (1998). *How do you know a child needs this therapy?* [On-line]. Available: www.attachmentcenter.org/

160. Ibid.

Evergreen Consultants in Human Behavior. (1998). [On-line]. Available: http://www.attachmenttherapy.com/evconsultants.html

Levy, Terry M., Ph.D. & Orlans, Michael, M.A. (1998). *Attachment, trauma and healing*, Pre-publication manuscript.

American Psychiatric Association (APA). (1994). Diagnostic and statistical manual of mental disorders (4th ed.). Washington, DC.

161. Mansfield, Lynda G. & Waldmann, Christopher H. (1994). *Don't touch my heart.* Colorado Springs, CO: Pinon Press.

Levy, Terry M., Ph.D. & Orlans, Michael, M.A. (1998). *Attachment, trauma and healing.* Pre-publication manuscript.

Cline, Foster W., M.D. (1992). Hope for high risk and rage filled children. Evergreen, CO: EC Publications.

Attachment Center at Evergreen. (1998). [On-line]. Available: www.attachmentcenter.org/

Welch, Martha G., M.D. (1988). Holding time (p. 25). New York: Simon and Schuster.

162. Keck, Gregory C. & Kupecky, Regina M. (1995). *Adopting the hurt child.* Colorado Springs, CO: Pinon Press.

163. Evergreen Consultants in Human Behavior. (1998). [On-line]. Available: http://www.attachmenttherapy.com/evconsultants.html

164. Payne, Roger, Ph.D. (1976, March). *National Geographic,* 325–39.

165. Attachment Center at Evergreen. (1998). [On-line]. Available: www.attachmentcenter.org/

Levy, Terry M., Ph.D. & Orlans, Michael, M.A. (1998). *Attachment, trauma and healing.* Pre-publication manuscript.

166. Attachment Center at Evergreen. (1998). [On-line]. Available: www.attachmentcenter.org/

167. Hughes, Daniel A. (1997). *Facilitating developmental attachment* (pp. 99–102). Northvale, NJ: Jason Aronson.

168. Keck, Gregory C. & Kupecky, Regina M. (1995). *Adopting the hurt child* (pp. 155–161). Colorado Springs, CO: Pinon Press.

169. American Psychiatric Association (APA). (1994). *Diagnostic and statistical manual of mental disorders* (4th ed.) Washington, DC.

170. Attachment Center at Evergreen. (1998). [On-line]. Available: www.attachmentcenter.org/

171. Ibid.

172. Mansfield, Lynda G. & Waldmann, Christopher H. (1994). *Don't touch my heart.* Colorado Springs, CO: Pinon Press.

173. Attachment Center at Evergreen. (1998). [On-line]. Available: www.attachmentcenter.org/

    Levy, Terry M., Ph.D. & Orlans, Michael, M.A. (1998). *Attachment, trauma and healing.* Pre-publication manuscript.

174. Evergreen Consultants in Human Behavior. (1998). [On-line]. Available: http://www.attachmenttherapy.com/evconsultants.html

175. Hughes, Daniel A. (1997). *Facilitating developmental attachment* (p. 236). Northvale, NJ: Jason Aronson.

176. Ibid.

177. Sensory Integration International. (1998). *Focus on sensory integration.* [On-line]. Available:http://home.earthlink.net/~sensoryint/

178. Ibid.

179. Ibid.

180. Ibid.

181. *Milwaukee Journal Sentinel.* (1998, Saturday, June 6). Frightened parents make a courageous call.

182. Tolman, Lani. (1998, June). Personal communication.

183. Ibid.

Index

About the Authors

Foster W. Cline, M.D.

Dr. Cline is an internationally renowned adult and child psychiatrist, lecturer, and author of eight books on parenting and working with difficult children. His best selling *Love and Logic* parenting series, co-authored with Jim Fay, has been translated into several foreign languages. *Hope for High Risk and Rage Filled Children* has become the classic reference on understanding and treating Reactive Attachment Disorder in children.

Dr. Cline is the cofounder of two clinics that specialize in the treatment of severely disturbed children. He is a popular speaker at workshops and seminars throughout the United States and has spoken in eleven foreign countries. Dr. Cline and his wife Hermie have three children by birth, one by adoption and several foster children. They live in the mountains of northern Idaho.

Cathy Helding

Cathy is a nationally known consultant, writer, and speaker in the field of special needs adoption and parenting of special needs children. Cathy comes from a background in special education and taught cognitively disabled middle school students in the 1970s. She is a former America Online Community Leader and newsletter editor for the Adoption Forum. She is a sought-after speaker for parent groups, agency trainings, and teacher in-service programs.

In 1998 she testified before a State Senate committee on fetal alcohol syndrome and was instrumental in the passage of legislation that recognizes the rights of unborn children of drug- and alcohol-addicted mothers. Cathy and her husband John have four children, three of whom were adopted as a sibling group with special needs. They live in a replica turn-of-the-century farmhouse on eight acres of restored native prairie in southeastern Wisconsin.

Notes

Notes

Notes

Notes

Need a Speaker for Your Group or Organization?

Dynamic Presentations by:

Foster W. Cline, M.D. and Cathy Helding

Authors of the new book *Can This Child Be Saved? Solutions for Adoptive and Foster Parents* and the *Cline Helding Adopted and Foster Child Assessment (CHAFCA)*.

Help and Hope . . . Practical and Fun . . . For Parents or Professionals . . .

Can This Child Be Saved? workshops and seminars by world renowned psychiatrist and author Foster W. Cline, M.D. and Cathy Helding, adoption specialist, author, and educator.

Custom tailored presentations for:

- adoptive and foster parents
- adoption professionals
- educators
- policy makers and administrators

For more information:

Phone: 414-835-2223
Fax: 800-932-3686
On the Web at:
www.cathyhelding.com
www.psychshop.com

Visit our websites for information about
books, seminars, workshops, reproducible articles
and handouts, contact information, and other resources:

www.psychshop.com

www.cathyhelding.com

Name:
Address:
City: State: Zip:
Phone:

Quantity	Title	Unit Price	Total Price
	Can This Child Be Saved? Solutions for Adoptive and Foster Families by: Foster W. Cline, M.D. & Cathy Helding	$24.95	
	CHAFCA (Manual plus 2 score sheet packets)	$19.95	
	Hope for High Risk and Rage-Filled Children by: Foster W. Cline, M.D.	$29.95	

	Purchase total:	Shipping cost:	
	Under $25	**$4.95**	
	$25.01–$50	**$5.95**	
	$50.01–$75	**$7.95**	
	$75.01–$100	**$9.95**	
	$100.01–$125	**$10.95**	
	$125.01–$150	**$13.95**	
	over $200	**by quote**	
Sales Tax: WI residents only, please add 5.1%			
		TOTAL	

Order from:

City Desktop Productions, Inc.

1-800-854-2344

Fax: 414-884-8889

☐ Check/Money order
☐ Visa
☐ MasterCard

CREDIT CARD NUMBER

EXPIRATION DATE

Hours: 8:00 A.M.–5:00 P.M. Central Standard Time